T0244128

Inaugural Ballers

Inaugural Ballers

The True Story of the First US Women's Olympic Basketball Team

ANDREW MARANISS

THORNDIKE PRESS
A part of Gale, a Cengage Company

GALE
A Cengage Company

LIBRARY OF CONGRESS CIP DATA ON FILE.
CATALOGUING IN PUBLICATION FOR THIS BOOK
IS AVAILABLE FROM THE LIBRARY OF CONGRESS.

ISBN-13: 979-8-88578-926-4 (hardcover alk. paper)

Published in 2023 by arrangement with Viking Children's Books, an imprint of Penguin Young Readers Group, a division of Penguin Random House LLC.

Printed in Mexico
Print Number: 1   Print Year: 2023

For Alison, Eliza, and Charlie
And for Linda, Sarah,
Pat, Mary, and Cathy

The inaugural ballers of 1976. Kneeling (left to right): Nancy Lieberman, Trish Roberts, Sue Rojcewicz, Juliene Simpson, Ann Meyers, Charlotte Lewis.

Standing (left to right): manager Jeanne Rowlands, trainer Gail Weldon, Gail Marquis, Cindy Brogdon, Lusia Harris, Nancy Dunkle, Mary Anne O'Connor, Pat Head, head coach Billie Moore, assistant coach Sue Gunter. (Women's Basketball Hall of Fame)

EVERLASTING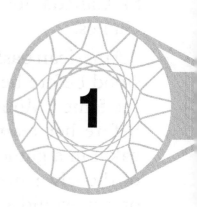

JULY 26, 1976
MONTREAL FORUM, QUEBEC, CANADA
SUMMER OLYMPICS

The locker room shook with music, women singing along with the Natalie Cole tape blasting from the small speakers in the corner.

THIS will be . . . an everlasting love
THIS will be . . . the one I've waited for

Someone turned off the tape player, and the room grew quieter. The only thing breaking the silence was the muffled murmur of thousands of spectators from around the world who had traveled

7

to Canada for the eighteenth Olympic Games.

American basketball coach Billie Moore stood before her players in the bowels of the famed Montreal Forum, just minutes before her team was to play Czechoslovakia in a game to determine the winner of the silver medal. The women in front of her would go on to become some of the most legendary names in the history of the sport, but at this moment they were still largely unknown.[1] For people who paid attention to women's basketball, it was a surprise this team had even made it to Montreal, let alone that it was in position to earn medals in the first women's Olympic basketball tournament ever played. The United States had placed a dismal eighth at the World Championships in Colombia a year earlier, only qualifying for the Olympics in a last-minute tournament for also-rans just two weeks before the opening ceremony. Heading into the Olympics, one sportswriter declared that the only positive thing anyone could say about US women's basketball in the past was that it wasn't the most inept program in the world. "Maybe the second or third worst," he wrote, "but not the worst."

A basketball coach must choose her words carefully in a pregame speech — just enough motivation, not too much pressure. As she scanned the room, locking eyes with the veteran co-captain from rural Tennessee, the brash young redhead from Long Island, and the quietly determined Black center from the Mississippi Delta, Moore sensed her players could handle a message that had been on her mind ever since the team's training camp in Warrensburg, Missouri, six weeks earlier.

The coach had confidence in this group, and though she didn't think much about politics, she understood the moment in time in which this team existed. In the summer of 1976, women were demanding rights and opportunities all over the world. The United States had just celebrated its bicentennial on July 4, a time for Americans to ponder whether all citizens were truly free.

Moore knew this game was an important stepping-stone on the journey to equality. Pat, Lusia, Annie, Nancy L., Nancy

D., Mary Anne, Sue, Juliene, Charlotte, Cindy, Trish, and Gail wouldn't just be playing for themselves but also for the women before them who had been denied opportunities. They would be playing for the little girls who yearned to hoop, and generations of athletes yet to be born.

Rather than calm her players' nerves by telling them to remember this was just another game, no different than any they'd played before, Billie Moore laid it all on the line.

"Win this game," she told her team, "and it will change women's sports in this country for the next twenty-five years."

BEGINNINGS

2

The young women, schoolteachers at Buckingham Grade School, were out for their daily walk to lunch when they heard a commotion coming from the gymnasium at the International YMCA Training School.[1]

The teachers opened the door, peered down at the hardwood gym floor below, and gasped at the strangest sight: two teams of men heaving a soccer ball toward an elevated peach basket. These women were the first "fans" ever to witness the brand-new sport of basketball. While James Naismith, a thirty-year-old instructor from Canada, invented his new

11

game as a diversion to keep the all-male student body in Springfield occupied during the snowy Massachusetts winter, women played and helped popularize the sport from the very beginning. It would take eighty-five years for the Olympics to include a women's basketball tournament, but that wasn't because the sport was new to women.

As word of Naismith's invention spread across Springfield, curious spectators crowded the elevated running track that hovered ten feet above the gym floor. The teachers came every day, so mesmerized by the exciting new sport they often skipped lunch entirely. After two weeks of watching, they approached Naismith with a question: Could they play, too?

"I don't see why not," he replied, arranging a time for them to have the gym all to themselves. Decades later, he wrote that he never forgot the sight of these women in their bustles and long dresses with leg-of-mutton sleeves. "In spite of these handicaps, the girls took the ball and began to shoot at the basket," he wrote. "None of the other fundamentals were observed; often some girl got the ball and ran halfway across the floor to shoot at the basket."

After several weeks of practice, the teachers yearned to play against real competition. Small problem: no other women in town had ever played basketball. Eventually the wives and girlfriends of college faculty members volunteered, including Naismith's future bride, Maude Sherman. Soon after this successful exhibition, Naismith recalled, "the game for girls began to spread almost as rapidly as the boys' game."

A pivotal development took place in 1892 when a Lithuanian immigrant introduced herself to Naismith at a physical education conference in Connecticut. Senda Berenson had read about the new game and was thinking about introducing it at Smith College, the women's college where she taught. Naismith encouraged her, sharing the news that women were playing the game in Springfield. Though team sports were "unheard of" at Smith, Berenson thought the game would improve her students' physical fitness. Smith women, using wastebaskets as hoops, considered basketball "great fun"

13

as soon as Berenson began teaching it, and the first official game was set for March 22, 1893, pitting first-year students against sophomores.

Players dressed in blue bloomers, and no men were allowed in the gymnasium. Students decorated the bleachers with colorful streamers, green for the sophomores and lavender for the freshmen. With women in the stands belting out dueling class songs, it was time for tip-off. Berenson stood at center court, tossed the ball skyward, and promptly dislocated the shoulder of the sophomore team's center, whose outstretched arm collided with Berenson's on the jump ball. Undeterred, Berenson found a substitute and proceeded with the thirty-minute game, which was ultimately won by the sophomores, 5–4.

As she worked to promote the game in the years that followed, Berenson — much like Naismith — valued basketball less for its competitive aspects and more as a source of exercise, fun, and teamwork. Perhaps because of the injury she caused in the first game, Berenson considered basketball a bit rough. She

Above: No one was more influential in the development of women's basketball than physical education instructor Senda Berenson of Smith College, a Lithuanian immigrant. (Women's Basketball Hall of Fame)

Left: Berenson developed special rules for women's basketball to remove some of the perceived "roughness" of the game. Her version of the game gained nationwide traction in part due to the influence of the popular Spalding rule book. (Women's Basketball Hall of Fame)

experimented with rule changes, dividing the court into three segments and requiring players to remain in their regions. She placed limits on dribbling, prevented players from stealing the ball from their opponents, and required players to wear their hair in feminine ribbons and braids.

Even with these concessions, at a time in American history when there were stifling restrictions on women in every aspect of life, Berenson understood the political statement made every time women stepped foot on the basketball court, drawing connections between athletics and equity in other areas of society.

"One of the strong arguments in the economic world against giving women as high salaries as men for similar work is that women are more prone to illness than men," she wrote, acknowledging a myth about female frailty if only to propose a way around it. "They need, therefore, all the more to develop health and endurance if they desire to become candidates for equal wages."

From its New England roots, the women's game spread across the country. Cal and Stanford played the first intercollegiate game in 1896 at the San Francisco Armory in front of seven hundred women who "roared until the glass doors in the gun cases shivered at the noise," and by 1897, physical education teacher Stella Vaughn had organized games for female students at Vanderbilt University in Nashville. The games were immensely popular — a boy from the Vanderbilt newspaper hid in the gymnasium's shadows to file a secret report on the first game (which men were barred from attending), and at Stanford, when word reached campus by telegram that their team had beaten Cal 2–1, students celebrated wildly and met their heroines at the train station, marching proudly alongside them all the way back to campus.

And how did Stanford's faculty members react to the news?

They promptly banned female students from competing in intercollegiate athletics.

When Billie Moore's team arrived in Montreal in the summer of 1976, they hadn't just overcome a series of opponents on the basketball court to reach the game's summit — they had climbed a mountain composed of nearly a century's worth of misogyny and obstruction.

A LADY'S BUSINESS

3

When Stanford faculty members responded to their women's basketball team's success in 1896 by banning further competition, it was among the first of many stops and starts for the sport, extending from those early games in Springfield all the way to Montreal eighty years later. For every advocate, there was a detractor. Every time the game grew, there was backlash.

By the 1920s, as women increasingly entered the workforce and first-wave feminists secured the right for white women to vote — most Black women weren't guaranteed suffrage until decades of courageous activism led to the Voting Rights Act of 1965 — participation in athletics increased, too. High schools added basketball teams for girls, and the Amateur

Athletic Union (AAU) held its first national tournament for women in 1926.[1] In Chicago, Izzy Channels led the all-Black Roamer Girls to six straight undefeated seasons in the 1920s while the *Defender,* the city's Black newspaper, heavily covered the team's exploits. Women's basketball historians Pamela Grundy and Susan Shackelford write that for young women in the late 1800s, "ideas of proper womanhood had been governed by modesty and self-restraint. By the 1920s, the emphasis was on a vibrant, adventuresome personality." For these women, female strength was a given: "Athletic competition seemed like fun, a fine place to channel youthful energy."

But by the end of the decade, backlash emerged. US First Lady Lou Hoover opposed the common practice of men's and women's basketball doubleheaders, leading a committee that concluded that women competing in athletic clothing in front of mixed crowds of men and women was inherently sexual in nature, noneducational, and unhealthy. Her solution was to ban women's basketball altogether. She found allies in both female physical education teachers and male sportswriters. Many teachers favored friendly, cooperative play for all girls over competition between the talented few, and the writers preferred lipstick to layups. "It's a lady's business to look beautiful," wrote New York sportswriter Paul Gallico in 1936, "and there are hardly any sports in which she seems able to do it."

At Delta State University in Mississippi that same year, Margaret Wade captained the school's women's basketball team. The next year, however, university officials dropped basketball, claiming the sport was "too strenuous" for women, even though they played by half-court rules and no player was allowed to dribble the ball more than two times. "We cried and burned our uniforms," Wade recalled, "but there was nothing else we could do." At Bennett College in Greensboro, North Carolina, the demise of women's basketball took about a decade longer. Basketball games had become a focal point of social activity at the historically Black college in the 1930s and a welcome public leisure activity in the segregated South. And the team was highly skilled, deemed the best in the country in 1937 by the *Chicago Defender*. But by 1941, in the name of "refinement and respectability," the program was disbanded, replaced with intramurals and noncompetitive "play days" with other institutions.

Across the country, coaches and players fought back against the threats to the sport. When state athletic officials in Iowa attempted to scrap girls' basketball, many coaches were livid. "Gentlemen," said one coach, "if you attempt to do away with girls' basketball in Iowa, you'll be standing in the center of the track when the train runs over." Girls' coaches broke away from their male counterparts and formed their own athletic association, creating the most wildly popular state basketball tournament in the country. By 1947, they were selling forty thousand tickets to the tournament in Des Moines (a spectacle that to one sportswriter felt like "a state fair and a World Series rolled into one"), with fans from small towns forming automobile convoys up to six miles long, escorting victorious teams' buses back home through farms and cornfields. "Basketball is the subject

A woman works on an airplane motor at the North American Aviation plant in California in 1942. (Library of Congress)

from morning until night; every one talks of it," wrote one Iowa high school journalist, declaring that whenever a group of girls gathered together, "you can guess they are talking about basketball."

Nationwide, the repression of the 1930s gave way to a rebirth in the 1940s as women entered the wartime workforce. If

Rosie the Riveter could build an airplane, how could you keep her off the basketball court?[2] While many factories and munitions plants sponsored women's basketball teams (such as Vultee Aircraft's "Bomberettes"), AAU and professional barnstorming teams also gained popularity. Players began to attract attention from fans and sportswriters for their individual skills. Women's basketball stars were born.

Alline Banks, known as the "point-a-minute girl" in the 1940s, outscored Nashville Business College's opponents all by herself in three consecutive AAU tournaments (once scoring 56 points in a national championship game) and earned All-American honors twelve years in a row. In the 1950s and '60s, Nera White, also of Nashville Business College, led her teams to ten national championships and earned AAU All-American honors for fifteen consecutive seasons. White was said to have "built her muscles while plowing and lifting feed sacks." She could do it all — hit a long-range jumper, finger-roll at the hoop, post up in the paint, float down the lane, knock down clutch shots, stifle

Nera White (top row, fourth from left) led the powerful Nashville Business College team to ten AAU national championships and was named an AAU All-American fifteen consecutive years in the 1950s and early '60s. (Women's Basketball Hall of Fame)

her opponents defensively, even dish out some fierce trash talk.[3] Sue Gunter, Billie Moore's assistant coach on the 1976 Olympic team, played with White in

Nashville and called her the best player of all time.

The barnstorming All-American Red Heads, a semipro team founded in 1936 to promote a chain of beauty shops in the Ozarks, drove tens of thousands of miles from town to town, playing — and beating — local men's teams in church basements, ice rinks, and school gymnasiums, splitting ticket sales with their hosts. The Red Heads were extremely talented players, but they were forced to clown around to make their mostly male audiences comfortable with the idea of watching women play ball.[4] They dyed their hair bright red, performed mid-game tricks, participated in sexist skits (one called for a player to beg the ref to call "a very personal foul" after an opponent pinched her butt), and were paid next to nothing. "These girls love basketball so much they don't care what they get paid," absurdly claimed the team's owner, a jarring example of the broader, chronic problem of the undervaluing of women's labor in the United States.

By the 1950s, as the country settled into post–World War II comfort and conservative social mores reinforced traditional gender roles, women's basketball took another blow. Advertising, television programs, and women's magazines portrayed the ideal mother of the era satisfying her family's every need without complaint and looking immaculate doing it. These "genteel" housewives, write Grundy and Shackelford, pursued "their daily affairs with smiles, spotless outfits and practiced ease. Such ideals lay far removed from the heated, sweaty competition of high-level basketball. Within this formulation, the qualities essential to athletic success — speed, strength, aggressive determination — were cast not as human traits but specifically masculine ones. Male athletes fit neatly into this picture. Female athletes did not."

The "popular girls" were cheerleaders, not ballplayers. By the 1960s, attendance at women's AAU games plummeted, sponsorships dried up, teams folded, and talented players gave up their hoop dreams. Colleges dropped competitive teams and instead scheduled "play days" with other schools, with mixed-together teams of women from both schools play-

The "popular girls" of the mid-twentieth century were those who adhered to conventional standards of femininity, such as cheerleaders and beauty queens — not athletes. For a girl to play sports required an independent spirit, thick skin, and a love for the game. (Getty Images)

ing friendly games followed by cookies and punch. Athletic women were often cruelly and homophobically labeled as "freaks." As phenomenally talented as Nera White was, men mocked her voice and physical appearance.

The casual sexism of the day was relentless in its ubiquity. In 1965, *Sports Illustrated* magazine sent a reporter to Provo, Utah, to write about the success of the Brigham Young University men's basketball team. At a time when the magazine's nearly all-male staff rarely wrote about the accomplishments of female athletes, the writer found one group of women — the BYU cheerleaders — worthy of his attention, practically drooling over his typewriter: "The swirl of brief blue skirts and flags and flashing teeth is so stunning that it frequently delays the halftime run on hamburger stands until after the teams resume play," he wrote. "'You know what this is?' shouted one sportswriter who came to watch them play and stayed to see them dance. 'All this is a big, wild, wonderful, gigantic peep show!'"

Over and over, women and girls were told that appealing to men was all that mattered. But that mindset was about to be challenged in a manner that altered the course of American history.

4

PAGEANT PROTEST

One by one, women walked up to the trash can and tossed in "items of oppression" and "instruments of female torture" — girdles, bras, high-heeled shoes, mops, brooms, false eyelashes, curlers, copies of *Cosmopolitan* and *Playboy* magazines, and cans of hairspray.

Busloads of women, mostly white and mostly from New York, had converged on the Atlantic City boardwalk to protest the Miss America beauty pageant taking place that night in the city's oceanfront convention center. Passing out leaflets (NO MORE MISS AMERICA!) and carrying signs (CAN MAKEUP COVER THE

Miss America Pageant protestors toss "items of oppression" into a "Freedom Trash Can" along the Atlantic City boardwalk on September 7, 1968. (Duke University Rubenstein Library, Alix Kate Shulman papers)

WOUNDS OF OUR OPPRESSION?), the women sought to draw attention to what they called a degrading and dehumanizing event that symbolized broader cultural attitudes toward women.

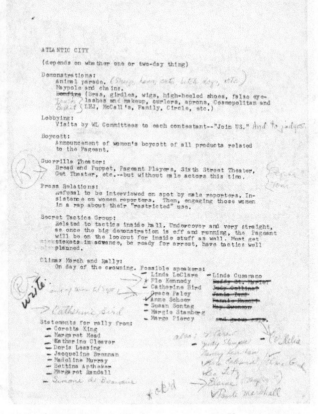

ATLANTIC CITY

(depends on whether one or two-day thing)

Demonstrations:
Animal parade. *(Sheep, hens, cats, little dog, etc.)*
Maypole and chains.
~~Bonfire~~ (Bras, girdles, wigs, high-heeled shoes, false eye-
lashes and makeup, curlers, aprons, Cosmopolitan and
LHJ, McCall's, Family, Circle, etc.)

Lobbying:
Visits by WL Committees to each contestant--"Join US." *And to judges.*

Boycott:
Announcement of women's boycott of all products related
to the Pageant.

Guerrilla Theater:
Bread and Puppet, Pageant Players, Sixth Street Theater,
Out Theater, etc.--but without male actors this time.

Press Relations:
Refusal to be interviewed on spot by male reporters. Insistence on women reporters. Then, engaging those women
in a rap about their "restricted" use.

Secret Tactics Group:
Related to tactics inside hall. Undercover and very straight,
so once the big demonstration is off and running, the Pageant
will be on the lookout for inside stuff as well. Must get
tickets in advance, be ready for arrest, have tactics well
planned.

Climax March and Rally:
On day of the crowning. Possible speakers:
- Linda LeClare   - Linda Cusumano
- Flo Kennedy
- Catherine Bird
- Grace Paley
- Anne Schoer
- Susan Sontag
- Margie Stamberg
- Marge Piercy

Statements for rally from:
- Coretta King
- Margaret Mead
- Katharine Cleaver
- Doris Lessing
- Jacqueline Brennan
- Madeline Murray
- Bettina Aptheker
- Margaret Randell
- Simone de Beauvoir

A planning document from the files of Robin Morgan, chief organizer of the Miss America protest. (Sallie Bingham Center for Women's History and Culture, Duke University, Robin Morgan papers)

The 1968 protest would be remembered as a pivotal moment in the public's recognition of a broader women's rights movement, the way Americans perceived women, and the way women viewed themselves. Members of the 1976 Olympic basketball team came of age in this era of great change and rising consciousness, watching women in all walks of life rebelling against the constraints of traditional gender roles and seeking the freedom to follow their individual interests.

For Americans in the 1960s, the live, nationally televised beauty pageant was a cultural touchstone, drawing more viewers than any other TV event all year. But a growing number of detractors believed that the pageant and the values it exemplified pitted women against each other in a sexist and demeaning way, illustrating the manner in which American culture valued women more for their sex appeal and conformity than for their intelligence, skills, or personality.

Comparing the pageant to a livestock auction, protestors, led by a group called the New York Radical Women, walked a live sheep down the boardwalk and held an impromptu ceremony for it, complete with sash and tiara. The scene attracted the attention they had hoped for — journalists showed up to interview and take photos of the protestors, spreading their message nationwide. Two protestors bought tickets to the pageant and took seats in the balcony. When the outgoing Miss America gave her farewell speech, they unfurled a bedsheet spray-painted with the words WOMEN'S LIBERATION and shouted, "No more Miss America!" Police escorted the protestors from the convention center as Judith Ford, a blond, eighteen-year-old lifeguard, gymnast, and trampolinist from Belvidere, Illinois, accepted her crown.[1]

Stories in the next morning's newspapers diminished Ford's athleticism and highlighted her measurements, the fact that she typically wore her skirts two to three inches above her knee, and her polite answers to questions such as "Are you a romantic girl?" ("It depends on whom I'm with") and "Do blonds have more fun?" ("I've never been a brunette to compare it with"). Ford had competed with a fear that her talent, trampolining, would be judged "too masculine." "Miss America," she had been warned, "is not supposed to sweat."

The protest received nearly as much coverage as Ford's victory, vaulting the

Judith Ford of Belvidere, Illinois, was named Miss America on the night of the protest. A trampolinist at the University of Southwestern Louisiana, Ford went on to become a PE teacher and basketball coach. (Wikimedia Commons)

women's liberation movement into the public consciousness and ushering in a new phase of feminist action in America. But it also revealed a persistent weakness in white feminists' strategy: a propensity for ignoring, disregarding, or minimizing the concerns of their Black contemporaries and the wisdom of a long line of brilliant Black feminists throughout American history, not to mention their complete erasure of Indigenous women and other feminists of color.[2]

When protest organizer Robin Morgan and her fellow New York Radical Women threw items into the trash can on the boardwalk, they sang "We Shall Not Be Used," a play on the civil rights anthem "We Shall Overcome." And among their criticisms of the pageant were the white standards of beauty at the heart of it. In the event's forty-seven years, no Black contestant had ever been a finalist.

But the Black press resented the white women's appropriation of "We Shall Overcome," especially since the New York Radical Women also opposed another beauty pageant taking place at the same time in Atlantic City, a Miss Black America contest intended to show that "black beauty is equal to that of the white woman." For many Black Americans, this measure of self-determination, Black pride, and equity in a society that conspired in countless ways against all Black people took precedence over the white feminists' concerns about male chauvinism.

Still, Black women understood the foundational idea that "the personal is political" better than their white sisters. Surveys in the early 1970s revealed that Black women held more progressive positions on issues involving day care, education, equal pay, and equal work than white women did. And there was no doubt that women's liberation advocates of all backgrounds were correct in their assessment of the inequities of American life and the second-class status of women.

Well into the 1960s, American pop culture bombarded girls with the message that their highest calling was to get married and raise children while their husbands worked, made political decisions, and developed other interests outside the home. "A girl who gets as far as her junior year in college without having acquired a man," reported *Harper's Magazine,* "is thought to be in grave danger of becoming an old maid."

When women looked for work outside the home, their prospects were limited. Most were steered toward clerical roles in office settings, waitressing, or cleaning homes, while a more privileged few became teachers, nurses, or librarians. In 1960, women made up only 9 percent of American doctors and dentists, 3 percent of lawyers, and less than 1 percent of engineers. Employers discriminated based on gender without fear of legal reprisal, and airlines ran "executive flights" for businessmen that barred women passengers entirely.

In 1960, a woman showed up at New York traffic court to pay her husband's fine and was sent home by an angry judge, ordered to put on "appropriate clothes." She had arrived at court in slacks and a blouse; he preferred a dress and heels.

In a society where all this was considered normal, the idea of a woman or girl choosing to lace up a pair of sneakers and spend her time on the basketball court went completely against the grain. "It takes a bold individual," said one successful female athlete, "to plunge aggressively into sports while much of society scorns her."

LIES, EXPOSED

5

In some ways, the march toward the Atlantic City boardwalk began in February of 1963, when writer Betty Friedan (who had been fired from a magazine writing position when she became pregnant) published *The Feminine Mystique,* a book that expressed many American women's immense dissatisfaction with the idea that fulfillment could only come as a housewife and mother. By 1964, Friedan had sold more than a million copies of the culture-shifting book, reaching number one on the nonfiction bestseller list, and launching the "second wave" in the American feminist movement. While first-wave feminists had focused on earning women the right to vote, second-wave feminists highlighted issues related to gender and family roles, workplace inequities, and sexuality.

Betty Friedan's landmark book The Feminine Mystique *captured the mood of a generation of women and helped lead to a new wave of American feminism. Friedan cofounded the National Organization for Women and lobbied for the Equal Rights Amendment. (Wikimedia Commons)*

Writing from her perspective as a highly educated, white, suburban wife and mother, Friedan articulated the question that millions of women like her internalized in the years following World War II: *Is this all there is?* Women who worked outside the home were made to feel guilty about it; those who stayed home knew there was more to life than baking potatoes, ironing clothes, and raising children. What had become, she wrote, of the hopes and dreams they held when they were younger? Further, when society valued women only in terms of their relationship to men — wife, mother, sex object — many felt it was their own fault if they were unhappy with this arrangement, that they were wrong for wanting something more, for desiring to be defined by their own thoughts and deeds. As they read Friedan's book, these women felt that at last they were understood and, equally important, discovered that they were not alone. The book was provocative, revolutionary, even subversive, exposing the deception that was the very foundation of America's male-dominated culture.[1]

"It meant that I and every other woman I knew had been living a lie, and all the doctors who treated us and the experts who studied us were perpetuating that lie, and our homes and schools and churches and politics and professions were built around that lie," she wrote. "If women were really *people* — no more, no less — then all the things that kept them from being full people in our society would have to be changed. And women, once they broke through the feminine mystique and took themselves seriously as people, would see their place on a false pedestal, even their glorification as sexual objects, for the putdown it was."

By 1966, Friedan had cofounded the National Organization for Women (NOW), a moderate group of professional women who, among other things, called for the federal government to investigate sex discrimination cases in the workplace.[2] Friedan and her supporters believed that women could achieve equality only by joining the decision-making mainstream of American political, economic, and social life.

But when younger, more progressive women joined the movement, they chafed at some of NOW's messaging and goals, deeming its brand of feminism too accommodating. "We in this segment of the movement do not believe that the oppression of women will be ended by giving them a bigger piece of the pie as Betty Friedan would have it," said one radical feminist. "We believe the pie itself is rotten."[3]

Despite differences in tactics and goals, Friedan's followers and the more progressive feminists existed on the same continuum, and their aims pointed in the same direction: toward freedom from arbitrary oppression. In Friedan's case, she believed that when women demanded the same rights and responsibilities as men and seats at the tables where decisions were made, it didn't mean women wanted to be men — it meant they wanted to be human.

In the case of women's liberation, advocates sought to dismantle repressive gender definitions and to replace them with the freedom for individuals to make their own choices about the direction of their lives.

Across the country, girls heard these calls for progress and freedom from older women, and though the feminists rarely mentioned sports, the message to the kids was clear.

Teenage girls of the early 1970s, including the ones who would go on to represent the United States at the 1976 Olympics, believed they should have the ability to choose their own interests, to be what they wanted to be.

Doctor, lawyer, teacher, politician, and even, perhaps, power forward or point guard.

ENTITLED 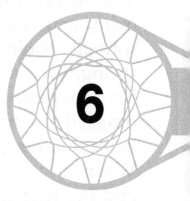 6

In Mt. Horeb, Wisconsin, fourth grader Jane Burns collected classmates' signatures in a spiral notebook to demand that her elementary school allow girls equal access to the gymnasium. The principal gave the girls Tuesdays.

In Paducah, Kentucky, fourth grader Sharon Shields asked her teacher and her principal if the girls could play softball since the boys played baseball. Both women told her no. Sharon had been playing the sport with her family in the backyard since she was six, so the women's rejection surprised her. "What are you going to do about it?" her grandmother asked, and Sharon went to work. She filled pillowcases up with sand, and her grandmother stitched them shut. Now she had bases. She asked her father how to organize a round-robin tournament, and she told her friends to ask for softball equipment for Christmas. By spring, the fourth-grade girls were ready for a tournament. On March 15, Sharon dragged a laundry bag stuffed with bats, balls, and her pillowcase bases to school. When it was time for recess, Sharon and her friends "stormed the field," and the tournament began, Sharon grinning from ear to ear.

Then her teacher called her over. Sharon knew she was in trouble.

"Did you organize this? I told you girls don't play softball."

Sharon admitted she was the instigator.

"Well," her teacher replied, "I guess you proved me wrong."

And the softball tournament continued.[1]

Burns and Shields were just two girls of the post–World War II era poking at inequities that were obvious to them, but that most adults still defended. In a typical school of the 1960s and early '70s, the era in which members of the 1976 women's basketball team and their contemporaries

46

grew up, boys and girls were separated in gym class, with boys learning how to play baseball, basketball, and football, while the girls practiced their cartwheels and somersaults.

Moving up to middle school, the boys had access to varsity, junior varsity, and intramural teams in multiple sports, while the girls might have one team in one sport. Even at high schools where boys and girls both had varsity teams in several sports, there was glaring inequality. The boys would play in the nice, new gym, the girls in the old, decrepit one. Boys would play baseball on the school's well-kept field; girls would have to walk over to a local park to play softball. Boys played tennis on the real courts, girls in the school parking lot, dodging cars. Boys' teams had multiple coaches, girls' teams just one — and that coach would be paid less, even though they did more because they had no help. Boys received new uniforms every year, girls passed theirs down from year to year, and used the same jerseys for both basketball and volleyball.

At the college level in 1971, universities spent just 1 percent of their total athletic budgets on women's sports, and the women's teams that did exist in the early 1970s were forced to obey any request made by coaches of men's teams. The women's track team at the University of Illinois had scheduled a meet a year in advance, inviting teams from all over the country to participate. But then a week before the event, the men's coach said he needed the track for a workout. The women's meet was canceled. At Michigan State, the women's swimming and diving team was forced to move its competition to a local pool after the men's team demanded the university's pool for practice. But the municipal pool was far too shallow, and the women divers suffered chipped teeth, scratches, and bruises.

But even with obvious athletic inequities and with the women's rights movement gaining momentum, feminists largely operated in entirely separate spheres from female athletes, coaches, and physical education instructors. "Many feminists," writes author Kelly Belanger, "saw . . . sports culture as . . . connected with all they found abhorrent in a patriarchal society that glorified competition, winning at all costs, and norms for masculinity rooted in 'misogyny, homophobia, and violence.'" Meanwhile, many female athletes, coaches, and PE teachers resisted association with feminism. Already viewed with great skepticism by men who resented the presence of women in "their" space, the last thing these women needed was another reason to be labeled a "man-hater" or to have their sexuality questioned.

But in 1970, a lawsuit concerned with ending discrimination against women in higher education, having absolutely nothing to do with sports, eventually led to the biggest game changer for women, and women's athletics, in American history.

It was a new law known as Title IX.

Bernice "Bunny" Sandler was a brilliant student, graduating with a psychology degree from Brooklyn College in 1948, a master's from City College of New York in 1950, and a doctor of education degree from the University of Maryland in 1969.[2] She had taught part-time at Maryland for seven years and had applied for

49

seven full-time faculty jobs there, and despite being highly qualified, she was turned down every time — all because of her gender. One time, her obituary noted, she was told she "came on too strong for a woman." Another time she was told the department didn't hire women because they missed too much work with sick children. Another time she was told she couldn't possibly be serious about her career; she was likely just a bored housewife wanting out of the house.

Sandler knew she wasn't the only one experiencing such discrimination. She gathered stories from scores of other women about the injustices they had experienced in higher education, collecting thousands of pages of documentation detailing how they had been denied jobs, graduate school admissions, scholarships, and other benefits because of their gender. With this information in hand, she filed a class-action lawsuit against every university in the country, alleging a pattern of discrimination against women in violation of federal law.

Sandler's advocacy led to Congressional interest in developing the language that became known as Title IX of the Education Amendments of 1972. She found Democratic supporters in the House of Representatives, including Martha Griffiths of Michigan, Edith Green of Oregon, and Patsy Mink of Hawaii, the first woman of color elected to Congress. In the Senate, Democrat Birch Bayh of Indiana led the charge, inspired by the experience of his wife, Marvella. She had been a straight-A high school student, class president, and president of Girls Nation. Yet when she applied to the University of Virginia, her application was rejected simply because of her gender.

The bias these advocates unearthed was so obvious and widespread that legislation prohibiting gender-based discrimination in education sailed through Congress with little opposition. Title IX, signed by Republican president Richard Nixon, declared that "no person in the United States shall, on the basis of sex, be excluded from participation in, be denied the benefits of, or be subjected to discrimination under any education program or activity receiving federal financial assistance."

Representative Patsy Mink of Hawaii, the first woman of color elected to the US Congress, was one of the strongest advocates for the passage of Title IX. (Library of Congress)

Because schools at all levels (and, by extension, their athletic departments) received federal money, these thirty-seven words were to change athletics history in the United States. But since the legislation made no specific mention of sports, most people in the sports world initially paid little attention to it, believing it had more to do with ending admissions and hiring quotas or enacting sexual harassment policies. Even outside of athletics, the new law appeared insignificant compared to the Equal Rights Amendment.

The ERA, which had first been proposed as an amendment to the Constitution in 1923 and more recently had been the focus of Betty Friedan and NOW, extended far beyond education into every aspect of American life, declaring that "equality of rights under the law shall not be denied or abridged by the United States or by any state on account of sex." The ERA had advanced through Congress with bipartisan support between 1970 and 1972, but it needed ratification by thirty-eight state legislatures to become law. Ratification seemed but a formality, a "kind of feel-good celebration of women's progress and the promise of even better things to come," wrote author Gail Collins. But while ERA opponents succeeded in blocking its ratification, Title IX became the law of the land when President Nixon signed it on June 23, 1972.

Upon Nixon's signature, the Department of Health, Education, and Welfare (HEW) still needed to solicit public comments and issue final recommendations on how — and when — the new law would be enforced. It was during this information-gathering period that an article in the June 11, 1973, issue of *Sports Illustrated* detailed the lousy status of sports for girls and women, focusing attention on Title IX's potential impact on athletics. In *The Feminine Mystique,* Betty Friedan had made the bold claim that day-to-day life in America was based on the lie of male superiority; in this article, titled "Programmed to Be a Loser," Bil Gilbert and Nancy Williamson exposed the big lie in American sports, eviscerating conventional wisdom by claiming it was not *women's* frailty that limited their athletic opportunities, but men's.

"The arguments most often used to justify discrimination against women in sports — that athletics are bad for their health and femininity, that women are not skillful enough or interested in playing games — have on the surface a nice paternalistic, even altruistic, quality," they wrote. "Recent studies indicate such assumptions are incorrect and self-serving nonsense. It simply happens to be in the best interest of the male athletic establishment to maintain the existing situation. Anything beyond token sexual equality in athletics represents a formidable threat to male pride and power."

Gilbert and Williamson pointed out that the large budgets for boys' and men's athletics were only possible because half the population — women — had been excluded from participating in sports, even though most school funding came from tax dollars paid by both men and women.

In the article, proponents and critics of Title IX legislation argued about the changes a new way of funding athletics might require. Some on both sides favored strict equality: if a school had a football team, men and women should be able to try out for it (football coaches and athletic directors especially liked this approach, because they figured no women would make the team). Another model called for more of a "separate but equal" philosophy, a dirty phrase to civil rights advocates but an approach that appeared most advantageous to women even for staunch women's rights activists. Funds should be divided equitably (if not equally) between the sexes, even if that meant football for boys and field hockey or soccer for girls.

James Bergene, a high school principal in Montana, spoke out strongly in favor of increased funding for girls' sports. "If athletics have a place in education, then they are as important for girls as boys," he said. "Any principal who is willing to support a strong boys' athletic program and is content to have a weak girls' one has no business calling himself an educator."

Dr. Kathryn Clarenbach, a professor at the University of Wisconsin, went further, arguing that providing girls greater access to athletics would have a far-reaching impact on American society. "By working toward some balance in the realm of physical activity, we may indeed begin to achieve a more wholesome, democratic balance in all phases of our life."

In response to the *Sports Illustrated* article, parents and students mailed a barrage of letters to HEW's offices complaining about inequitable funding for girls' athletics at their schools. Soon, HEW attorneys announced that athletic programs at all levels would be subject to Title IX. Schools would not be required to provide equal funding for men's and women's sports, but to provide equally consequential opportunities for both men and women. "The goal of the regulation in the area of competitive athletics is to secure equal opportunity for males and females," HEW acknowledged, "while allowing schools and colleges flexibility in determining how best to provide such opportunity."

Advocates for women's sports understood the opportunity this presented, and so did the many powerful opponents of Title IX. College football coaches, athletic directors, and the NCAA itself, which spent $300,000 lobbying against the legislation and purposely misrepresented its intent, resented the idea of sharing money, facilities, and other resources more equitably with women. They had benefited from a rigged system for so long that they perceived anything approaching fairness as unjust.

"It would really put us in a financial bind," complained BYU athletic director Stan Watts, "if we were required to give equal opportunities to women." NCAA executive director Walter Byers said Title IX foreshadowed "the possible doom of intercollegiate sports." University of Maryland athletic director Jim Kehoe attached no such qualifiers, calling the new law ill-advised, unrealistic, impractical, and irrational, claiming it would bring about chaos that would lead directly to "the ruination of college athletics."

The complaints from men failed to change any minds at HEW, which viewed the doomsday predictions as absurd. "We can't allow any school to discriminate against members of minorities or against women or against men for the reason that it costs too much to not discriminate," said HEW attorney Gwen Gregory. "The regulations will call for equal opportunity. But that doesn't mean equal expenditures as the NCAA would have everyone believe . . . We're not interested in getting a hundred women out for football, but we are interested when the women's track team has to run through the neighbor-hoods because the men's team is using the track."

Three months after the landmark *Sports Illustrated* article ignited public discussion of women's athletics, the subject fully caught fire. In an exhibition tennis match on September 20 at the Houston Astrodome, the world's best female player, Billie Jean King, was set to take on Bobby Riggs, a washed-up, fifty-five-year-old former pro who had taken on the persona of the ultimate male chauvinist, yapping that women "belong in the bedroom and the kitchen, in that order." Though King was at the top of her game — she'd been named *Sports Illustrated*'s first Sportswoman of the Year in 1972 — and Riggs was well past his prime, Americans were fascinated to see whether a woman could compete with, let alone beat, a man in an athletic contest. Riggs had already soundly defeated the world's second-ranked woman, Margaret Court, in a May match dubbed the Mother's Day Massacre, an infuriating defeat for women.

King knew what it felt like to be embarrassed on the tennis court, and she was also the most prominent athlete to embrace the feminist cause. As an eleven-year-old, she had proudly worn a new pair of shorts her mom had sewn for her to compete in a tennis tournament. When officials told her she couldn't join the other kids for a group photo because she wasn't wearing a tennis skirt or dress, she felt a burning humiliation. By the time she was ready for college, she had already gained international attention by winning the Wimbledon doubles championship, yet she had to pay her way through Los Angeles State College by working as a playground attendant. There were no athletic scholarships for female tennis players in the early 1960s. A decade later, when she discovered that the 1970 Pacific Southwest Open would pay its men's champion $12,500 and its women's champ just $1,500, King and other players boycotted the tournament and quickly organized another, the first step in creating a separate professional tennis circuit — sponsored by a cigarette brand, Virginia Slims — for women.

When they were escorted onto the Astrodome court — King carried on an Egyptian-style cart by topless men and Riggs in a rickshaw pulled by female models — Riggs was just there to have fun and make some money; King felt the weight of the women's rights movement on her shoulders, believing it would "set the movement back fifty years" if she lost. This was must-see TV. In Wisconsin, Jane Burns had just been fitted for a full-body brace, meant to treat her scoliosis. She hurried home to watch the match. In Tennessee, twenty-one-year-old college basketball player Pat Head sat as close as she could to the TV set, not wanting to miss a thing. Burns and Head joined an estimated 90 million worldwide television viewers; anticipating the massive interest in the spectacle, ABC had paid $750,000 for the broadcast rights at a time when NBC paid only $50,000 for the right to air Wimbledon.

King won the match in straight sets, topping Riggs 6–4, 6–3, 6–3. In Tennessee, Head screamed, "Yes!" at the top of her lungs when the match was over, ecstatic to have witnessed "the grand-

Tennis star Billie Jean King is carried onto the court at the Houston Astrodome on September 20, 1973, for her historic match against Bobby Riggs. King's victory in the "Battle of the Sexes" was one of the first visible examples of the connections between athletics and the women's liberation movement. (Associated Press)

est example of competitive ferocity and performance under pressure I'd ever seen from a woman."

Impressed by King's strength, courage, and cool demeanor, Head was profoundly influenced by the outcome of the match. Growing up in the rural South, she'd encountered plenty of sexism and inequality. But she never felt an affinity with feminist protestors — carrying a sign wasn't her style, and she didn't think it was effective, anyway. In this regard, she had more in common with King than she might have understood. Though she advocated for Title IX and later became a champion for a range of women's rights issues, at the time, King believed that her performance on the tennis court was the most valuable statement she could make. "Tennis helps the women's movement just by *doing*," she said. "If people see us out there every day, that changes people's minds, not *talking* about it."[3] In King's prowess, Head saw an approach to gender equity that appealed to her, one that would drive her to earn a spot on the 1976 Olympic basketball team and later to become the most successful coach in basketball history. "Billie Jean, now there was an influential force," she wrote decades later. "Was there anything more equalizing than her sheer toughness, her combination of smarts and muscle? I wanted to influence, and to change. But there was only one way I could see that changed things: winning. You changed things for women by winning."[4]

HEAD'S START

7

Pat Head sat nervously on a Pan Am jet bound for a basketball tournament in Moscow. As elegant stewardesses in baby-blue pillbox hats and heels strolled the aisles, Pat fidgeted in her seat, imagining what might go wrong on her first trip out of the country. Would she get trapped behind the Iron Curtain? Would she ever make it back to her family in Tennessee?

Leaving home had stirred unusual emotions in Pat, who had just finished her junior year at the University of Tennessee at Martin, a small West Tennessee branch of the main UT campus. Her father, Richard, rarely spoke, never hugged his kids, never showed any affection. But before she left on this trip, she felt the need to tell her dad that she loved him. With a lump in her throat, she went in for an awkward hug and muttered something close to those words. He grunted. Pat never cried — her older brothers would not allow it under any circumstances — but she wept all the way to the airport in Nashville.

Tense as she was, this journey to the 1973 World University Games was all part of the transformation of a young woman for whom the game of basketball made a world of difference. A Tennessee farm kid once picked on for her awkward height, unstylish clothes, and country grammar, she had earned the right to represent the United States in the biggest international tournament in which any American women's basketball team had ever played, an important first step in building a program capable of competing in the 1976 Olympics. Her life had not been easy, but the hardships, she believed, had prepared her for this moment. She was a competitor, and basketball gave her purpose.

Pat had grown up on a farm forty miles west of Nashville, learning to drive a tractor by age seven, milking cows twice a day, and riding horses in the rodeo.[1] She and her three brothers arm-wrestled and fought constantly — throwing dinner rolls, hedge clippers, baseball bats, and butcher knives at each other, frequently drawing blood.

Her father, who stood six foot five, physically abused his children. When she was five, Pat's brothers had taught her a silly song about farting. She sang it at the dinner table one night and Richard exploded, smacking her with the back of his hand and flipping her head over heels to the floor. As she grew older, Pat considered her fearsome father a "towering, unsmiling patriarch," a man who would whip disobedient kids with a belt, a switch, a tobacco stick, whatever was close by. When he entered a room, everyone's stomachs clenched; everyone stopped talking.

For Richard and for Pat's mom, Hazel, life was all about work. There was no distinction between work and "hard work" — it was all the same. There were no short-cuts on the farm; you were done working when the work was done. Cows and crops knew nothing of weekends, summer vacations, birthdays, or bad weather. Pat did as she was told, but she resented it. It felt like torture.

Not that the distribution of work was equal. Pat noticed that while her father and brothers never helped around the house, her mother milked the cows, tended to the garden, made beds, mowed the lawn, cooked dinner, and washed clothes. "Looking back on it," she recalled, "I don't think anyone in the family worked as hard as my mother or got less credit for it."

The chauvinism was especially glaring at the dinner table. Whenever one of the boys had finished a glass of iced tea, they would hold up the cup and shake it, the sound of rattling ice a summons for Pat or her mother to refill their cups. The "insistent, unthinking, and demanding" behavior began to grate on Pat, until finally one day she snapped, "Get it yourself!"

If there was one source of joy on the Head farm, it was in the hayloft, where Richard had shown a rare glimpse of love for his children by building them a basketball court complete with wooden backboards and lights strung by a rope so they could play deep into the night. Needing a fourth player for a game of two-on-two, Pat's older brothers included her, and they cut her no slack. Their games were full of hard knees, clenched fists, and sharp elbows; firm boxouts; and blocked shots. But Pat held her own. It didn't hurt that she had grown to five foot nine by the time she was in third grade and developed muscles to match, able to carry a hundred-pound sack of feed in one arm and a sixty-pound bag of dog food in the other. Pat hated to lose so much that she simply would not allow it to happen, even if it took all night up in that barn loft, ten feet above the hay bales below. "We'd play until I was on a winning side," she said, "because I had no intention of going to bed in second place."

The rough-and-tumble games suited Pat's rebellious style as a teenager. Though she never missed a day of school from kindergarten through high school, she smoked cigarettes, drank beer, played cards, and drove way too fast down drag strips and country roads. Turning corners on two wheels, she would turn to her friends and smile: "Are you skeered?!"

But it was on the basketball court where she felt the most freedom. She played for the eighth-grade team as a third grader, growing into the kind of player who lived for the sound of sneakers on wood, the smell of sweat, and the feel of the ball in her hands. The girls played by the old six-player rules — three on one side of the court, three on the other, a system that made no sense to Pat. "Gym teachers in those days didn't believe girls were capable of running full court," she once wrote. "We were capable of heavy farmwork, and of absorbing whippings, but for some reason, they didn't think we could run ninety-four feet without getting the vapors and passing out, or damaging our ovaries." Still, for a girl so tall and skinny her friends nicknamed her "Bone," these basketball games gave her a welcome sensation of confidence. "You gain such a sense of command over your own arms and legs that it can almost feel like flying, and you begin to crave that sensation daily," she wrote. "Everything else is just an interruption until you can return to it. That was me. I played, quite literally, in my sleep."

Basketball in her dreams? Indeed. At her high school? Not a chance; her school didn't offer a team for girls. And this is where Richard Head demonstrated another measure of love for his daughter. He announced that the family would move to an old clapboard house six miles across the county line in Henrietta, just so Pat could attend Cheatham County Central High School in Ashland City, where they had a girls' basketball team. "The best, most valuable thing my father gave me," she recalled, "was an equal opportunity."

Pat excelled on the team at Cheatham County High. She loved the beauty and movement of the game and the fact that that beauty emerged only through "hard work, sweat, and pain," the same elements that fueled the rest of her existence. She was unafraid of the blunt lessons the game revealed. Don't run away from your deficiencies, she believed; run toward them. Take ownership of self-improvement. Keep striving even in the face of potential failure.

These were the valuable lessons basketball taught Pat Head, but as she approached high school graduation, there were few opportunities for her to continue playing in college. In the state of Tennessee, she knew of only two schools that offered varsity women's basketball, Belmont College in Nashville and UT Martin, and neither provided athletic scholarships. She had played ball up in that hayloft just like her brothers, had starred in high school just as they had, but Austin Peay State gave Tommy and Kenneth full athletic scholarships, and nobody gave her a dime.

UT Martin was just an unassuming country school in the middle of nowhere — 135 miles northeast of Memphis, 150 miles west of Nashville — but to Pat, it felt like the most sophisticated place in the world. The girls wore makeup and miniskirts and talked with refined Southern drawls. All the traits that had gained her respect back home — her physical strength and her skills on the farm — were looked down on here. Girls made fun of her unstylish clothes with hemlines drooping below her knees, her hick accent, and her naivete, the way she called her suitcase a "soup case" and dressed in her dorm room closet out of modesty.

"I fought a running battle with embarrassment and insecurity every day," she recalled. "But I learned that overcoming fear is the most broadening thing in the world, if you make yourself do it."

She asked her sorority sisters to help her pick out clothes, to help her improve her grammar. She enrolled in speech classes, forced herself to make friends, gained confidence.

Even as she overcame her insecurities as a woman on campus, she never lacked for confidence on the basketball court. The program at Martin was hardly elite — it had just been elevated from intramural status a year before she arrived — but it provided a platform for her to excel. There were no real basketball uniforms; players just sewed their own numbers on PE jerseys. Pat couldn't sew, so she fastened her numbers with safety pins. Players washed cars and held bake sales to raise money for travel expenses, which were minimal, anyway. The team drove to road games in two station wagons, ate homemade bologna sandwiches, and brought sleeping bags so they could spend the night on their opponents' gym

Before becoming the winningest coach in the history of women's basketball, Pat Head played at the University of Tennessee at Martin in the pre–Title IX era of nearly nonexistent support for women's athletics. (UT Martin Athletics)

74

floors to save the cost of hotels.

At first, Head thought little about the miserable support for her team and the disparity with the men's. But her attitude changed after the women won a Tennessee state championship, when the only reward the athletic department provided was an invitation to the men's team's banquet. "While we went 16–3, the guys had gone 3–20," she later wrote. "Yet we sat for hours, watching guys receive plaques and awards and congratulations for their efforts. Finally, they paused the proceedings to briefly introduce us. That was our recognition; we got to stand up for a minute."

Head and her teammates may have gone largely unrecognized by their own university, but her skills on the basketball court did not go unnoticed in the larger world of women's basketball. After excelling in a tournament in Boone, North Carolina, she drew the attention of basketball officials putting together tryouts in the summer of 1972 for the team that would compete at the 1973 World University Games in the Soviet Union.[2] She was one of just sixty-eight women invited to participate. Her coach, Nadine Gearin, drove her to tryouts in Fairfield, Iowa, at her own expense.

All the way from Tennessee to Iowa, Head had just one thought on her mind. "I burned," she wrote, "to be on the team." She wasn't the best shooter or the most gifted athlete at the camp, but nobody worked harder or was more competitive — she dove for loose balls, crashed the boards for rebounds, and played skin-tight defense. By the end of tryouts, she was one of twelve players invited to a second camp in Boston the following summer, where she was selected for the team and sent to Moscow.

Now she sat on that Pan Am plane, ready to make history — for herself, and for women.

TIME TRAVELERS

8

Twelve players, two coaches, and a team manager arrived in Moscow ready to make history at the 1973 World University Games. But first they needed a smaller victory — permission to leave their dormitory at Moscow State University.

Identification badges for the Americans had mysteriously gone missing, so the US delegation was confined to the dormitory — four to a room — for two days. Some players were even denied entry to the dining hall. The stone building was dark and cavernous, so imposing that Marsha Mann, a center from the University of North Carolina, imagined it as the home of the "Wicked Witch of the West."[1] Those who could eat weren't too thrilled with the Russian food, mostly vats of borscht and big bowls of broth with fish heads floating on the surface. They ate rolls and potatoes instead, along with ice cream and small packs of vanilla wafers.

The extended time together in the dorm presented a welcome opportunity for the American players to bond. They'd only been together for the monthlong training camp in Boston and were still getting to know one another. Cherri Rapp was the team leader, the captain and most experienced player. A three-time All-American and two-time AAU national champion at Wayland Baptist College, where she graduated number one in her class with a degree in math, Rapp had toured internationally with the US national team since 1969.

Juliene Simpson was the emerging leader, a fireplug of a point guard who walked and talked with a New Jersey swagger. Growing up Catholic, she had once dreamed of becoming a nun. But she told her mom her knees couldn't handle both praying and basketball — and she chose hoops. For college, she picked John F. Kennedy College in tiny Wahoo, Nebraska, in part because of the team's full slate of basketball games and in part because of the sparkling swimming pool and other amenities featured in a color brochure.[2] It wasn't until she arrived in Wahoo, a town with one blinking stoplight and a corner store that sold bib overalls, that she realized none of the photos were of things actually on campus. But she loved the school anyway and won two AAU titles.

Nancy Dunkle had grown up in Southern California, attracted to basketball more for the joy it brought her in the moment than for any long-term opportunities the game might provide. She envisioned a future in which she learned plumbing skills, lived on a farm, or worked on a yacht or as a forest ranger — something that gave her independence and the freedom not to depend on anyone else to solve her problems.

Two days in the dormitory allowed the women to get to know each other better than ever. And when their ID badges appeared, the players were finally able to leave the hotel and go sightseeing in Moscow, descending long escalators to the subway to visit Red Square and Lenin's

After winning two national championships at Wayland Baptist College, Cherri Rapp played on the US national team for seven years and captained the gold-medal-winning Pan American Games team in 1975. (Cherri Rapp)

Tomb along with their Russian guide and translator, Slava.

Head dubbed her teammate Theresa Shank "Pennsylvania" because she hailed from Philadelphia's Immaculata College, while Shank called Head "Tennessee." Brenda Moeller, a five-foot-ten center from Wayland Baptist College in West Texas, loved peering out the windows of the team bus and observing people on the street — old women sweeping sidewalks with straw brooms, wearing clothes that would have been twenty years out of style in America. "Everyone was very friendly," she said, "but it was like stepping back in time."

The Boston tryout camp where the team had been formed was historic. It was the first time an American women's basketball team had been assembled to play in the World University Games, an international event established in 1959 for college students.

The camp took place at Northeastern University, led by head coach Jill Upton of Mississippi State College for Women (nicknamed "The W") and assistant Billie Moore of Cal State Fullerton (who would not become head coach of the national team until 1976). Jeanne Rowlands, the women's basketball coach at Northeastern, served as the team manager, handling administrative details so Upton and Moore could keep their focus on the court. Upton, thirty-three, was a product of the juggernaut team at Nashville Business College, where she had twice earned All-American honors as a player. As a coach, she'd built a powerhouse at The W, a small school in Columbus, Mississippi, with an enrollment of less than three thousand. The college offered no basketball scholarships and didn't even have a regulation-sized court, making it all the more remarkable that Upton led the Blues to a national championship in 1971.

Moore may have been the assistant coach, but she wasted no time asserting herself running practices. Watching the players lumber up and down the court during the team's first workout, she turned to Upton and told her that the players needed to get in better condition. In a hurry.

"I had this vision of what we needed to be," Moore recalled, "and of course I was young and a maniac. I probably came pretty close to killing the players in Boston. I always thought we should be in the best shape. Somebody could be better than we were, but they shouldn't be in better shape."

Upton, who had played against the Soviets during their US tour in 1961, agreed with Moore's assessment. She knew international basketball was rougher than anything her players had ever experienced. She told Moore to keep the pressure up in practice, make the games seem easy compared to the workouts — three practices a day, two hours each.

"Billie was the most demanding person I'd met since my father," Head recalled. "She had a very alive coaching style; loquacious and high energy, she talked and gestured with her hands, which made her short blond hair bounce up and down. If you didn't do something exactly right, she snapped, 'Again.' And then she'd stalk down the court after you, with her hair flopping. If you didn't get it right again, you ran. And ran. And ran."

As the final practice of each day drew to a close, Moore would gather the players at the free throw line. Every woman, already exhausted, took two free throws. "You make the two shots, I'll see you tomorrow," Moore would say. "You miss one shot, start running. You miss the two shots, you really start running."

At one point, the team's trainers told Moore to back off. She was pushing the players too hard; their knees were aching. Moore obliged — to an extent. If the hardwood court was hard on the players' legs, they'd run somewhere else. "She put us in a swimming pool and she made us run under water," Head recalled. "We spent so much time in the pool we told her, 'We're going to be able to qualify as a water polo team.'"

Moeller said that by the end of camp, she was in the best shape of her life. But she was so sore she asked herself a question every night at bedtime, one that had no correct answer: Jump in bed and have her whole body hurt at once, or creep in and hurt little by little?

Head had never been pushed this hard on the basketball court, and she loved every minute of it. Moore's ability to lead this group of women with "no discernible traces of fear or self-consciousness" fascinated her. "She was forceful, uncompromising, strong voiced, and she didn't seem to think she had to demand less of us just because we were women," Head recalled. "If anything, she suggested that

84

she intended to demand *more* from us because we were women."

By the end of the Boston workouts, the team had rounded into shape. Still, Upton knew her players were about to face the best competition any of them had ever seen. The World University Games, she told Boston sportswriter Leigh Montville, would be the "biggest basketball games any team of women from the United States ever has played."

Rain fell on Central Lenin Stadium on August 15, 1973, as four thousand athletes from seventy-two countries paraded into the stadium for the opening ceremony, presided over by Soviet leader Leonid Brezhnev. More than ninety thousand fans packed the stadium for the start of what was known as the Little Olympics, a warm-up for the 1980 Olympic Games, which Moscow had bid on and was expected to win. The crowd cheered wildly for the Soviet delegation and teams from other Eastern Bloc countries, but they also gave a loud ovation to the Americans. When the Israeli team marched in, however, many in the crowd loudly jeered the Jewish athletes, whistling and shouting epithets while Soviet police officers ripped down Israeli flags and good luck signs held aloft by Russian Jews in the grandstand. It was an ugly display of anti-Semitism made more shocking given recent history. These World University Games marked the first international appearance by an Israeli team since the 1972 Olympics in Munich, where terrorists killed eleven Israeli athletes and coaches.[3]

When the American women marched in wearing their ragtag uniforms — blue men's windbreakers and white golf skirts — team manager Jeanne Rowlands stifled a laugh. She recalled how the team had not been provided shoes until Dexter Shoe Company came through with a donation a week before the team left Boston — bulbous white bucks that reminded her of the shoes worn by the popular but straitlaced singer Pat Boone. "They were the biggest shoes I had ever seen," she recalled. "It looked as though we were wearing the boxes."

The scene was colorful, loud, and crowded with humanity. It was unlike anything Head had ever experienced before, and she felt overwhelmed by the sights and sounds. Again, she wondered if she'd make it home alive.

Head had more to fear on the basketball court than she did from the unfamiliar surroundings in Moscow. The United States had been a nonfactor in recent international women's basketball, failing to medal in the four previous FIBA World Championships dating back to 1959, including a last-place (eleventh) finish at the 1967 World Championships in Prague. At that tournament, the American women won just one game and lost six, and were outscored by an average of 16 points per game. While American women's basketball was only just beginning to emerge from the six-player game meant to protect women's supposedly fragile bodies, the international game was rough by contrast. Carla Lowry, who competed on American teams internationally in the 1950s and '60s, joked that the best way to prepare for these tournaments was to fill tires with concrete and swing them into players as they dribbled toward the basket.

The first opponent for the Americans might as well have been carrying those cement-filled tires onto the court at Moscow's Palace of Sports. It was the team from the host country, the Soviet Union, a team that was tall, strong, fast, and highly motivated.

Coach Lidia Alexeeva's team hadn't lost a game in international play in five years. Her center, Uljana Semjonova, stood a towering seven feet two inches tall and could score at will.

At a time when the United States and the Soviet Union were locked in a bitter Cold War feud, when every aspect of life in each country was held up to the world as an indication of the superiority of either capitalism or communism, Soviet women's basketball stood head and shoulders above the rest.

BIG RED MACHINE

9

For decades after the Communist revolution of 1917, the Soviet Union refused to participate in the Olympic Games, viewing the entire enterprise as a plaything of imperialist European aristocrats. When the USSR took over the Baltic states of Lithuania, Latvia, and Estonia during World War II, Soviet leaders viewed sports administrators in those countries as suspicious, in one case arresting two Estonian Olympic officials and executing them.

But beginning in the 1950s, athletic venues became Cold War battlefields. A popular billboard in the USSR spelled out the new attitude: ALL WORLD RECORDS MUST BE TAKEN BY SOVIET ATHLETES. In 1952, the Soviets made their Olympic debut in Helsinki, faring quite well in men's basketball: they won six of eight games and earned a silver medal, with their only two losses coming against the gold-medal-winning United States. While the Americans had a seven-foot-tall player and three others who were six foot eight or taller, the Soviets' tallest player was just six foot two. Coming out of Helsinki, Soviet basketball officials believed the only thing preventing them from competing for a gold in the next Olympics was height. They went looking for tall teenagers wherever they could find them, scouting on playgrounds and schoolyards and enrolling tall players in Soviet sports academies. The Soviet men took silver again in 1956, 1960, and 1964, bronze in 1968, and finally upset the US to win gold in Munich in 1972, in the most controversial basketball game in American Olympic history.[1]

Ironically, given the Soviets' initial hostility to Baltic sports officials, they relied heavily on basketball talent from the region, especially in Lithuania and Latvia, where the game had gained its earliest foothold. Lithuania had won European championships in 1937 and 1939 after the game was popularized there by Frank Lubin, a Lithuanian American member of the first US men's Olympic basketball team in 1936.

The search for height wasn't limited to just the Russian men's teams. Spotting an opportunity to quickly dominate in women's basketball, a sport the US did not yet take seriously internationally, Soviet sports officials set out to assemble a powerhouse team. In 1965, coaches from the most successful girls' club team in Latvia, TTT Riga, were out driving the countryside, looking for tall young women to join their program. They found Uljana Semjonova, a thirteen-year-old who had already grown to six foot two and would grow to seven feet by the 1973 World University Games.

Semjonova was an unstoppable force in international women's basketball. She was so much taller than opposing players that any time she received the ball near the basket she was virtually guaranteed to score. And she was far from the only talented player on the Soviet national team. Most American observers considered Soviet captain Nadezhda Zakharova to be the best guard in the world.[2]

Head coach Alexeeva believed the best approach in coaching women was to do what the men did — push the ball on the break, make quick cuts and sharp passes, play stifling defense, and find big, tough players who could score and rebound on the inside. From an American perspective, her teams were ahead of their time, a vision of what was to come in the US decades later. And they were practically unbeatable in international tournaments, not just winning games but winning them by outrageous margins.

When the Soviets and Americans faced off in the first game of the tournament in Moscow, it wasn't the first time they'd met. American college and AAU teams had played exhibition games in the Soviet Union dating back to 1958 (the Russian press dubbed Nera White a "dangerous sharpshooter"), and the Soviets returned the favor in '59, touring the US to take on teams such as Wayland Baptist. While American sportswriters were impressed by the Russian women's defensive prowess and relentless drives to the basket, they couldn't resist succumbing to the sexist tropes that defined their coverage of women's sports. *Sports Illustrated* dubbed the "Russian gals . . . fresh-faced charmer[s] . . . who looked so sweet and pleasant" and were a "visual treat," simultaneously undercutting the Soviets' basketball abilities and taking a sexist jab at their American counterparts.

Stepping onto the floor for the first game in Moscow, Pat Head took one look at the towering Semjonova and knew she was in for a long night. No "charming treat" awaited. "I knew I had to figure out a way to box her out," she said, "or I'd be sitting on the bench with the coaches." Brenda Moeller felt the same way, realizing her only hope was to try to force the seven-footer as far away from the basket as possible. "She could practically touch the rim just standing there," Moeller recalled. Equally impressive were Zakharova and the other Soviet guards, women who controlled the pace of the game from the opening tip. "They were a well-oiled machine," Moeller said. "Anything you'd do to change things up, they had an answer for. You could tell they had played together for a long time."

Watching from the bench, American assistant coach Billie Moore observed the Soviets for the first time and thought back to her high school days in Kansas, when her dad would drive her to St. Joseph, Missouri, to watch elite teams such as Nashville Business College and Wayland Baptist compete in the Amateur Athletic Union national tournament. She thought those teams were good, but the Russian women were the best she'd ever seen.

"It was eye-opening," Moore recalled nearly fifty years later. "It told me something about how women could play. They were inspiring. It told us, if you want to compete internationally, here's where the bar is. They did everything well. They had size at every position. They checked every box." And they beat the US easily, 92–43. After this opening defeat, the Americans knew that if they wanted another crack at the Soviets, or a shot to earn a medal, they would have to win their next two games just to stay alive in the tournament.

One of Moore's responsibilities as Upton's assistant was to scout upcoming opponents. In these days before coaches could watch film to break down other teams' tendencies, scouting reports could only be prepared by watching games in person. With a game against Mexico coming up third, Moore attended their game against the Soviet Union to observe the Mexican players and their style of play.

She learned nothing. The Soviets dominated the game so thoroughly she left with a blank notepad. All that stood out was the fact that Semjonova came back from the locker room at halftime showered and dressed in her street clothes. It was the ultimate flex by Coach Alexeeva: her team was so far ahead, she didn't even need her star in uniform. Moore made a mental note: if the Americans played the Soviets again, their goal would be to force Semjonova to keep her uniform on the entire game.

After beating France 54–43 and slipping past Mexico 52–47, the US advanced out of round-robin play. But early in their next game, against Bulgaria, Pat Head took a hard elbow to the face, dislocating her jaw. The blow hurt so badly she felt like her skull had been cracked in half; her face hurt every time she blinked her eyes. Officials rushed her to an ambulance, bouncing through the dark streets of Moscow in search of a doctor who could treat her on a Sunday night, jolts of pain shooting through her body with every bump. Unable to find an open clinic, the ambulance dropped her off at the host university, where a team doctor reset her jaw with his hands. She was unable to eat or speak much of the rest of the trip, losing fifteen pounds and emerging with an offset jaw that became one of her trademark physical features. Still, after beating Romania 54–47, the US advanced to the medal round. The only thing standing between them and a rematch with the Soviet Union for the gold medal was a semifinal game against Cuba.

The Cubans entered the game without a loss in the tournament and were favored to advance, but American team captain Cherri Rapp dominated the game with 16 points, and scrappy point guard Juliene Simpson led a second-half comeback with

12 points and several key rebounds to earn the US a 59–55 upset victory. After the game, Upton told reporters she was proud of her team's fifth straight win — and admitted the run would likely come to an end in the gold medal game against the Soviets, who'd advanced with an easy 98–60 drubbing of South Korea — the Koreans had no players taller than five foot ten, and Semjonova dominated with 45 points. "We are a more experienced and poised team now," Upton said. "We may not win, but the Russians will know they've been in a fight."

Maybe, maybe not. The Soviets cruised to an 82–44 win over the US to collect the gold medal, but the Americans did take away a bit of a moral victory. Before the game, Moore had given the players one of the most pragmatic pep talks in history. The Soviets were the most flawless team she had ever seen. Competitive as she was, she still knew the USA had no chance to win. "I wanted to be honest with our players," she said. "I couldn't realistically say that if we did A, B, C, we'd win the game. So I just said to them, 'Let's be competitive enough that Semjonova has to stay dressed for the second half.'" When the Soviets emerged from their locker room after halftime and the Russian giant was still in uniform, the American bench erupted as if they had won the game. Moore understood that the ascension of US women's basketball would be a gradual process. This moment was an important step along the way.

After the game, the American players lined up to receive their silver medals. Theresa Shank inspected hers and was amused to see that her name was already inscribed on it, even though the game had just ended. "I'm thinking, 'Wow, I wonder if they knew who was going to win this game or not.'"

The event ended with closing ceremonies back at a rainy Lenin Stadium. Participants from each country were supposed to march in orderly lines around the track, but a group of British athletes broke through a phalanx of guards and began dancing in the middle of the field. Athletes from other countries followed, forming a long conga line that snaked its way through the Red Army band, with the Israeli athletes at the center of it all.

Pat Head received a hero's welcome when she returned to campus after the 1973 World University Games in Moscow. (UT Martin Athletics)

Pat Head had entered this stadium two weeks earlier, startled by the scene, afraid she might not make it home alive. Now she had a broken jaw, a silver medal, and a newfound, life-changing confidence.

Returning to the UT Martin campus, she noticed that people treated her with more respect. "Men looked at that silver medal like I'd come home from a war with a battle flag," she wrote. "The university administration even honored me on the field at halftime of a football game. Me, a woman. At a football game. The example was clear: that medal earned me a respect I couldn't have acquired in any other field."

Until this point, she was unsure how she felt about the movement for women's rights.

She was uncomfortable, she said, with the "tenor of complaint" she heard from many activists. But she shared similar goals. "I wanted to change things in the most solid, demonstrable way for young women like me, help broaden their lives and choices, through athletics," she wrote. "I wanted to help other women be . . . strong. If I had to sum up my feelings at the time, I'm not sure I could have. But the writer Nora Ephron would say it years later for me. 'Above all, be the heroine of your life, not the victim,' she said. That, right there, was the heart of my conviction."

FAIR GAMES

10

Ten young women from Montana arrived in Missouri by train. The girls, ages fifteen to nineteen, had come for the St. Louis World's Fair, also known as the Louisiana Purchase Exposition, a white man's celebration of his presumed "manifest destiny" to expand westward across the North American continent. The fair also included the Olympic Games as one of its attractions, with a dozen countries sending 651 athletes (645 of whom were men) to compete in sixteen sports — including just one official event, archery, for women.

The girls left the train station carrying heavy suitcases, for this was to be no quick visit; they would stay at the fair for six months, not to take in the sights, but to *be* one.

These teenage girls, led by captain Belle Johnson, were Native Americans from the Fort Shaw Indian Boarding School, and they were sent to St. Louis to join thousands of other Indigenous people from Asia, Africa, and the South Pacific to create a massively racist "human zoo." Fairgoers could stand behind fences and watch these "exotic" brown-skinned people from across the globe live in their "natural habitats," a monument to supposed white supremacy that positioned the displays as a living illustration of the progress of mankind.

When the girls reached the St. Louis fairgrounds, they set down their bags in the "Indian village," where members of fourteen tribes ate, slept, attended school, and entertained the four million people who visited these anthropological tableaux. The chief human attraction in this demeaning spectacle was the Apache freedom fighter Geronimo, a federal prisoner who would observe his

102

seventy-fifth birthday in the fairgrounds the day after the girls arrived. But there was another curious feature in the Indian village, and it was the reason Fort Shaw school superintendent Fred C. Campbell had sent these ten girls to Missouri: a basketball court. In their suitcases, these women packed traditional tribal clothing and crafts, school uniforms — and their basketball gear.[1]

Girls at Fort Shaw had played basketball since 1897 as part of the school's destructive mission to strip Native Americans of their language (students were required to speak only English), religion, and customs while indoctrinating them in white culture. Fort Shaw was just one of many such schools, a network of reeducation camps — notorious sites of physical, emotional, and sexual abuse — where many students were held against their will. With white Americans fascinated by the idea of Native American assimilation, leaders of Indian residential schools used their sports programs as public relations tools to show off their "successful" efforts. But while school administrators believed that teaching Native American children

A team of Native American women from the Fort Shaw Indian School traveled to St. Louis for the 1904 World's Fair. The women defeated the St. Louis All-Stars and were named "champions of the fair." (Picryl.com)

sports was an effective way to teach them to be white, many Native American students saw participation in athletics as an opportunity to create connections with other students, to find moments of peace outside the toxic confines of the school, and to assert their individuality and excellence.

104

Indigenous people from around the world, including these Native Americans, were put on display in the grossly racist "human zoo" at the 1904 World's Fair in St. Louis. One reason organizers wanted the Fort Shaw girls' basketball team at the fair was to demonstrate their assimilation into white culture in contrast to other Native Americans. (Picryl.com)

The Fort Shaw girls earned a reputation as one of the best teams in the West, winning barnstorming games against white girls and insisting on playing full-court — they would have none of the half-court rules. In addition to attending a "model school" during the fair and demonstrating their mastery of poetry, song, and literature, the girls were to show off their skills in two exhibition basketball games each week, as well as two crowning games against the St. Louis All-Stars, an undefeated group of white alumnae from the city's Central High School.

One of the purposes of the "human zoo" was to illustrate white supremacy in athletics. Not only could fairgoers gawk at the "natives" going about their daily routines, they could also watch them get beat in a series of athletic contests the Indigenous people had never heard of before — including the high jump, long jump, and shotput — which were designed to make them look like fools. Though their basketball games weren't officially part of the Anthropology Days schedule, which featured only male participants, the women from Fort Shaw understood the concept and refused to go along with the conceit. With Geronimo watching their games, they played to win.

The St. Louis All-Stars' coach, who had scouted the Fort Shaw girls' fair-grounds exhibition games for more than two months, brought his team to the Indian village on September 3 full of confidence for the first of the two scheduled games. But "to the great surprise of several hundred spectators," wrote the *St. Louis Post-Dispatch,* the Native American girls proved to be "more active, more accurate and cooler than their opponents," demolishing the All-Stars 24–2.

The teams were scheduled to play again a week later, but the All-Stars begged off, requesting a delay of several weeks to get their act together. But when they returned to the fair on the afternoon of October 8, they were soundly beaten yet again (17–6), and the Fort Shaw girls were named champions of the World's Fair. Since the Olympics also took place as part of the fair, this group of Native American women were the among the first to participate in — and win — an Olympic exhibition of basketball.[2]

A men's demonstration of the game also took place at the St. Louis World's Fair, won by a group of boys representing the Kansas City Athletic Club. One of the stars of that team was Forrest "Phog" Allen, who would go on to fame as the head coach of the University of Kansas Jayhawks. It was Allen, more than any other person on the planet, who worked hardest to see basketball added as an official Olympic sport for men, lobbying international Olympic officials throughout the 1920s and '30s. He finally succeeded when men's basketball first appeared on the Olympic program at the 1936 Olympics in Berlin.[3] James Naismith himself presented gold medals to the victorious Americans at those Nazi Olympics, and the US would win gold in every successive Olympics until they fell to the Soviets in 1972.[4]

It was the USSR, as an emerging basketball power in the 1950s, that first called on Olympic leaders to officially add women's basketball to the program as a medal sport, a half century after the Fort Shaw girls demonstrated the game in St. Louis. Their first attempt came during a June 1955 meeting of the International Olympic Committee in Paris, where the Soviets asked delegates to vote on adding women's competitions in volleyball, basketball, speed skating, and rowing, all of which were already open to male athletes. Rules required that two-thirds of the fifty IOC delegates — all of whom were men — vote in favor of a new sport for it to be added. With thirty-four votes needed, the Soviets' bid for gender equity failed spectacularly in each case; only four IOC members voted in favor of rowing and speed skating, five for volleyball, and ten for basketball.

The issue came up again at IOC meetings in 1965 and 1969, but again failed both times. Finally, at a 1970 IOC gathering in Munich, a motion was brought forth to launch women's basketball at the 1976 Olympics in Montreal with six teams (though there would be twelve for men). Inequitable as the proposal was, FIBA, the international basketball governing body, voted to accept this plan two years later in 1972. FIBA leaders also determined that the six-team women's Olympic field would be composed of the host nation (Canada), the top three finishers in the 1975 World Championships in Colombia, and two teams to be determined at a last-chance qualifying tournament.

As far as rollouts go, there couldn't have been less fanfare or more muddled communication about a historic addition to the Olympic Games. During the Boston workouts prior to the 1973 World University Games in Moscow, American coach Jill Upton told reporters she was skeptical. She'd heard rumors about women's basketball and the Olympics before, but nothing ever materialized. FIBA president R. William Jones arrived in Montreal in late August and was surprised to discover that local reporters had no idea women's basketball was being added to the slate — an embarrassing situation considering that Naismith, the game's inventor, had been born in Ontario and attended college in Montreal. The IOC was compelled to make a final announcement confirming the news during an October 1973 meeting in Varna, Bulgaria.

But finally the word was out, and it was time for administrators across the globe to

110

prepare — hiring national team coaches, assembling rosters — with an eye first on international qualifying tournaments in 1975. In the US, this responsibility fell on Mildred Barnes, a pioneering athlete, physical education instructor, and coach who was so steeped in the game's development that one might say she had written the book on women's basketball.

Literally.

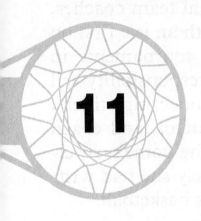

11   BIG GUNS

It was 1934 in upstate New York, and four-year-old Mildred Barnes struggled to breathe. Battling pneumonia, her lungs filled with fluid so quickly her parents took her to the hospital, worried she might not survive. Nurses told Mildred that a boy in another bed had the same illness. They wheeled in two big machines for each kid, asking Mildred and the boy to blow water from one tank to the other.

"And that's where I developed my competitiveness," Barnes recalled more than eighty-five years later. "I wasn't going to let that boy beat me."

When it came time for the United States to build a basketball team that could potentially compete in the 1976 Olympic Games, it turned to forty-five-year-old Mildred Barnes to lead the way. As an accomplished former multisport athlete and current head coach at Central Missouri State University, she was one of the most respected administrators in all of women's athletics. It would be her job to hire coaches and develop a process to select players to represent the US, first for the World Championships and Pan American Games in 1975 and then, should the team qualify, for the Olympics in Montreal.

Barnes's family moved from the Albany, New York, area to Pittsfield, Massachusetts, in the 1940s, when she was in junior high. Though her school only offered intramural sports for girls, she was the type of kid who always had a ball in her hands, and her parents fully supported her athletic interests. One time in high school, she learned of an AAU basketball tournament taking place in town. She put together a team of friends from school, but organizers refused to let them in, claiming they weren't old enough to compete. But when another team dropped out of the tournament, "they came begging for us to play," Barnes recalled. "And then we won the tournament."

Barnes attended Sargent College at Boston University, an esteemed health and physical education school. Though Sargent offered no varsity sports for women, Barnes again put together a basketball team for an AAU tournament — and won it. She played field hockey and lacrosse, too, lugging her sticks through subways and trolleys to the fields at Wellesley College just to play — earning All-American honors for twelve consecutive years and a spot on the US national lacrosse team. She also competed nationally in tennis and badminton, and was drafted by a professional women's baseball team.

Barnes stayed in shape by jogging — at a time when hardly anyone else did. For local police officers, the sight of a woman running down the street in the late 1940s and early '50s was so alarming that cops interrupted her runs on at least three occasions to see if she was OK. "They thought I was crazy," she recalled.

As a part-time student teacher at two schools in the Boston area, Barnes coached baseball at an elementary school, and tennis, softball, and field hockey at a high school where she eventually accepted a full-time job teaching physical education. She loved attending Celtics games at Boston Garden and Red Sox games at Fenway Park, and she treasured an autographed photo of the legendary slugger Ted Williams. One day during her lunch period at Winchester High, she was shooting hoops by herself when three guys showed up to play. When they asked if she wanted to join them, she realized that two of the men were Celtics players Bill Sharman (a future Hall of Famer) and Jim Loscutoff, getting in a preseason workout before training camp opened. Barnes joined them for a game of two-on-two, teaming up with Sharman. "He set picks for me, and I just loved it," Barnes recalled. "When I took one shot, I took several. One time I faked Loscutoff out of his shoes. He couldn't believe it."

After earning her master's and doctorate degrees, Barnes accepted a job at the University of Iowa in 1966, where she taught PE, introduced the sport of lacrosse (building the goals herself out of PVC pipe), and launched the women's basketball program. With no budget and no scholarships, players paid for everything on their own — tuition, housing, and uniforms — and without a conference to compete in, they played against whoever they could find. When her team qualified for a national tournament, Barnes asked the men's basketball coach if he had any old warm-up suits her players could borrow. He obliged, but the black-and-yellow suits were enormous. "We had to turn up the cuffs on the shirts and pants," Barnes recalled, "but at least we had warm-ups."

Barnes was amazed by the popularity of the Iowa high school girls' basketball tournament but frustrated that the girls still played by the old half-court rules. When former Iowa high schoolers tried out for her team, she recalled, "they either knew how to guard or to shoot, but not both." In 1969, she moved on to Central Missouri State in Warrensburg, Missouri, attracted, at a time of great social unrest, by the school's relatively sedate student body.

Barnes had served on numerous national sports committees since her days at Winchester High, and she continued to devote time away from her job to help build a national infrastructure for women's athletics. As a member of the American Alliance of Health, Physical Education, Recreation and Dance, Barnes served on the organization's Division for Girls' and Women's Sports (becoming president in 1974), working to establish physical education programs and competition between schools rather than noncompetitive play days. She served on the organization's women's basketball committee as a rules interpreter, answering questions from coaches and officials — including basic ones from PE teachers who had never coached the game before.

She was also named vice president of the organization that oversaw the US national basketball teams, known at the time as the Amateur Basketball Association of the USA (ABAUSA); she was the first woman ever named to the board. "I was trying to get them interested in basketball for women," she recalled. "But I was outnumbered."[1]

In 1972, Barnes chaired a national rules committee that finally ushered in the full-court, five-player game for girls and wrote an instructional book for coaches and PE teachers. Maddeningly for Barnes, female PE instructors who bought into the idea that the full-court game was too strenuous for girls were some of the biggest sources of opposition to the new rules.

"It made no sense to me," Barnes said. "We played thirty-minute halves in lacrosse and field hockey, with no timeouts or substitutions, two or three times a day. In high school basketball, we played eight-minute quarters with timeouts and as many substitutions as you wanted." Barnes also battled the perception that competitive team sports were unladylike. "The badminton people, the tennis people, the horseback riders — they were looked on as OK for females," she said. "They weren't as aggressive or in contact with other players."

On January 19, 1975, a newspaper in Springfield, Missouri, ran two articles that illustrated the state of flux in women's basketball. Steps forward here, steps backward there. One story mentioned that Barnes had been selected chair of the ABAUSA's first-ever

Olympic women's basketball committee, charged with holding tryouts for the
1975 World Championships and Pan Am
Games. But another described an embarrassing incident at the University of
Cincinnati, where a women's basketball
game in progress between the Bearcats
and Miami of Ohio was whistled to a stop
so that the men's teams could warm up
for their game, which wasn't scheduled
to tip off for another thirty-five minutes. "Athletics offers the same values
— character-building, teamwork, and
patience — to women as well as men,"
Miami coach Elaine Hieber told reporters. "But apparently some people still
don't take that very seriously."

When Barnes went looking for a head
coach for the US national team, she
turned to the most successful woman in
the game: Cathy Rush, a stylish twenty-
seven-year-old from Immaculata College
near Philadelphia. A small Catholic wom-
en's college that attracted mostly working-
class white students from Philly's all-girls
Catholic high schools, Immaculata had
won three straight national basketball
championships between 1972 and 1974,

despite offering minimal financial support for a program that had existed since 1939.

Rush had grown up in Egg Harbor Township, New Jersey, believing her boy neighbors and cousins "had it easier" because they didn't have to wear dresses or play with dolls. Her mom once told her if she kissed her elbow, she'd turn into a boy. "I tried very hard," she recalled, "but nothing happened." She was self-conscious about her interest in sports, but her father encouraged her to keep playing — she clearly had talent. She starred as a freshman at Oakcrest High School, leading her conference with 30 points per game and earning the nickname "Big Gun," but when the school dropped girls' sports entirely her sophomore year, she enrolled in gymnastics lessons.

After graduating from Philadelphia's West Chester State College — where she played two years of basketball — in 1968, Rush taught physical education and coached basketball, lacrosse, and field hockey, first at a local high school and then at a junior high. Her husband, Ed, was a referee in the National Basketball Association, spending much of the winter and spring on the road.[2]

When Immaculata posted a job notice for a basketball coach, Cathy applied. With Ed traveling and a new baby at home, she liked the idea of getting out of the house and spending time on campus. The job paid just $450 a year and the school had no gymnasium (the old one had burned down), offered no scholarships, had no PE major, and owned just a few rubber basketballs. Not ideal, but no pressure, either, for a twenty-two-year-old coach with a baby in tow.

Rush took the job and began building a program. With her son sleeping in a portable crib on the edge of the court, she ran early morning practices in the college's novitiate — after the nuns had finished roller skating and bouncing on pogo sticks, their habits flying in the breeze. With no real court for home games, she drove the team to opponents' gyms in a tank-sized station wagon, earning the nickname "Queen of the U-Turn" for her questionable driving skills.

Because the Catholic university forbade women from wearing shorts on campus, her team played in old-fashioned wool frocks with white blouses and pleated skirts. One opponent offered to steal the hideous uniforms so they'd be forced to get new ones. Immaculata players declined that offer but, because their own basketballs were so lousy, did get in the habit of leaving one of their rubber balls in the rack and walking away with one of their opponents' real leather ones.

The program was lacking in every way but talent. While girls' high school athletics went unsupported in many public school districts around the country, the strong network of all-girls Catholic schools in the Philadelphia area sent experienced players to Immaculata every year. Rush's first great player was Theresa Shank, a six-foot center who drew comparisons to the best men's players at the time (*Sports Illustrated* called her the "female Bill Walton"), starred at the 1973 World University Games in Moscow, and would eventually earn a spot in the Women's Basketball Hall of Fame.

With Shank at the post, Rush ran a style similar to what her husband officiated in the NBA — traps, screens, man-to-man

Known for their outdated frocks, the Catholic women of Immaculata College won AIAW national championships in 1972, 1973, and 1974, but the team was never a contender after the implementation of Title IX. (Women's Basketball Hall of Fame)

defense. It worked, and after each victory, Rush called local newspapers and radio stations with the results. Ed joined the publicity push, too, asking his friends in the media to publicize his wife's unusual program. Reporters were fascinated by the talented Catholic girls in tunics, the cheering nuns in the stands. "The more exposure we can get," Rush believed, "the more women's basketball will catch on in the country."

Rush also played up her conventional femininity, which appealed to male sportswriters during a time when many of them felt threatened by the women's liberation movement. She asked not to be called "coach" or "Ms." but "Mrs. Rush." She paced the sidelines not in athletic gear but in tight plaid pantsuits, splashed on Jean Naté perfume before games, and shaped her blond hair in popular styles.

"I like clothes. I love to dress. I have a pretty good wardrobe," she told the *Philadelphia Inquirer*. "I know I'm sort of onstage. People are looking at me. It really bothers me, one thing about women's athletics, there's just too many women who dress and act like men. So, I probably go to the opposite extreme . . . No one will ever call me dainty. But at least you can be feminine, and you can look nice and dress well and still be involved in sports. I hate to see pictures of women athletes in junky-looking clothes — real short hair, very mannish. I don't think you have to look like that to play a man's game. After all, I don't want to compete with men. I just want to compete."

Her comments could be interpreted two ways. At one level, she was a strong woman, a working mother in a traditionally male field choosing to do things her own way. But at another, her comments could be viewed as expressing internalized sexism, propping herself up at the expense of other women, denigrating their appearance, their motivation, and by extension, their sexuality — not to mention conceding that basketball was a "man's game." In so doing, Rush set herself and her program apart from others by contributing to the misogyny and homophobia that plagued women's sports.[3]

By her second season, in 1971–72, Rush's Immaculata team had already become one of the best in the game, earning an invitation to the inaugural AIAW national championships in Normal, Illinois. The Association for Intercollegiate Athletics for Women was an alternative to the NCAA founded in 1971 to administer championships for nineteen women's

125

sports at hundreds of institutions. The nuns who ran Immaculata, however, had no money to pay for the team's travel to the tournament, so players sold toothbrushes and pencils to earn enough money for airfare. When they came up short, only eight of the eleven members of the team were able to make the trip. Author Julie Byrne wrote that for most of the Immaculata players, just traveling "was a really big deal." They were "more excited about staying in a hotel than playing in the national tournament" and "stayed up most of the night watching television" in their rooms, playing the first few games of the tournament "on almost no sleep."

Well rested or not, Immaculata pulled off a shocker, advancing to the championship game and beating crosstown Philly rival West Chester in the title game. When Rush called campus to deliver the good news, one of the nuns told her to fly first class on the way back home — the school would figure out how to pay for it later. Though only five people had come to Illinois to support the team, five hundred jubilant fans greeted the returning champs at the airport. A phenomenon was born. Rush's winter hobby had blossomed into the most visible program in women's basketball.

While a new gym replaced the one that had burned down, it included no bleachers for spectators. Instead, players helped set up hundreds of folding chairs around the perimeter before games. Nuns and students filled the seats and passionately supported their champs, banging wooden blocks on metal buckets purchased at a local hardware store owned by the father of one of the players. The Bucket Brigade was born, lifting the Mighty Macs of Immaculata to two more AIAW titles in 1973 and 1974.

With its cheering nuns, attractive coach, small campus, quaint uniforms, NBA connection, and unprecedented run of success, Immaculata became as much of a media sensation as any women's team in American history. In 1975, they were part of the first nationally televised women's basketball game, a January 26 game at the University of Maryland. Four weeks later, they were part of the first women's college game ever played at the legendary Madison Square Garden in New York,

Cathy Rush (center) and members of the Immaculata basketball team return to Philadelphia after winning their first AIAW national championship in 1972. The small school's improbable rise to the top inspired the 2009 movie The Mighty Macs. *(Women's Basketball Hall of Fame)*

facing the powerful Queens College team coached by Lucille Kyvallos, who had been Rush's coach at West Chester.

All told, it made perfect sense that when Mildred Barnes sought a coach to lead the US National Team to the 1975 World Championships and Pan Am Games, Rush would emerge as the right woman for the job. Newspapers reported that the

1975 tournaments would be a stepping-stone for the '76 Olympics, where Rush, they said, would lead the US women should they qualify.

Behind the scenes, however, Rush understood the improbable success she'd achieved at Immaculata was already on its way to becoming an anachronism. Title IX was ushering in a new era of women's athletics, one where small schools offering no scholarships could no longer compete. Rush had gone to the nuns asking for more money for her program and they refused, claiming Immaculata did not "want the image of a sports college." The tiny school had played an enormous role in creating a new level of visibility and potential for women's basketball, but in this new era, there was no room for an Immaculata.[4]

Within two years, Rush would retire from coaching at the age of twenty-nine, never to return to the sidelines. But for now, it was time to fly to Colombia for the World Championships and a possible berth in the 1976 Olympics.

12

DEEP TROUBLE

SEPTEMBER 1975
CALI, COLOMBIA
FIBA WORLD CHAMPIONSHIPS

The American basketball players had checked into their hotel in Cali, Colombia, for the World Championships. Roommates Juliene Simpson and Ann Meyers were settling into their room for the night when the phone rang.

Simpson picked it up.

"Tomorrow," said a male voice in Spanish-accented English, "you will no longer be."

The caller hung up. Simpson stared out her window to see if anyone was watching her from the office building across the street and thought about the threat.

"In other words," she believed, "I was going to be shot."

Rushing to the window, she closed the drapes and turned to Meyers. "Can you believe that?

Then she looked outside her door and saw a pineapple sitting in the hallway. Was a bomb inside it? Police arrived to look. It was just fruit.

From the moment Cathy Rush and her players arrived in South America for the tournament, they felt under siege. While they competed in relative anonymity in the United States, their status as Americans earned them visibility and derision in Cali. American interference in Colombian politics, the recent war in Vietnam, anti-imperialist sentiment, and tremendous economic disparity combined to create a stew of hostility toward Rush and the players. Focused on basketball and generally unprepared for the anti-American atmosphere, the US contingent was surprised to come under such intense fire.

Whenever the American women boarded a bus to practices or games, soldiers carrying submachine guns joined them. When assistant Billie Moore needed to leave the hotel to buy something she'd forgotten to pack, she was told to dress in plain clothes (nothing designating her as an American) and to exit through the hotel kitchen accompanied by two escorts from the American embassy.

Mildred Barnes, who accompanied the team, was confused by the team's hotel arrangements. Players were given rooms on the exterior of the building, while staff members were segregated far away in the interior. "I said, 'That's not going to work,'" Barnes recalled, "but I didn't win that battle." Colombian organizers, Barnes learned, had placed team officials in more secure interior locations "to protect us from any protests or abduction attempts." Barnes recalled Colombian protestors rocking the Americans' team bus as they boarded. "With the armed guards lining the sidewalks and the protestors, it was a little scary."

The challenge for Rush and Moore was to keep their players' minds focused on basketball and earning a spot in the Olympic Games. Only the top three finishers in the tournament would receive invitations to Montreal. Before leaving for South America, the team had practiced for a month at Adams State College in Alamosa, Colorado, the Rocky Mountains location chosen specifically to help the women acclimate to the thin air they'd breathe in Colombia. As camp progressed, Pat Head believed the team had greatly improved from the World University Games in 1973. "We have better shooters," she said, "we are stronger on the inside, and with our quickness, we can apply pressure both on offense and defense."

Rush felt a similar sense of optimism. "We're not expected to do well by other teams because the US women's teams have never done well, but I think we'll surprise them this year," she said. "The girls are at their peak, and we have come together as a team." She expected Carolyn Bush, team captain Cherri Rapp, and Juliene Simpson to lead the team's offensive attack: "All three are experienced, international-style players and have been leading during practice. I expect about 45 points out of them each game. That's one of our strengths — their combined ability to come through on scoring instead of just having one girl who is a star."

There had been moments of dissension at camp. Players could see that Rush and Moore had very different personalities and did not always agree on strategy. And as the youngest player on the team, sixteen-year-old Nancy Lieberman's immaturity annoyed some of her teammates. "She was just this New Yorker who was brash," Moore recalled. "She was so eager and there was no question she had the talent, but I used to tell her that if she didn't learn to grow up, they were going to do a raffle to see who got to take her out first."

Lieberman used any perceived slights from the other women as motivation at the Colorado camp. In her autobiography, she claimed to have been rebuffed by Ann Meyers when she asked for an autograph prior to the first workouts. "I couldn't believe it," Lieberman wrote. "How could someone be so cocky as to turn down an autograph? At that point, I decided that Ann Meyers was going to be my personal mission at tryouts."

For her part, Meyers does not recall the autograph request, and other teammates describe her as anything but cocky. She had grown up under the long shadow of her brother Dave, a former All-American at UCLA who was just beginning his NBA career with the Milwaukee Bucks.[1] Dave was merely the most famous in a family full of athletic kids; Annie was the sixth of eleven, including a sister, Patty, who was eight years older and had played for Moore at Cal State Fullerton.

Annie's parents had moved several times as she was growing up, following her father's jobs. The constant upheaval made her a "nervous wreck" in school, and she repeated second grade. In her large family, she played the role of the peacemaker, offering to help her mom with any chores without even being asked. "Little sweet Annie," her mom called her.

But the sweet little girl was full of energy and competitiveness. In a family of athletes, the best way to get the attention of her father, Bob, a former college basketball player at Marquette University, was by performing some athletic feat. She played baseball, basketball, and football with her brothers and their friends, and by the time she got to high school, she added volleyball, field hockey, tennis, badminton, and track to her repertoire. Whether it was a game of cards, hide-and-seek, or Monopoly, Annie played to win. On weekends, she'd watch NBA games with her siblings, and then go outside and mimic the moves of Bill Russell, Jerry West, and John Havlicek, her favorite.

Many teachers considered her athleticism and love of sports inappropriate by the standards of the 1960s. Boys let her join them on the playground because she was good, but otherwise resented her presence. Girls gave her the cold shoulder because she played with the boys. Schoolmates called her a tomboy. "I'd go home crying," she recalled, "but it made me stronger."

At recess one day, a teacher demanded she stop playing football with the boys, lecturing Annie that it wasn't "ladylike." In her autobiography, Meyers described the teacher's comment as a punch to the gut. "I wanted to scream," she said. *"Who am I hurting? What's the point of being ladylike on a playground?* Having been raised to be respectful, I said nothing. But her rebuke elicited a powerful sensation of shame. *'Not ladylike' means she thinks I'm acting like a boy. But why are jumping, running, competing, winning, and all of those fun things, strictly allowed for boys?* I wouldn't dare ask. Instead, I lowered the ball, along with my head, and simply walked away." Another time, she broke "the cardinal rule of school playgrounds everywhere," beating a boy in a footrace. The boy claimed that it had been a tie, and Meyers learned a truth she'd encounter throughout her life: the lengths to which some men would go to deny losing to a woman.

In fifth and sixth grades, Annie played on an after-school boys' basketball team (but only after all the other parents agreed to allow it), leading the team to a city championship as a sixth grader. In middle school, pressure from other parents and teachers kept her off the boys' team, so even though she played with — and beat — the guys at lunchtime, she could only play the six-person game with girls after school.

As a freshman at Sonora High, Annie played seven sports and set a record in the high jump at the Junior Olympics, while her brother Dave was a senior and the star of the boys' basketball team. Despite her own athletic success, Annie said she felt "small and inconsequential," only worthy of anyone's attention because she was Dave's little sister.

To chart her own course as a sophomore, Meyers transferred to an all-girls Catholic school, Cornelia Connelly High. One of her teammates was Nancy Dunkle, the six-foot-one center who would later join her on the US national team. The volleyball coach and driver's education teacher was Ann's sister, Patty. Even as a teen, Annie understood that she was living out her sister's unfulfilled dreams. So much had changed in just eight years.

"Patty Meyers . . . wouldn't have called herself a feminist or a groundbreaker. She wouldn't have called herself anything," Meyers wrote in her autobiography. "She was just who she was; the oldest, toughest, brashest, most passionate, and most athletically talented of all the Meyers. Unfortunately, Patty had been born too early. Doors that had been closed to her were suddenly opening for me, and

*A tremendous all-around athlete in her own right,
Ann Meyers often felt she existed in the shadow
of her older brother Dave, a star at UCLA and
then with the Milwaukee Bucks of the NBA.
(Getty Images)*

I wanted to walk through every one." Annie was a huge success at Connelly, but after her brother graduated from high school, she yearned to take on the challenge of returning to Sonora and playing with the boys.

Between her junior and senior years, she showed up for tryouts for the boys' summer league team. The gym was packed with parents. During one scrimmage, she made a layup, then stole the inbounds pass and scored again. "You gonna just let some GIRL do that?!" screamed one of the boys' parents. Every time Annie made a good play, the crowd jeered the boys rather than celebrating her success.

Female classmates questioned her motivations. One told her if the ball hit her too hard in the chest, she'd get breast cancer. Another said that girls thought if she wanted to play boys' basketball so bad, she must be gay. "The term was never used in our house. I wasn't completely sure of its meaning, but I had an idea," Meyers recalled. *Why would they say that? . . . Was I gay because I wanted to play competitive basketball . . . ?"* She questioned the cultural assumptions that said girls are passive and boys are aggressive. "What's the definition of feminine? Is it to be weak? There are a lot of men who cry and show emotion. Is there something wrong with that? Why are we put into categories?"

In burdening a young basketball player with their homophobic presumptions, Meyers's classmates and their parents were thrusting her squarely into the middle of a hackneyed conversation.

"Almost every female sports star in U.S. history, with the exception of an occasional outstanding beauty, has been rumored to be [gay] at some point in her career," wrote Lynn Rosellini in a landmark series on gay athletes for the *Washington Star* in the mid-1970s. "And almost every female sports star — gay and straight alike — has resented the automatic label . . . In a culture in which plain features, a muscular build and a competitive instinct in women often are equated with lesbianism . . . lesbians in sports have yet another reason to stay in the closet."

While Meyers asked herself philosophical questions about gender, sexuality,

141

sports, and stereotypes, many parents in her community asked simpler but less honest ones. If she played with the boys' varsity team in the winter, where would she dress for games? Where would she shower after? "The questions were smoke screens," Meyers recalled. "I'd use the girls' bathroom and wait until I got home to shower. It didn't take a rocket scientist to figure that out." The truth, she believed, was that the boys' parents didn't want her on the team, not because of any concerns about bathrooms or showers but because they didn't want their sons to lose playing time, or a roster spot, to a girl. "Their jeers might have inspired me a few years earlier, but not now," Meyers admitted. "I was just as attuned to what others thought and said about me as every other teenager on the planet." She knew she was good enough to make the boys' team. But she didn't want to "cause problems." She gave up her quest and played with the girls instead.

But Meyers refused to let the narrow-mindedness of other people derail her dreams, becoming the first woman to receive a full athletic scholarship to UCLA in 1974. And she wasn't the only history-maker on the US national team. When she and her teammates posed for a photo before the World Championships, the picture was unlike any other in history. There were Black players in it: Carolyn Bush, a forward from Wayland Baptist in West Texas; Lusia Harris, the powerful center from Delta State in Mississippi; and Charlotte Lewis, a high-jumping center from Illinois State. These were the first Black women's basketball players to represent the United States in international competition.

Black women had been playing basketball since the beginning, of course. Black women's teams had squared off in front of paying crowds at least as far back as 1910, when the "New York Girls" took on the "New Jersey Girls" at a Harlem casino. And just as Philadelphia was a hotbed for white women's hoops, Philly had also been the center of Black women's basketball since the early 1930s, when a team known as the Germantown Hornets, led by star Ora Washington, captured the Black national championship.

Members of the 1975 World Championship and Pan Am Games team pose before heading off to South America. Kneeling (left to right): Rita Easterling, Juliene Simpson, Nancy Dunkle, Mary Anne O'Connor, Charlotte Lewis, Cherri Rapp, Lusia Harris. Standing (left to right): Nancy Lieberman, Sue Rojcewicz. (Women's Basketball Hall of Fame)

Many historically Black colleges in the South sponsored women's basketball teams, too, part of a long tradition of support for women's sports at HBCUs. When Alice Coachman won the high jump at the 1948 Olympics in London, becoming the first African American woman to win an Olympic medal, she was still known to many as a former basketball star at Tuskegee Institute in Alabama.[2] The first Black team to compete in an AAU national tournament came from Philander Smith College in Little Rock in 1955. Their star, Missouri Arledge, became the first Black woman named an AAU All-American; it wasn't until 1969 that Sally Smith became the second. The supposedly level playing field of sports was routinely tilted against Black teams by racist tournament organizers. White AAU officials mostly prevented Black teams from competing in their tournaments, and when they did let Black teams in, they gave them unfavorable draws and instructed referees to favor white opponents in order to eliminate the Black teams as quickly as possible.

Along the way to the US national team, the lives of Bush, Harris, and Lewis had intersected with many key moments in the civil rights movement. Born within a year of the landmark 1954 *Brown v. Board of Education* Supreme Court decision that declared the concept of "separate but equal" unconstitutional, their lives spanned the ascendance and assassinations of Martin Luther King Jr. and Malcolm X, the lunch counter sit-ins and the freedom rides, the passage of the Civil Rights and Voting Rights Acts, the birth of the Black Panthers, and the raised fists of American Olympians Tommie Smith and John Carlos in Mexico City.

For Black women growing up in the South during this period, these broader social changes played out in the particularities of their daily lives and basketball careers. Harris was the first Black player at Delta State, Bush the first at Roane County High School in Tennessee.

Bush had been raised by her grandmother in Kingston, Tennessee, attending school through sixth grade in a segregated, two-room schoolhouse. Her teacher, Miss Gertrude, spent money out of her own pocket to make lunch for her students each day — bologna sandwiches and fruit — and advised them that life in America was not fair. As Black boys and girls in America, she told her students, they'd have to make two steps for every one the white kids did — and work twice as hard.

Ora Washington (standing, fourth from left) led a team sponsored by the Philadelphia Tribune *to eleven straight championships and was considered the best Black player in the country during the 1930s. Also an outstanding tennis player, Washington was prevented from playing in tournaments sponsored by the segregated United States Tennis Association. Washington was inducted into the Women's Basketball Hall of Fame in 2009. (Women's Basketball Hall of Fame)*

Because white families would not allow Black children to play at the city's municipal park, local Black parents built their children a playground of their own

Carolyn Bush in her trademark Afro puff hairstyle. A star at Wayland Baptist, Bush was named to the inaugural Kodak All-American team in 1975. In 2019, she was inducted into the Women's Basketball Hall of Fame. (Cherri Rapp)

deep in the woods, complete with a see-saw, swings, a horseshoe pit, and a wire-rim basketball hoop, where Bush, who despised playing with dolls, shot hoops with neighborhood boys. "They said, 'If you want to play with us, you'll have to learn how to play and be tough,'" she recalled. "I got knocked down and I cried and hollered, but they didn't have any sympathy. My uncles told me, 'You better get up!' "

The town's middle school desegregated just as Bush arrived. She said she and her white basketball teammates got along well, "no problems whatsoever," but with other girls there were tensions. One white girl thought Bush liked the same boy she did and harassed her through an entire class period, sitting behind her and repeatedly bumping her chair and whispering a racial slur at her. Finally, when the class bell rang, Bush followed the girl out into the hall, grabbed her by the collar, and slammed her against a locker. "Who's the n——, now?!" When the principal saw the girls fighting, she demanded they sit together on the same gymnasium bleacher for the rest of the day until they apologized to one another.

When Bush became the first Black player at Roane County High, white coach Freddie Paul Wilson told her grandmother that Carolyn "won't have to worry about anything." He quickly had a chance to prove it. Bush had grown up with the dehumanizing, racist custom of Southern segregation that demanded

Black customers order their food from the back door of a restaurant, either eating in the kitchen or taking their food to go. But when her team stopped to eat on the way home from a road game, she walked in the front door with the rest of her teammates.

"I'm sorry, Coach, but she can't come in here," the restaurant manager told Wilson.

"If she can't come in, we can go somewhere else and eat," Wilson replied as he ordered his players back on the bus. As her teammates hugged Carolyn and told her they loved her, the manager came running over to the bus. "We've changed our mind."

Wilson saw promise in Carolyn's game. At this time in Tennessee, girls still played the half-court brand of basketball, so Bush, with her outstanding leaping ability, was assigned to defense, where she was told to rebound and push the ball out for the offense. "I could not walk and chew gum at the same time," she said. "Coach Wilson saw something in me and kept working to help me get better."

During her senior year in high school, two small Tennessee colleges recruited her: St. Mary's School of Nursing in Knoxville and Hiwassee College in Madisonville. Bush chose Hiwassee and starred there for two years, during which she was named a Junior College All-American both seasons and MVP of the National Junior College Tournament. Her success caught the attention of Harley Redin, coach of the legendary Wayland Baptist Flying Queens of Plainview, Texas.

The team, which traced its success to a run of AAU championships and a 131-game winning streak in the 1950s, had earned its nickname because a wealthy donor had provided a fleet of four-seat Beechcraft planes to transport the women, dressed in heels and conservative skirts, from game to game. A recruiting visit to the school also provided Bush the first flight of her life. She was petrified, sweating so much one of the flight attendants gave her a cooling towel to place over her eyes. She didn't take it off until the plane landed in West Texas.

"I'm used to all these trees and hills and mountains, and everything is green in

The Flying Queens of Wayland Baptist College traveled to road games aboard small Beechcraft airplanes. The Queens won 131 straight games, including four national championships, in the 1950s. (Women's Basketball Hall of Fame)

Tennessee," Bush recalled. "They open the airplane door in Lubbock, and it's flat and dusty and I can see straight into three different cities. I turned around and sat back down and said, 'I want to go home. I don't like this.'" The flight attendant told Bush she had to get off the plane, but she refused until one of the Wayland players came out of the airport to practically drag her off. "I got off the plane and said, 'What have I gotten my little country bumpkin self into?'" But Bush ended up enjoying her visit and soon became a Flying Queen.

The Queens were enormously popular, so much so that when university trustees unanimously voted to disband the team in 1961 to cut costs — in a stark example of the perceived disposability of even highly successful women's sports — outraged citizens and alumni raised enough money to cover the cost of twenty-seven scholarships. The trustees reversed their decision, and the team, which had won six AAU championships the previous eight years, was saved.[3]

When Bush arrived at Wayland, she was initially dismayed to learn that the women played their games immediately after the school's men's team. "Well, God," she said, "there won't be nobody there." What she didn't realize was that in Plainview, fans showed up throughout the men's game to be sure they were in their seats in time for the warm-ups of the women's game, which were an elaborate production. Dressed in satin warm-up suits, the Queens would line up in a football formation to the tune of "Sweet Georgia Brown," the theme song of the Harlem Globetrotters. One player would kick the basketball as if for a field goal, knocking it off the backboard and starting a procession where each player would run toward the basket, catch the ball, and knock it off the glass for the next player. Tap, tap, tap, tap, and then Bush would come in last, leaping high, catching the ball, dunking it through the hoop, and sending the crowd into a frenzy.

Bush turned heads in the games, too, earning a spot on the first-ever Kodak All-American women's basketball team in 1975 along with Wayland teammate Brenda Moeller, Immaculata's Mari-anne Crawford, eventual World Championship teammates Ann Meyers, Lusia Harris, Nancy Dunkle, and Sue Rojcewicz, and three others. That recognition caught the attention of Barnes, Rush, and Moore, earning Bush a tryout and an eventual spot on the national team. The girl who had grown up playing on a makeshift dirt court in segregated East Tennessee was now wearing the red, white, and blue, representing the US on the world stage.

In the round-robin opening stage of the World Championship tournament in Colombia, the US would play Japan, Australia, and Czechoslovakia, needing to finish in the top two of the group to advance to the next stage. It would be no easy task in an environment where the American women felt danger at every turn.

The start of the opening game was delayed forty-five minutes to allow security to search fans for weapons. When the Americans were introduced for their opening game against Japan on September 23, spectators heated coins with cigarette lighters and hurled them onto the court, accompanied by boos and whistles. Aware of the death threats made against Simpson, the other American players came up with a strategy to protect her during team introductions. When the public address announcer called out Simpson's name, every American player on the bench stepped forward and waved, making any would-be assassin's job more difficult.

To Cathy Rush, it appeared the entire gym was allied against her team from start to finish. And the small but quick and talented Japanese team was tough, too, ultimately winning a back-and-forth game 73–71. The clinching points came on a miraculous thirty-foot shot that sank through the net as the final buzzer sounded. After the US beat Australia 65–52, their chances of advancing to the next round depended on the outcome of their game against a bigger and stronger team from Czechoslovakia. Win the game, and there would still be an opportunity to qualify for the Olympics. Lose, and there were no guarantees.

The US lost, 66–65. Two losses by a total of three points could keep the Americans from earning a bid to Montreal.

Then there were consolation games left to play, and the Americans split the first two, beating Hungary 78–55 and losing to Canada 74–68.

Resentments floated to the surface. Some players thought Lieberman was in over her head. Others considered Head — out of shape after suffering a knee injury that required surgery in her final season at UT Martin — deadweight on the end of the bench. Others pointed fingers at Cathy Rush's coaching and communication methods, while Rush quietly seethed that she hadn't been able to select her roster herself, instead relying on US officials to pick players she didn't believe suited her style of play.

Heading into the final game of the tournament against two-time defending champion Brazil, the players called a meeting to air their grievances. "Don't get me wrong. Cathy tried to do what she thought was right," Simpson told a reporter. "But she played favorites. She had her own system, a run and gun game, and never took the starters out, no matter how many mistakes they made." After the meeting, Rush made some adjustments, and her players went out and demolished Brazil, 104–72.

Even with the big win over Brazil, and even though the US team's losses had all been closely contested, the tournament had been an enormous failure. Not only had the Americans blown an opportunity to qualify for the Olympics, but they had also finished eighth in the world, an embarrassing position for the country where basketball had been invented, and where the men's team routinely won gold medals.

"As an American you have this attitude that we're supposed to be the best, and then we didn't even qualify for the Olympics," Meyers recalled. "I was heartbroken. It was like, 'Wow. We're not that good.'"

MEXICAN GOLD

13

With the 1975 World Championships complete, four of the six spots in the Olympic basketball tournament were set: the top three finishers in Colombia (the Soviet Union, Czechoslovakia, and Japan), along with Canada, which received an automatic bid as the host country. The final two entries in the six-team Olympic field would be determined at a last-chance qualifying tournament for also-rans in Hamilton, Ontario, taking place just weeks before the opening ceremony. But to even earn an invitation to play in that tournament, the US women would need to regroup just eight days after and win the Pan Am Games in Mexico City.

The Pan Am Games were a sort of mini-Olympics, bringing together the nations of North, South, and Central America every four years to compete in events ranging from athletics (track and field) to wrestling. The 1975 US delegation included four hundred athletes representing nineteen men's and women's sports. As in Colombia, the US teams were unpopular guests in Mexico. Track coach Roy Griak complained that his athletes were booed, jeered, shoved, and spat on. Walking the streets in their red, white, and blue sweatsuits, the American basketball players, Ann Meyers recalled, "found out quickly what the rest of the world thought of us: we were arrogant, and we were rich."

Charlotte Lewis, the American forward from Illinois State, had grown up in public housing projects in Peoria, but she was shocked by the poverty she witnessed in Mexico City, which was far from the paradise she'd seen promoted on American game shows. "It was nothing like a *Let's Make a Deal* vacation," she recalled. "We would walk around and people would be washing dishes in sewers and stuff like that, and it kind of disheartened me because the hype was always sunny Mexico, la-di-da. On the street, people were very poor."

The tension between the American athletes, the Mexican fans, and the athletes from other developing countries was predictable. Just four months earlier, Mexico City had hosted thousands of delegates from around the world for a United Nations conference marking the "International Year of the Woman," an event that revealed the vastly different priorities of women from wealthy countries, who demanded equal pay with men, and women from poorer countries, who sought necessities such as food, water, and medical care. Intended to bring the women of the world together in a spirit of shared sisterhood, the conference instead exposed the stark economic and social inequities that transcended gender and the ways in which the past and present actions of wealthy countries fueled global poverty.

American women entered the UN conference in a state of anxious uncertainty, experiencing simultaneous steps forward and back. *Time* magazine accentuated the positive in a broad and paternalistic fashion, declaring that in 1975, "an im-

To commemorate the fiftieth anniversary of women's suffrage in the United States, women march along Fifth Avenue in New York on August 26, 1970. Five years later, women of the world met at a United Nations conference in Mexico City, but it was far from a united gathering. (Getty Images)

mense variety of women [were] altering their lives, entering new fields, functioning with a new sense of identity, integrity and confidence." It compared them to "a new immigrant wave in male America. They may be cops, judges, military officers, telephone linemen, cab drivers, pipefitters, editors, business executives — or mothers and housewives, but not quite the same subordinate creatures they were before."

But politically and economically, there were distressing developments. Ratification of the Equal Rights Amendment was stalled in state legislatures, facing powerful conservative backlash. Many women in the political middle, sympathetic to the economic and social arguments of women's rights advocates, were turned off by the more militant participants' criticisms of marriage and motherhood. A declining American economy, bad news for men and women alike, hit low-income women the hardest. Typically the last hired, they were also the first fired. Statistics from the US Department of Labor showed that for every five dollars earned by a man, a woman earned just three dollars, a wider gap than ten years earlier. On average, a Black woman with three years of college didn't earn as much as a man with an eighth-grade education.

But the problems of the American woman appeared inconsequential compared to the life-and-death concerns of their global counterparts at the UN gathering. "To those who have lived on scraps of food from a city dump," said a Colombian delegate, "talk about sexism and demands for equal pay for equal work seem meaningless." An Indian representative continued the theme. "We of the poorer developing nations are not interested in the psychological liberation of Western women," she said. "If you American ladies paid more attention to the imperialist economic policies of your government, women throughout the world would not have to worry about such unfashionable problems as starvation and homelessness."

The attacks came largely as a surprise to the American delegates, who considered their work for equal pay and equal rights to be revolutionary, and who had centered their own concerns over the plight of poor women around the world.

"They found themselves simply unable to accept the third-world position that the status of women will rise automatically with economic development and independent of a militant movement aimed specifically at female liberation," wrote one Chicago journalist. "American women were loath to admit that their own goals — such as equal pay for equal work and the right to control their own bodies — were any less important, either for themselves or any other group of women."

The mood was disorienting to those who arrived expecting to set the agenda rather than to defend their presence, exposing a measure of privilege and fragility. "I was frightened," the Chicago journalist wrote. "The anti-American feeling is so strong. It's no fun being hated. I take 'Imperialist!' quietly. But not, 'Pig!' They hate the press, too. At one point I put my hand over my press card to hide it. I kept thinking of final words to say to my children."

Even within the American delegation, there was tension. Some women resented that Betty Friedan still attracted the media spotlight on this international stage, even as her star had faded back home. Lesbian attendees called for greater representation on panels. And African American women felt a surprising sting, treated as indistinguishable from white women in the minds of delegates from developing countries in Africa and Asia.

"It's doubly ironic to be stereotyped as an American — not only because I think of myself as being Black and being proud of it," said a delegate from Los Angeles, "but because Black women in America have been saying for years that they find it difficult to relate to the feminist movement because it articulates the preoccupations and frustrations of the white middle class — and now we're being lumped in right along with them."

In the eight-team Pan Am Games tournament, the US expected to face its stiffest competition from four countries: host nation Mexico, which had finished ahead of the Americans at the World Championships in Colombia; Cuba, which had given the US a scare at the World University Games in Moscow; Canada, which had beaten the US at the World Championships; and Brazil, the two-time defending Pan Am champions.

While Ann Meyers, as the little sister of an NBA star, and Nancy Lieberman, the high school sensation, attracted the most curiosity from the few American media members who paid attention to women's basketball, Coach Rush knew her team's chances of winning Pan Am gold rested on the broad shoulders of her six-foot-three center, Lusia Harris of Delta State University. And in Harris's story was evidence that the surprise white feminists felt when confronted by the global poor was proof of how little they understood about the connections between racism and economic justice at home. In the Mississippi Delta, Black people lived in poverty because racist people and policies worked, for centuries, to keep them poor.

Harris had grown up in Minter City, a tiny and impoverished town in Leflore County deep in the heart of cotton country. There in the Mississippi Delta, the legacy of slavery echoed louder than a thunderclap. Between 1877 and 1950, whites in the county lynched forty-eight African American men, women, and children, the most of any county in a state where lynchings occurred more frequently than in any other. In fact, one of the most infamous lynchings in American history took place there when Chicago teenager Emmett Till was murdered by two white men while visiting relatives in 1954. It was a vicious attack provoked by a lying white woman, followed by a farce of a trial that found Till's killers innocent. Leflore County was where the kidnapping and violence began.

In the early 1960s, college students arrived in the Delta to combat the voter-suppression tactics of white Mississippians that left only around 2 percent of eligible Black voters registered. White citizens responded to these efforts with violence and cruelty, attacking Black churches where voter-registration drives were held, arresting student organizers, and blocking federal food subsidies to poor Black families. In 1963, US attorney general Robert F. Kennedy visited the Delta to see Black residents' living conditions with his own eyes. He was brought to tears as he witnessed the inhumane conditions that systemic racism and injustice wrought, meeting families with no running water or electricity, kids starving from malnutrition, dilapidated houses infested with rats. In 1966, civil rights leader Stokely Carmichael came to the area and popularized the term "Black Power," calling on Black citizens to organize and fight back against the ravages of white supremacy.

The tenth of Willie and Ethel Harris's eleven children, Lusia grew up picking cotton after school, sewing her own clothes, and washing laundry in the Tallahatchie River. Her parents worked long, hot days on white men's farms for meager wages, preaching the value of education to their children. In their small home, all the boys shared one bedroom and the girls another. They had no telephone for much of her childhood, and their small black-and-white TV set picked up only one station. Her parents didn't talk much about the racism of the Delta, but the lessons they shared were all about survival in a capriciously violent world: keep your mouth closed, don't say anything, stay out of trouble. Lusia listened. "My father was kind of small in stature, but very demanding," she recalled. "I mean when he told you to do something, it was best to go ahead and do it. Let's just say you didn't want to test him."

After the backbreaking, finger-pricking days in the fields, Harris and her siblings spent long nights shooting baskets in the backyard with neighborhood kids who congregated there. A tall and uncoordinated kid, Lusia struggled to learn the basics of the game — she was the one nobody wanted on their team. But no one outworked her. After all the other kids went home, she'd still be out back developing her skills deep into the night. "I'm going to make this shot," she'd tell herself, hurling the ball toward the bent rim hoisted on a wooden pole. "I'm going to beat my sister." And sometimes at night, when she was supposed to be in bed, she'd hang a blanket over the TV and watch basketball.

Schoolmates picked on Lusia for her towering frame — "long and tall, that's all," they'd taunt as they lined up by height before class. She hated being the tallest kid in middle school, but one of the

A 1960s basketball scene in the Mississippi Delta. Lusia Harris grew up playing ball in a similar environment and became the first Black player at Delta State University and the first woman to score a point in an Olympic basketball game. (Getty Images)

basketball coaches saw something special. All the work in the backyard was starting to pay off. From the moment coach Molly Parker first saw Lusia bank in a shot in the paint, she knew she had the potential to be great. But first she had to convince Ethel Harris to let her daughter join the girls' basketball team. Mrs. Harris didn't want her daughter to get hurt. "I told her that we would never know what would happen unless she let Lusia play. I said it wouldn't be too hard on her," said Parker. When Parker wouldn't let up, Ethel finally surrendered. "I just gave in," she recalled. "I had watched her brothers and sisters playing every night after supper, and I didn't want another girl playing. But [Molly] was a pretty good talker and I just said 'yes' to get her to shut up."

After developing her game and her strength in middle school, Harris gained a reputation as the "tower of power" at Amanda Elzy High School in Greenwood, Mississippi. "I loved seeing the ball go through the basket," she said, "and that just kept my interest up." Intrigued by the phenom from Minter City, local sportswriters chronicled Harris's every success: team captain, all-state, three-time MVP, 46 points scored in one game. Once a week, it seemed, there was an article on the unstoppable Lusia Harris. She clipped the stories from the newspaper and placed them in a scrapbook, but never read them. She didn't want to know how many points she scored or how many rebounds she grabbed; it just made her nervous. All she wanted to do was play the game for as long as she could. And as far as she knew, that meant until the end of high school. She planned on attending Alcorn State University, and the historically Black college did not sponsor a women's basketball team.

But then Margaret Wade from Delta State University in Cleveland, Mississippi, approached Harris, telling her the school planned on reviving its team, which had been disbanded back in 1933. (Wade had been one of the players who burned her jersey in protest.) Wade had a budget of just $5,300 and couldn't offer Harris a basketball scholarship, but between academic aid and work-study, Harris could scrape by. She would be the centerpiece of the new team, but she'd also be one of the few Black students — and the only Black basketball player — at Delta State. Emerging from a world of constant, brutally enforced segregation, Harris said, diplomatically, that her arrival at predominantly white Delta State "was awkward at first." She had seen white people before, she said, but had never talked to them until arriving on campus. And many of her white classmates had never questioned the racist society in which they grew up, never treated a Black person as an equal. One Saturday morning, Lusia rode her bike twenty-six lonely miles along Highway 8 back to Minter City for a dose of the comfort only her mother could provide.

When she was on the court, opposing fans yelled racist slurs at Harris and opposing players scratched, clawed, and pinched her. Harris said she felt support from her white teammates and coach. Wade hid a button reading GIVE 'EM HELL under her jacket, flashing it at Harris and her teammates during time-outs. Harris decided the best way to get back at those who denigrated her was to beat them. With her size, strength, rebounding ability, and nearly automatic bank shot, she lifted Delta State to the top of the women's basketball world. As a sophomore in the 1974–75 season, she powered the Lady Statesmen to an undefeated 28–0 record, scoring 32 points and grabbing sixteen rebounds in a national championship victory over Cathy Rush's Immaculata team. "She is more than a superior basketball player," said Delta

Lusia Harris was the biggest thing ever to happen to tiny Minter City, Mississippi. Here she poses with her parents and Margaret Wade, the legendary Delta State coach. (Delta State University)

Lusia Harris earned Kodak All-American honors in 1975, 1976, and 1977, and led Delta State to AIAW national championships all three seasons. (Delta State University)

State president Kent Wyatt. "She is a B+ student, a campus leader, and goodwill ambassador for our university, the state of Mississippi, and the country."[1]

A goodwill ambassador, perhaps, but still a target at the Pan Am Games in Mexico City.

When the United States team took the court for their opening game against Mexico at the Sports Palace, fans of the home team hurled insults, bottle caps, and flaming matchbooks toward the women on the American bench. Accustomed to the abuse from the World Championships, the Americans dominated the game from start to finish, demolishing Mexico 99–65.

They even started to have a little fun with the Mexican crowd. When the jeering resumed prior to the next game against Canada, center Nancy Dunkle came up with a way to return fire. Before tip-off, protocol called for both teams to walk around the perimeter of the court and wave to fans. "Nancy said, 'They're cussing us out and here we are waving at them,' so she starts cussing back," teammate Carolyn Bush recalled. "She said, 'They don't know what we're saying,' so we did it every time. We'd march around and then we'd come together at half court and exchange gifts with the other team. But Lord have mercy, Nancy starts letting [the curse words] fly, so quite naturally a few of us others start letting it fly, too. Smiling, waving, saying stuff."

After beating Canada 75–56, a redemption after losing to the Canadians in the World Championships, the Americans began to relax further. Charlotte Lewis hung out with some of the players on the US men's team, including future NBA stars Tree Rollins and Robert Parish, telling them about the braces she had worn on her legs as a child and a doctor's prediction that she would never be able to run.[2] Pat Head joined the coaching staff for poker games, annoyed that Rush always seemed to quit playing whenever she had won a pot of money. Dunkle posed for photos in her room dressed in a trench coat, imitating Inspector Clouseau of the *Pink Panther* movies. Cherri Rapp and Pat Head took advantage of a day off to go sightseeing, taking a bus tour downtown. After "piddling around" and missing the bus back to their hotel, Rapp wanted to hail a cab, but Head preferred to save money and hitchhike. The prospect of standing on the side of the road in downtown Mexico City hoping for a ride in a stranger's car initially scared Rapp. "But I realized that no one was going to [bother] Pat," she said. "She'd just beat them up. So we end up hitchhiking in the middle of Mexico City."

When the Americans won their third straight game, a 116–28 thrashing of El Salvador, and then followed it up with a 70–64 victory over highly regarded Cuba, there was more cause for celebration. Some of the players told Mildred Barnes they wanted to stop in a bar to listen to music and have one drink. Barnes invited USA Basketball executive director Bill Wall to join them. He hated the idea, certain the women would stay too long and drink too much. "Bill, they're going to be OK," Barnes assured him, but Wall refused to come in, storming off down the street. But thirty minutes later, after enjoying some music and sipping on one drink each, the women ran into Wall while walking back to their hotel. "He was astonished," Barnes recalled. "He said he never would have gotten the [men's basketball team] out of there."[3]

One player, however, later admitted she spent too much time in the cantinas of Mexico City. Still working her way back into playing shape while recovering from knee surgery, Pat Head had gained nearly thirty pounds before the tournament, and she spent more time in Mexico drinking with Ernie Grunfeld of the men's team than she did on the basketball court.

"I joked that I played end, guard, and tackle," Head recalled. "Sat on the end of the bench, guarded the water bottles, and tackled anyone who came in there who wasn't supposed to be there."

Slow, hobbling, and "swallowing her pride," Head's most important contribution to the team was mentoring the younger players. As embarrassed as she was to sit at the end of the bench, she understood that maintaining a positive attitude was crucial to the team's chemistry. The only other player who saw as little playing time as she did was Nancy Lieberman, the teenager known for her unpredictable and immature ways.

In the US's next game, a 99–50 win over the Dominican Republic in which Head remained stuck on the bench, she found an opportunity to contribute to her team by counseling Lieberman. "It would have been very easy for me to lean over and whisper complaints in her ear. But I decided that if I ever wanted to amount to anything as a professional, I had to be an example for Nancy," Head later wrote. "She and I were invariably the last players to get in the game, and one afternoon it got particularly humiliating. The USA was up by more than 30 points and there were just a couple of minutes left when Cathy Rush finally looked down the bench and pointed at Nancy and me. It was time for the scrubs to mop up. Nancy was furious."

Lieberman turned to Head. "I'm not going in."

"Why?"

"This is embarrassing. I'm not going in."

"Oh, yes, you are. And I'll tell you one thing. You better not pass me the ball, because if you do, you'll never get it back."

After beating Colombia 74–48, the US completed a run of seven consecutive victories in the tournament by defeating Brazil 74–55 in the championship game, a convincing win against a powerful team that had beaten the Americans in their last three PanAm matchups. Along the way, the Mexican crowd had begun to appreciate the American players' skills. When the players were introduced before the final game, Juliene Simpson received a standing ovation.

After receiving their gold medals, the Americans jubilantly made their way back to the locker room. "Everyone was jumping around, hugging, and kissing each other, just like you see on TV," Lieberman recalled. "It's such a different feeling because you tried out for yourself, but you're winning for the USA. Everyone back home is a teammate, and you pull energy from that feeling."

Even Bill Wall let loose. When the players and coaches went out to celebrate at a restaurant, he covered the cost of champagne, thirty dollars a bottle — and more than just one drink per person.

REGIME CHANGE

14

Cathy Rush sensed it back in Colombia: her run as US national coach was toast as soon as her team finished eighth at the World Championships. The Pan Am gold medal in Mexico, she believed, would amount to little more than a parting gift.

Confiding in Philadelphia sportswriter Dick Weiss, she complained about the players who had been selected for the team by Mildred Barnes and her committee members. "This is the last time I'll ever coach somebody else's team," she said. "I coach a certain style. I have to get players who can play that style. There are certain things I look for. Some so-called supers are just not quick enough for me."

Weiss predicted that while Rush was

"easily the most qualified person to coach a US team in international competition," she would be "gently led to the gallows" because of the disastrous finish in Colombia, a decision Rush believed was shortsighted.

"We lost to Japan and Czechoslovakia by a total of three points," she said. "That's three points away from finishing in the top three and qualifying for one of the six spots in Montreal. What ticks me off is that this team is so much better than the last US team to play in the World Championships. That team finished eighth too, though, so I know what people are going to say."

Less than two months later, Mildred Barnes said it: Rush was out, and her assistant Billie Moore was in as the new head coach. Given the friction that had developed between Rush and Moore over the course of the two tournaments, Moore's appointment could be seen as a victory in a power struggle. Mel Greenberg, a *Philadelphia Inquirer* sportswriter who created the first national women's basketball poll, said Rush resented the close friendship between Moore and Head. More than

Intense and direct, Billie Moore enjoyed tremendous success as head coach at Cal State Fullerton, winning a national title in 1970. She was named US national team coach in 1976 after serving as an assistant the previous three years. (Getty Images)

forty years later, Barnes said she simply felt Moore was the best person for the job at the time, and that it was common for the head coaching position to turn over year to year.

While Weiss's claim that Cathy Rush was the most qualified woman to coach the US national team had unquestionable merit, Moore was also supremely qualified. She had amassed a record of 112–8 as a collegiate head coach, including seven conference championships and a national AIAW title. She had gained international experience as an assistant at the World University Games, World Championships, and Pan Am Games.[1] Now it was her responsibility to propel this team to the Olympics, an assignment she viewed with gratitude and trepidation.

"It took me a while to come down from the ceiling when I got the phone call with the news," she said. "I felt very honored and very fortunate to be selected. I was almost smart enough to understand the magnitude of what the job was going to be. You've been named to coach a team that's not qualified for the Olympics. So that's a tremendous challenge ahead of you."

Moore believed that the difference between "pressure" and "opportunity" was a state of mind. And the potential to compete in the world spotlight in Montreal presented a tremendous opportunity for the future of women's basketball in the United States. "Having coached for a few years at the collegiate level, the thing you were always battling was to get recognition," she said. "To get media to cover us, to get people to pay attention, to get the marketing going. You needed certain things to happen to cause things to springboard. One thing that helped women's sports springboard was Title IX. I thought with the Olympics being [nearby] in Montreal, that could have another big springboard effect if people could just see us play."

Barnes gave Moore the freedom to choose her assistant coach, a decision she spent little time contemplating. Her pick was Sue Gunter, the highly successful coach at Stephen F. Austin State University in Nacogdoches, Texas.[2] Moore understood that Gunter, an old friend and respected opponent from Moore's days playing softball for the legendary Raybestos Brakettes of Stratford, Connecticut, would provide a necessary balance to her demanding ways. "[Sue] always said I used to knock people down," Moore recalled, "and she'd come along behind and put them back together."

Not that the chain-smoking Gunter was a pushover. She had grown up riding horses on her parents' farm in Walnut Grove, Mississippi, and brought a country-strong work ethic to the basketball court. As a teammate of Nera White's at Nashville Business College, she'd helped lead her team to two national AAU championships and two runner-up finishes. As a coach, she had an innate ability to connect with anyone at their level, equally at home drinking cold beers in a roadside shack or sipping red wine in a fine restaurant discussing world history. She knew how to communicate with any player, whether to push or coddle, and she understood basketball at a minute level, seeing the patterns and tendencies of her opponents before anyone else did. She showed her players not just what to do but why and how to do it, then had them practice over and over and over until they didn't have to think anymore, just react. Practice didn't make perfect; perfect practice did.

US assistant coach Sue Gunter was a highly successful head coach at Stephen F. Austin State University at the time of the 1976 Olympics. She went on to coach at LSU and retired in 2004 as one of the winningest coaches in college basketball history. (Stephen F. Austin State University)

Gunter had fought the same battles as many of her contemporaries, struggling for support from male administrators who had no interest in women's sports and felt no obligation to fund them. Her teams at Stephen F. Austin wore red, white, and blue uniforms because those colors were cheaper and easier to buy off the rack than the school's official colors of purple and white, which the school was only willing to special-order for its men's teams.

When Gunter begged the chair of the women's physical education department for more money for her program, the professor took Gunter with her to meet with unsympathetic university officials.

"We started off with one of her superiors, and we went to a couple of the deans of the college, and we finally wound up in the president of the university's office," Gunter recalled. "I left that building, and there were tears running down my cheeks because I was so angry. But she had made the point."

"Sue," the professor told her, "this is what I fight every single day."

Still, Gunter refused to temper her own expectations for the sport she loved. "She was a visionary," recalled Bob Starkey, a longtime coaching colleague. "She always thought there would be full arenas, television, pro basketball for women. It was something she talked about." And as Moore's assistant, striving to participate in the first women's Olympic basketball tournament, Gunter saw the historic opportunity at hand. "You were truly the footprint on the surface of the moon," Starkey said. "She used that as motivation. They would all be the first person to do anything."

Gunter, in fact, would be the first member of the new coaching staff to lead this team in competition. With the US national team scheduled to tour Taiwan and Japan for a series of exhibition games in April 1976 and Moore unable to attend due to obligations in California, Gunter assumed temporary head coaching duties. She, in turn, picked Bessie Stockard of Federal City College in Washington, DC, as her assistant, with Stockard becoming the first Black woman to serve as a US assistant coach.[3]

Stockard was a pioneering figure in women's athletics, playing basketball and tennis at Tuskegee Institute in Alabama, becoming one of the first Black woman to compete on the Virginia Slims women's professional tennis tour, and launching the women's basketball program at Federal City in 1969. If Cathy Rush's success at Immaculata was improbable, Stockard's was impossible. Federal City had no campus — just classrooms in buildings around the District of Columbia. No

191

gymnasium. No scholarships. No uniforms. But by 1974, Stockard had built a juggernaut, ranked preseason number one in the country, recruiting players primarily from DC-area high schools and leading with Black pride. Stockard paced the sidelines in stylish wide-brimmed hats, while her players wore tall Afros; fans and players alike rocked to beats played on a boom box before each game. Gunter had met Stockard at an AIAW national tournament and was impressed by her team's conditioning, relentless defense, and unlikely success. Stockard was just the kind of woman she wanted by her side.

Along with Barnes, team manager Jeanne Rowlands, trainer Marjorie Albohm, and referee Chuck Osborne, the team departed Los Angeles on China Airlines Flight 007 on April 3, the first leg of a two-week journey through Asia that would provide another chance for the players to test themselves against international competition prior to the Olympic qualifier.

From the moment the plane touched down in the Taiwanese capital of Taipei, the Americans were made to feel at home,

Bessie Stockard built a national power at Federal City College from scratch. Stockard had played basketball at Tuskegee and was the first Black woman to play on the Virginia Slims women's professional tennis tour. (University of the District of Columbia Athletics)

Barnes recalled in a diary of the trip. After unpacking their suitcases at the Inn of the Sixth Happiness, the team admired the city's architecture and attended a welcome dinner where their "first efforts with chopsticks demonstrated we had much to learn."

The next day began with sightseeing with members of the Air China basketball team, including a visit to former president Chiang Kai-shek's estate and a lavish thirteen-course lunch (with six dishes per course). Playing before a friendly crowd of seven thousand fans that evening ("we appreciated the cheers instead of whistles," Barnes remarked), the US team beat Air China 81–66 and then enjoyed ice cream and hamburgers at an American-style restaurant with their opponents after the game.

The visit included more sightseeing — a boat ride across a large lake, a dance party, visiting children at an American school, admiring the jade and ivory at the National Palace Museum — and relatively easy victories over Taiwanese teams, with the Americans using their height advantage to shoot over 50 percent from the field in 86–64, 76–48, and 85–52 victories.

Before a game on April 10, Carolyn Bush and several teammates were out walking with tour guides through a shopping area known as Jade Alley. Bush noticed an elderly woman following them, "talking and pointing, talking and pointing." Bush asked one of the guides to find out if there was a problem, then watched as the guide spoke briefly to the old woman and walked back toward her. "She wants to touch your puffs." Bush was wearing her hair in the Afro puff style popular in the 1960s and '70s, with two large balls of hair on either side of her head. The idea of a non-Black person asking to touch a Black woman's hair was a cringeworthy violation back in the US. But as a guest in Taiwan, Bush was willing to let the old lady satisfy her curiosity. "I guess she had never seen a Black woman before, so she patted my puffs for about five minutes," Bush recalled. "I was bent over because I was too tall for her to reach up." Moved by the experience, the old woman bowed and walked away with tears in her eyes.

That night, an enormous crowd of eighteen thousand turned out to watch the US take on another Taiwanese opponent, with the Americans taking a 42–24 lead at halftime. The friendliness of the Taiwanese fans evaporated in a hurry when the American official Chuck Osborne blew an over-and-back call, whistling a turnover according to the American rule when he should have been following international rules. The fans went ballistic, throwing marbles, oranges, and shoes on the floor, even a rolled-up newspaper that had been set on fire. Writing in her journal, Barnes noted that "it was twenty minutes before order was restored and the game could resume." More than forty years later, Osborne recalled the scene with mixed emotions. On the one hand, he said it was the only time in his career he wondered if he'd get out of an arena alive. On the other, he knew he'd made a bad call and couldn't help but be impressed with the spectators' passion for women's basketball. "The fans," he deadpanned, "sure took it seriously."[4]

After beating the Cathay Pacific team 69–55 the next night, completing a streak of six straight victories in Taipei, the Americans boarded a two a.m. flight to Osaka to begin a three-game series against the Japanese national team, which had beaten the US by two points at the World Championships in Colombia. After a reception and shopping near the hotel, the first "anxiously awaited game arrived." With the US trailing 44–37 at halftime, Gunter made some quick adjustments for the second half — which paid off as the US came back to win 76–70. "It was a great come-from-behind win and demonstrated that the US team is world class caliber," Barnes wrote. "The press interview after the game was short and tense. We were not expected to beat a team that had been in training for six months. It was a happy evening for the US."

After a quick flight to Tokyo the next day, the Americans practiced, shopped ("stereos and amplifiers were among the acquisitions . . . We seemed to have increased our baggage by some eight or nine pieces"), and were pleased to discover American fast food staples McDonald's, Pizza Hut, and Baskin Robbins on the streets of the Japanese capital. But the home cooking did them no favors, as they lost 73–60 and 77–63 in their final two games of the trip.

After playing nine games in eleven nights, the US delegation welcomed a stop in Honolulu on the way back to California, staying at the Dynasty Hotel on Ala Moana Boulevard. The players swam and sunbathed on Waikiki Beach, and Ann Meyers introduced teammates to NBA star Wilt Chamberlain, who had an apartment nearby. One night, everyone gathered aboard a party boat for a dinner cruise with live music.

When the band struck up the "Tennessee Waltz," Pat Head, the farmer's daughter from Cheatham County, turned to Chuck Osborne, the referee, seated next to her.

"Get up," she demanded. "You're going to dance with me."

"You win," Osborne replied. "Let's go."

SUMMER CAMP

15

There was the iron bridge, where teenagers would sit and drink beer while their legs dangled toward the water. There was the old limestone quarry, easy to sneak into at night for a swim. There was the roller rink, with its panels pulled up on summer evenings so kids outside could cruise by and see who was skating. There was the burger joint, where you could carve your name into the old wooden booths, and the annual lawn mower races on the Fourth of July.

But for most teens in sleepy Warrensburg, Missouri, sixty miles east of Kansas City, summer fun meant one thing: hanging out on the deserted campus of Central Missouri State University.[1] With its basketball courts, baseball fields, swimming pools, bowling alley, and pool tables, the entire campus became the kids' playground.[2]

Vic Bozarth, a tall and skinny fifteen-year-old, had spent most of his adolescence at the university. Every day in the spring and summer of 1976, Vic carried his basketball to campus looking for a pickup game. If nobody was playing in one gym, he'd move along to another. He loved basketball and he loved Warrensburg, but as a sixth-generation resident of the town, he was also the first to admit there wasn't much else to do.

One day in early June, he carried his ball into sweltering hot Garrison Gym, drawn to the familiar sounds of a basketball practice. He walked inside and took a seat in the bleachers. There was something unusual about this practice. All the coaches and players were women, and none of them were local.

When Billie Moore needed a place to hold tryouts for the 1976 US national team, she came to Central Missouri State. The main reason was that Mildred Barnes was the coach there, and she'd convinced university administrators to let the national team use the facilities for free. But Moore liked Warrensburg for another reason: there was nothing to do. With no distractions, her players could focus all their energies on preparing for the Olympic qualifying tournament in Hamilton, Ontario.

The day Vic Bozarth walked into practice, he struck up a conversation with the only other spectator in the gym, a summer intern from the *Kansas City Times* named Lloyd Grove. Grove didn't care much about sports, but as an intern he covered whatever stories his editors assigned. Along with a photographer, he had driven over from Kansas City to learn more about this wannabe Olympic team practicing in the city's backyard.

Moore had gathered her players around her in the un-air-conditioned gym, blistering mad. In a scrimmage against a team of boys in suburban Kansas City the night before, she'd been disgusted by what she considered a lack of hustle by several players who failed to get back on defense. Moore hadn't said anything at the time, but sitting on the bench, Pat Head, who hung out more frequently with Moore and Gunter than with the other players, knew by the look in Moore's eyes that she'd teach the team a lesson. "We'd all better get to bed early tonight," Head warned teammates who had planned on going out for pizza after the game, because "tomorrow she's going to kill us." But some of them went out anyway. They were about to learn why they'd made such a big mistake.

"There was absolutely no excuse for what happened yesterday," Moore said. "You have to decide you want to play every minute, or you don't play at all. I'll go to Ontario with only nine players if I have to; I don't care if I go with six if there are only six of you who'll give 100 percent. For the rest of you, there will be box seats in the front row."[3]

"And so began," Grove wrote, "the most rigorous practice of the US Women's Olympic team to date." And by "practice," he meant running. And running more. And running some more, puking up pizza, and then running some more. Then running, puking, and more running.

Moore eventually gave her players three minutes to catch their breath and gulp down some Quickick, an electrolyte drink. Several women fell to the ground, drenched in sweat. One collapsed onto the stage at the end of the court, sobbing. "Hands up over your head," shouted team manager Jeanne Rowlands. "Move your body, move your body, do not collapse."[4]

Rowlands and assistant coach Sue Gunter approached Moore. "That's enough. They've had enough."

But Moore's lesson was not complete. For an hour they ran, never touching a basketball. Grove asked Rowlands to explain the method behind Moore's madness.

"These women," she said, "are proving to themselves that they can get beyond pain — and you must be able to get beyond pain."

Grove interviewed more players and coaches and said goodbye to Bozarth. He asked Vic whether, after the carnage he'd just witnessed, he'd watch another practice.

"I think I'll come back tomorrow," the teenager replied. "I don't have anything else to do."

By the time Bozarth and Grove watched a practice they'd never forget, tryouts for the 1976 women's basketball team had already progressed through two significant steps. Though the twelve players who had competed on the 1975 World Championship and Pan Am squads had a significant advantage to make the team that would travel to Hamilton, USA Basketball executives Mildred Barnes and Bill Wall believed it was important, especially in the bicentennial year, to offer any woman in the country a chance to try out.

Barnes placed advertisements in newspapers across the country, encouraging women to attend regional tryout camps in one of seven venues from California to Iowa to Maryland. Directors of each regional then sent their camp's best few players to Warrensburg, where a group of thirty-four finalists would be whittled down to twelve active members of the roster and three alternates ready to be called on in case of illness or injury.

> "Any amateur player possessing United States citizenship who believes she has international playing ability and who wishes to attend a regional trial, should write the trial director for an application. Competitors must qualify for the final trials through selection at a regional site of the competitor's choice. Competitors are responsible for funding their expenses to the regional trials."

Talent levels at the regional camps were wildly divergent, some women showing up just to be able to someday tell their grandkids that they had tried out for the national team, others blissfully unaware of their ineptitude. There were even a few surprise stars. Ann Meyers attended a camp in Sacramento along with Juliene Simpson. Neither had anything to prove, but there they were on the court with 250 hopeful women, some giving their all, some just getting in the way.

A simple layup line was enough to weed out dozens of candidates. On the second day of camp, Meyers went up for a layup and was undercut by a defender, landing awkwardly and spraining her ankle. She was unable to play for the rest of the try-outs, but when officials announced that she would be advancing to Warrensburg anyway, some of the other contestants complained.

Simpson would have none of it.

"Annie Meyers could beat any one of you hopping around on one foot," she said, putting an end to the protest. No doubt, Meyers was one of the most talented players on the planet, but Simpson's words of support still mattered. Meyers had felt pangs of guilt for making the cut without playing, doubting whether she really deserved it. "I could hear what they were saying, and it did make me sad," she recalled. "I was insecure in a lot of ways. For somebody to speak up for me like Juliene meant a lot."

Pat Head showed up at a regional camp in Nashville in the best shape of her life, having lost twenty-seven pounds. The previous summer, she'd been warned by both Wall and Moore that if she didn't dramatically improve her conditioning there was no way she'd make the team. Head took the advice to heart, working out five or six hours a day, running long distances, playing pickup games with men, and spending long hours in the weight room at the University of Tennessee at a time when women weren't too welcome there.

But Head wasn't alone in her determination; everyone had a story and an Olympic dream. Marianne Crawford Stanley of Immaculata was considered one of the top guards in the country and would have likely made the World Championship and Pan Am rosters, but she had been seven months pregnant at the time of the tryouts for those teams and couldn't compete. Now she was back and ready to reestablish herself. Brenda Moeller had been teaching at a junior high in Iowa, staying in shape by working out in the school gym. Gail Marquis had supported herself by selling concessions at the New York Mets' Shea Stadium, patrolling the ballpark with crates of soft drinks, hot dogs, and peanuts. Mary Anne O'Connor slept on her sister's sofa bed, waking up early to work a six-to-three shift at a gas station, refereeing high school games, and helping coach at her alma mater, Southern Connecticut State.

When the thirty-four finalists arrived in Warrensburg, Moore asked them to pose for a group picture outside the gymnasium. This was before the age of coordinated athletic gear, whether from sponsors or the Olympic committee. Instead, the women posed in whatever clothes they'd packed for the trip, a colorful mishmash of ringer T-shirts, flip-flops, high-top sneakers, rugby shirts, striped socks, and tank tops.

Wrangling a bunch of young people together for a group activity was nothing new for Billie Moore. It hadn't been all that long ago that she was teaching PE classes at a junior high school in Topeka, Kansas, prepared to pass out jump ropes and mend skinned knees for the rest of her career.[5] But a chance invitation to a basketball clinic changed everything. She met successful coaches, impressed them with her knowledge of the game, and

Olympic hopefuls convened at Central Missouri State University in Warrensburg, Missouri, for the final tryout camp to determine the 1976 US national team roster. (Mildred Barnes)

found herself rising the ranks in college basketball and traveling to Moscow, Cali, and Mexico City with the US national team.

It may have been an improbable journey to the top for Moore, but with the possible exception of a softball field, there was no place on earth she felt more comfortable than on a basketball court. As a kid growing up in tiny Westmoreland, Kansas (population: 500), she tagged along with her dad, also named Billie, to every game he coached, holding her own clipboard and mimicking her father by scribbling imaginary plays during timeouts. When she was old enough, she set down the clipboard and picked up a ball, playing with such skill that the men in town begged her dad to let Billie Jean play on the boys' team in eighth grade. And she would have if her mom hadn't squashed the idea.

So Billie Jean played ball with the girls, which kept her close to her father since he coached their team, too. Billie Moore was hard to please — infamous for his piercing stare — and Billie Jean felt she could never live up to his high expectations. But at least he had them. All over the country, moms and dads discouraged their daughters from playing sports — the sweat, the competition, the bumping and bruising, it was all so "unfeminine." But Billie supported his daughter's interest. When she injured her back and hip playing ball, he didn't ask her to quit, but instead drove her to Lawrence, home of the University of Kansas, to see a specialist who could heal her pain and get her back on the court.

There was some poetry to Moore assembling the team in Warrensburg, Missouri, of all places. Dr. Allen, the Lawrence osteopath who treated her bad back as a kid, was Dr. *Phog* Allen, the legendary Kansas men's basketball coach who as a young man had won the men's basketball tournament at the 1904 World's Fair in St. Louis. Allen coached at Kansas from 1919 to 1956. But before that, he had cut his teeth at a place called State Normal School No. 2 — later known as Central Missouri State, where he practiced medicine and coached basketball and football. Eventually the school's board of regents, which included two doctors in competition for Warrensburg's patients, gave him an ultimatum: focus only on coaching or get out of town. He left for Kansas, developed the Jayhawks into a college basketball power, lobbied for basketball to be included in the Olympics, and set up an osteopathic clinic in Lawrence, passing away two years before one of his former patients became head coach of the US women's national team.

With no time to waste, Moore made the most of every minute in camp, putting the players through two or three grueling workouts a day. She understood an important part of her job was convincing her players to do things they wouldn't do on their own. At one level, that meant suppressing their egos for the good of the team. She told the players they'd all need to become interchangeable "chameleons," willing to do whatever was in the team's best interests. This was a mental challenge, one the players were willing to accept.

The physical challenges Moore presented were more difficult. Knowing her team would not be as talented or as deep as the Soviets, the only way the US could compete, she believed, was by outrunning them. "I thought there was a certain way we had to play, a certain level of shape we had to be in, so I was a pretty tough taskmaster," Moore recalled. "If you don't demand from people how hard you want them to practice and play and leave it up to them to decide, you're not going to like what you get. It will be inconsistent, and they will pick and choose when they play hard. So you try not to let those decisions be theirs." Mostly, that meant making the players run to the point they couldn't feel their legs anymore. Again. Again. Again. "I think they thought I was going to kill them," Moore recalled, "and that was probably true."

Writing in her journal at lunch one day, Lieberman described the brutal session she'd just endured. "We went 2 hours this morning — I believe they're crazy — yes, the coaches — we ran 3-man weave, 5-man weave, 3 on 2, 2 on 1, 11-man drill, shooting, man defense, zone defense — deny, head on ball, full court 1 on 1, then, 'Ladies, let's scrimmage.' Scrimmage — I can't breathe or walk. Need some sleep. Next practice session at 2:00."

Beyond the sheer physical demands, Moore's abrupt style — no praise to soften a critique — took some players aback. With the Hamilton qualifying tournament just a month away, Moore made her points directly, with no sugarcoating. She didn't scream — just a glare, a scowl, the unvarnished truth. "I didn't have a lot of time to soft-pedal it," she recalled. "I used to say, 'I might not have time to say, "I like your blue eyes," however, that was the worse excuse for a pass I've ever seen.'"

For Moore, Gunter, and the selection committee, the workouts provided an opportunity to see how the new players stacked up against the veterans.

Marianne Crawford Stanley had been the point guard on Immaculata's most successful teams, winning championships in 1973 and '74, and playing in the nationally televised game at Maryland and the first women's game at Madison Square Garden. There was no denying her talent and court savvy, nor would the international stage be too big for her.[6]

Carol Blazejowski was one of the most electric players in the college game, a sweet-shooting jump shooter and strong rebounder from Montclair State College in New Jersey. Though her high school didn't offer girls' basketball until her senior year, she developed her game so

Assistant coach Sue Gunter, head coach Billie Moore, team director Mildred Barnes, and team manager Jeanne Rowlands in Warrensburg, Missouri. (Mildred Barnes)

quickly that she earned All-American honors as a sophomore at Montclair in 1976, averaging over ten rebounds and nearly 30 points per game, tops in the nation.

Michelle McKenzie arrived in Warrensburg from Bessie Stockard's Federal City College team in Washington, DC. She had dropped out of school for a semester to focus entirely on training for

215

the Olympic tryouts. One of the last cuts for the World Championship team a year earlier, she'd been determined to make the team this time, doing so much swimming, cycling, and running in the months leading up to the Warrensburg camp that Moore's drills hardly bothered her. "It was right up my alley," she recalled.[7]

Then there was Cardte Hicks from San Pedro, California, one of the most intriguing athletes at the tryouts, a phenomenal leaper with international experience as a volleyball player. Growing up with five brothers and two sisters, Hicks developed her basketball prowess at a young age, a "tomboy" and neighborhood hustler. Her brothers would challenge their friends to take on their sister in a game of one-on-one, the loser handing over their sneakers to the winner. Hicks won a lot of shoes for her brothers. By age fifteen, she was dunking in playground pickup games. "Alley-oop to my sister, alley-oop to my sister!" her brothers would shout. "Most of the other girls were just trying to learn how to shoot and dribble, but I was slapping the backboard like it was nothing," she recalled.

When her older brother Marc came down with the mumps, Hicks cut her hair, taped down her chest, put on his uniform, and impersonated him in a game, just for fun. "I looked exactly like him," she said. "No one knew. Everyone was yelling at me, 'Gimme the ball, Marc.' I had to remember I was supposed to be Marc." None of the coaches or players caught on, but they were impressed when "Marc" scored 18 points.[8]

The biggest wildcard of all, however, was one of the "experienced" players, seventeen-year-old Nancy Lieberman, still so immature and full of energy she continually irritated the other women. "Her verbal gun," wrote one sportswriter, "is always drawn — and likely loaded." In one of the first practices, Lieberman crashed into Simpson while going up for a rebound, giving Simpson a concussion that left her suffering from dizzy spells for a week. "Moore didn't know whether to reward [Lieberman] for her aggression or lock her up in a cage," wrote another sportswriter. Her teammates would have preferred the cage. Even after exhausting workouts, Lieberman bounded around

For teenaged Nancy Lieberman, throwing herself fully into basketball was a means of escaping family dysfunction. Her youthful energy propelled her success but grated on some of her teammates. (Women's Basketball Hall of Fame)

the dormitory with a football, begging anyone to play catch with her. "Shut the hell up!" the women would reply. Lieberman's roommate, Charlotte Lewis, sought sympathy from the others. "I need a break," she'd moan. "I need a break."

Lieberman had grown up in the Far Rockaway neighborhood of Queens. Her father was the grandson of Jews killed in the Holocaust, and his parents' arms bore the tattooed identification numbers of a Nazi concentration camp. Her mom was an Irish Catholic daughter of former vaudeville performers.

When she was a kid, Nancy's parents fought all the time. One day she was playing outside, trying to get away from the screaming, when she heard the crash of a breaking window as a glass milk bottle shattered through and fell to the ground. Her parents separated when she was ten, and finally divorced when she was twelve, leaving Nancy with her mom and brother. Her father would promise to come visit, and Nancy would sit on the front steps waiting, but he'd never arrive. She'd cry and cry, and even decades later, she said that she was unable to find the words to describe the disappointment she felt on those lonely afternoons.

Nancy's brother, Cliff, was a studious and quiet asthmatic child who read books and played the piano, the apple of his mother's eye. He was a good boy, while Nancy was "worse than ten boys." She brought home stray dogs and cats, quit piano lessons, ordered an alligator that arrived in the mail, and dribbled her basketballs so loudly in the house her mom punctured five of them with a screwdriver just to shut her up.

"I'd get her dolls, she'd want balls," her mother once said. "My kid and sports, you wouldn't believe. I yelled. I screamed . . . 'Stop it already. Sports aren't for girls. Why don't you be a secretary? A nurse? Put on a dress?' Nothing worked. She thought it was a challenge having everybody against her. She'd fight the world if she had to."

Nancy refused to wear the dresses her grandmother bought her. Instead, she saved money from her paper route and went shopping for a pair of canvas Chuck Taylor basketball shoes. The salesman gave her a funny look. "It's not a shoe for girls," he said. But she bought them anyway. When her class took a field trip to the Bronx Zoo, Nancy stopped at a newsstand along the way and bought a copy of *Sports Illustrated*. "Everyone looked at birds and I read about Oakland and Green Bay in the Super Bowl," she later wrote. "There was no road map for someone like me. What there was? A lot of bullying and judgment."

She searched her school library for books on women athletes and found none. Instead, her role models became the basketball players she watched on TV, guys like Willis Reed and Clyde Frazier of the New York Knicks — and a loudmouth boxer from Louisville, Kentucky. "Muhammad Ali represented everything I wanted to be in sports," she recalled. "He was bold, brash, confident and cocky, but he backed up everything that he said he was going to do."

For Lieberman, sports were an escape from for her anxiety and depression, a chance to get away from her brother who wouldn't play with her, rebel against her mother, and fight back against an absent father. Any happiness in her life came from playing with boys in the neighborhood. "I needed basketball more than basketball or sports needed me," she said. At age nine, she was a good enough baseball player to make the boys' Police Athletic League team as the starting left fielder. But the day before the team's first game, her coach told her the league wouldn't allow a girl to play. She turned to basketball and fell in love with the freedom of the game and the improvisation it required. She had no patience for the noncompetitive PE activities girls were restricted to at her school.

If she was going to play, she wanted to play with the best. And in New York City, that meant taking the subway to Harlem's Rucker Park. She'd stuff extra T-shirts into her jacket to look bigger and tougher on the train and then prove herself on the court, a redheaded white girl earning acceptance from young Black men in the unlikeliest of circumstances. "Rucker Park saved my life," she recalled. "It was a safe place and nobody profiled me or made fun of me . . . All that mattered was street cred and if you could play." On the basketball court, twisting and turning and elbowing and rebounding, she could forget about her absent father. Holding her own with the boys at Rucker Park, earning the nickname Fire, she could escape her brother's shadow and her mother's disapproval. "My childhood fears and insecurities were channeled into being the best — not by a little, by a lot," she said. "I felt like I wasn't noticed at home, and so it became very important for me to be noticed, period."

Fire became a legend in Harlem, invited by an AAU coach named LaVozier LaMar at age thirteen to play for his team for boys, the New York Chuckles. "Nancy was the queen of Harlem," LaMar recalled. "She would roar down the court left, right, turning, spinning, flying in the air. You know, getting it all done."

As a sophomore at Far Rockaway High, Lieberman led the Seahorses to the city championship game, her team losing by one point in double overtime. New York sportswriters and US national team coaches took notice of the red-headed phenom, and she earned an invitation, at only fifteen, to try out for the national team in 1974. She played well enough at a regional camp in Queens to advance to the final tryouts in Albuquerque. But her mom told her she couldn't go; she didn't have the money for airfare. When friends, neighbors, and high school teammates in Far Rockaway learned that Nancy wasn't going to be able to pursue her basketball dream, they came to the rescue, raising enough money to send her to the tryouts.

In New Mexico, Lieberman felt at peace surrounded by other elite players. Here she wasn't "different" or a "tomboy," but a respected female athlete. She had grown tired of people telling her that her love for sports was merely a phase she'd outgrow. Now, for the first time, she understood not only that her interests were legitimate but also that a lot of other women shared them, too.

The coach of the camp was Alberta Cox, a legendary former AAU player who had first coached the US national team in 1965. Cox, Lieberman recalled, ran the site like a "boot camp," requiring players to carry a basketball with them at all times — to the cafeteria, to the bathroom, to bed. On the third day of camp, Lieberman fractured her ribs and bruised her spleen after colliding with another player in a rebounding drill. She'd have to return home.

Cox drove Lieberman to the airport, wishing her a speedy recovery and challenging her to continue working toward a spot on the 1980 Olympic team. Lieberman took that as an insult. "I told her I was thinking more about making the 1976 team. She just smiled at me and gave me a look that said, 'Not a chance.' "

But now here Lieberman was in Warrensburg — young, loud, aggressive, and skilled — on the verge of proving her doubters wrong.

For a city girl like Lieberman, Warrensburg could not have been more boring. In New York, the landmarks she was accustomed to were among the tallest buildings in the world, the most famous stadiums. In Warrensburg, everyone knew the Triangle, notable as the spot where a dirt road converged with a paved one. New York was the concrete jungle; Warrensburg the birthplace of the riding lawn mower. On one bus ride to a scrimmage in Kansas City, Pat Head gazed out the window, admiring the long stretches of green. "Look how pretty the grass is," she said. In her autobiography, Lieberman recalled the country girl/city girl comedy that followed.

Lieberman said it was just grass, nothing to get excited about.

Head said it reminded her of the farm where she grew up. Lieberman said she grew up surrounded by cement and sky-scrapers.

"What did you do on the farm?" Lieberman asked.

Head explained that she used to bale hay and slop the pigs.

"I pointed out that we did have something in common," Lieberman recalled, telling Head that she slapped people just like Head slapped pigs.

Head was exasperated. *Slopped* pigs. Fed them. Not slapped them.

"You didn't punch a pig?!"

Exhausted as they were, the players weren't content to just gaze at the grass during their off-hours in Warrensburg. Barnes organized an outing to Kansas City for a Royals game, and Moore and Gunter took several women golfing — a frustrating experience that found them still putting on the second green after what seemed like two hours. Head played five-card stud with the coaches. Towns-people ran into the players at the grocery store, walking along the main drag near campus, or eating at restaurants thanks to the coupons the coaches had earned by speaking to civic groups. A few of the local guys were smitten with some of the players, and one invited Pat Head over to his parents' house for dinner. She accepted, and decades later, his friends recalled their "summer romance."

On May 19, Mildred Barnes posted a list in the hallway of the dormitory. If a player's name was on it, she was still alive; if not, she'd been cut from the team. The hall became a confusing stew of emotions — tears of joy and pain, wails of anguish and delight, hugs of celebration and solace. The names of all twelve returning players from 1975 were on the list (Bush, Dunkle, Easterling, Harris, Head, Lewis, Lieberman, Meyers, O'Connor, Rapp, Rojcewicz, and Simpson), as were ten others: Carol Blazejowski, Cindy Brogdon, Tara Heiss, Cardte Hicks, Gail Marquis, Dorothy McCrea, Michelle McKenzie, Brenda Moeller, Trish Roberts, and Marianne Crawford Stanley. The final roster, it was announced, would be revealed in just three days. The last few practices in between would be the most intense of all.

One way the coaches compared the remaining players was by matching them up for full-court battles. "There's nothing like going one-on-one to find out who wants it most," Moore said. Lieberman was matched up with Crawford Stanley, believing that "the committee was paying special attention" and may only select one of them for the team.

Head recalled that "with a gleam in her eye," Moore ordered her to take on the blond eighteen-year-old from Buford, Georgia: Cindy Brogdon. Brogdon arrived at camp with a reputation as a deadly shooter, having grown up playing by herself in the backyard, bouncing passes off pecan trees and shooting at a hoop mounted on a wooden backboard. She joined her school's eighth-grade basketball team in seventh grade because she was the tallest kid in gym class and scored 52 points in her first game. She went on to win four state MVP awards in high school and became the first Georgia high school girl to earn a full basketball scholarship, to Mercer University in Macon.

Aware of Brogdon's reputation, Head set out to deny her opportunities to shoot. "I told myself, 'She can't score if she doesn't have the ball,'" Head recalled. Brogdon missed her first shot, and from then on, every time she shot and missed, Head blocked out hard, preventing any offensive rebounds or second shots. After five minutes, Head was on top 5–0, and Brogdon, at least in Head's mind, was demoralized. "She was so strong you could not get around her to follow your shot," Brogdon admitted. "She was the most aggressive person I ever met on a basketball court."

But the night before the final cuts, Head uncharacteristically succumbed to anxiety. She realized that with "very little difference between the players' ability," the selection committee was looking for the tiniest flaws. "I felt the pressure then," she recalled. "It was all mental." In a scrimmage open to the people of Warrensburg, she was fouled and stepped to the free throw line. All she could think of was how badly she wanted to be on the Olympic team. Her knees trembled; her body went weak. Even before the ball left her fingers, she knew what was going to happen. Air ball. "I choked," she said. "I could not physically get the ball to the rim." Her Olympic dreams, she believed, were over.

Gail Marquis felt the same way. All the work she'd put in, all the sacrifices she'd made, even the skills she'd shown during the first days of tryouts were meaningless when she fell apart in the final scrimmage. "I was so nervous, I played terribly the whole time," she said. "My defense was weak; I was missing my shots from the outside and I wasn't showing my court sense." Matched up defensively against Blazejowski, Marquis allowed Blaze to "go off," giving up 10 points in rapid succession. On her way back to her dorm, Marquis was convinced she'd blown her chance, blaming herself for getting her hopes up in the first place.

When she got back to her room, her bunkmate Trish Roberts also believed she'd botched her opportunity, not so much through poor play as through a lack of confidence. She had never been coached by someone as demanding as Moore and found herself intimidated.

"All she had to do was look at me and I'd start crying," Roberts recalled decades later. "I was so afraid of her. I had never had anybody push me so hard. She yelled at me all the time. Even after practice, I couldn't sit anywhere near her. I couldn't look her in the eyes. I always had my head down."

That night, as the selection committee made its final determination, Marquis and Roberts packed their suitcases, certain they'd be sent home in the morning.

Barnes, Stockard, Rowlands, Wall, and the coaches stayed up late, running through the strengths and weaknesses of each player. Moore considered Charlotte Lewis the "most physical presence" on the team, a tremendous rebounder, and the only player with the muscle to compete with the Soviets and Eastern Europeans. Nancy Dunkle was "smooth as silk" on her good days, too prone to self-doubt on her worst. Cindy Brogdon was a born shooter. Mary Anne O'Connor could force turnovers and score on the fast break. Play Trish Roberts too tight, she'll drive past you; play her too loose, she'll shoot. Juliene Simpson never backed down from a fight. Annie Meyers wanted to play every minute of every game and hated to lose. Sue Rojcewicz had great vision and was unselfish. There were no limits to Lusia Harris's potential. Marianne Crawford Stanley had matched up well against Meyers and Rita Easterling in one-one-one scrimmages — some considered her the smartest player on the floor. Carol Blazejowski could score at will. No one was more athletic than Cardte Hicks, no one more experienced than Cherri Rapp. Moore and Gunter didn't have a vote, but Moore told the committee that with the twelfth and final roster spot, someone who wouldn't play much anyway, she'd like a young player, someone who could gain experience for 1980. There were no easy decisions.[9]

Waking up early the next morning, players anxiously waited for Mildred Barnes to post the list. "The tension in the dorm was unbearable," Nancy Lieberman remembered. "I can never recall being as fidgety or nervous in my entire life." Some women wondered if the decisions would be based purely on talent or if politics would play a part. Would an existing relationship with one of the coaches make a difference? Would the Black players have an equal opportunity? And, absurdly, had Lieberman's father, so absent in her life, bribed the committee to ensure his daughter made the team?

Finally, a shout went out. Barnes had posted the list of names on the wall: the twelve members of the team and the three alternates. "There was screaming and crying all at once as players registered their emotions after looking at the list," Lieberman recalled. Roberts and Marquis remained in their room, too nervous to look, too certain they hadn't made it. As happy as she was to see her name on the list, Nancy Dunkle felt deep sympathy for those who didn't. They'd all worked so hard. Frustrations rose to the surface. "One of them hollered out, 'Why didn't I make the team?'" Marquis recalled. "They said, 'You didn't rebound your shots.' 'I didn't have to; they all went in.' Another one said, 'Why did so-and-so make the team? I ate her lunch!'"

When Lieberman learned she'd made it, she called her mother in New York and then placed a collect call to Alberta Cox, the coach who had told her to focus on making the 1980 Olympic team. "I said, 'Coach Cox, this is Nancy. Remember you said I was going to make the '80 group? I'm at tryouts and I just made the '76 team, and I want to thank you for inspiring me. And thanks for accepting the collect call!'"

Roberts finally emerged from her room, daring to look. Women were coming down the hall toward her, some crying, some practically skipping with happiness. "Everybody was patting me on the back," she recalled. "I didn't know if it was a good pat or a bad pat." Not only was Roberts's name on the list, but her roommate Marquis's was, too. As stunned as she was by the news, Roberts was equally surprised that Carol Blazejowski hadn't made the team. Blaze walked over to Marquis, tears in her eyes, and congratulated her. Brenda Moeller was less surprised that she hadn't made the team than that none of the Wayland Baptist players had — Cherri Rapp was an alternate, and Carolyn Bush was cut. Immaculata wouldn't be represented, either — Crawford Stanley had been cut.

Cardte Hicks was stunned to see her name only on the alternate list, believing she had earned a roster spot but had been denied because she was Black. Rather than continue as an alternate, she confronted Moore with her theory and asked for a ticket home. Althea Gwyn, who was cut outright, also believed race was a factor, certain that only a limited number of Black players would be acceptable, as did Michelle McKenzie of Federal City College, who was named an alternate. The idea of a quota for Black players was not far-fetched; previously all-white teams in men's sports had discriminated in this way for years. Nor did any Black guards make the Olympic team — another pattern seen in men's sports, where white coaches favored white ball handlers.

Moore, Barnes, and Stockard, McKenzie's coach in Washington, DC, all denied that race had been a conscious factor in their decision-making and said they put together what they believed would be the most successful team, including four Black players and two Black alternates. Still, there was no denying the role of systemic racism, including the fact that opportunities for Black women to play college basketball, and thereby put themselves in position to try out for the team, were far more limited in 1976 than at any other point since. Stockard also said the network of coaches and officials who spread word about the entire tryout process was mostly white. So the funnel of Black players leading to Warrensburg was narrow to begin with.

"We tried to be as fair and honest as we could," Stockard said. "I just wish we could have taken them all. You have sympathy for a girl that tries so hard to make a team and then she doesn't make it, but you have to understand you can't have but so many. It's up to you to impress the committee. Some of the people were not pleased, but I felt it was well done."[10]

The fact that the committee cut three players — Rita Easterling, Cherri Rapp, and Carolyn Bush — from the previous summer's teams came as a shock to their former teammates. "When we learned that they hadn't made the team, it was heartbreaking," Meyers said. "But the three new players were just as deserving."

Along with Roberts and Marquis, Cindy Brogdon was the third newcomer.

Carolyn Bush believed she'd been given a fair chance, but she still was devastated by the thought of telling her friends and family that she hadn't made the team. So many people had invested in her life: the parents who built a playground when white parents refused to let Black children play in the city park, the grandmother who raised her and told her she'd need to be twice as good to succeed in a racist country, the white coach who defended her humanity in the face of Tennessee bigotry. She cried all the way home, asking herself what she could have done differently.

"I had some difficult feelings for certain people," she admitted. "Something like that will make you take a good look at yourself. What could I have done better to make the team? It wasn't all the selection committee's fault. It was something I didn't do, too." When she arrived home in Kingston, her grandmother would not let her wallow in her sorrow. "Honey, I'm sorry you didn't make the team," she said, "but you can't stay here and do nothing."

It was her way, Bush believed, of making her "dust [herself] off and start pursuing other things. She had always taught me that when disappointment comes, you can't fall apart."

With her final roster set, Moore's mantra to her players was "learn to adjust," imploring them to set aside their individual desires for the good of the team, to learn what made each other tick on and off the court. This would not be a team that relied offensively on strict adherence to set plays, nor would it mimic the style of play the women were accustomed to on their college or high school teams. Lusia Harris was used to a more methodical pace of play at Delta State, where the team's guards waited on her to gain position under the basket. "You aren't in Cleveland, Mississippi, anymore," Moore told her. "The Russians aren't going to wait for you." Learning to adjust also meant reacting to the defensive sets their opponents gave them in any particular game. Moore wanted her players prepared for anything. "Ask questions now," she said. "Now is the time. Not when we're in Canada."

'GOT TO BELIEVE'

The Story Of The Olympics

Star-Journal Photos By Wally Emerson

The Women's Olympic Basketball Players, in Warrensburg since May 16, are confident they will win a gold medal in Montreal this summer. They know the secret of success is attitude. As team member Pat Head explained this week: "You've got to believe in yourself." That "got to believe" spirit is drummed into the team by coach Billie Moore in the photo at right during a recent scrimmage. Below, Charlotte "Peach" Lewis trash talent busters as Nancy Dunkle relieves pre-game tension with lively conversation.

The US women's basketball team's tryout camp was big news in Warrensburg, Missouri, home of Central Missouri State University. Local kids watched the team's practices in blazing hot Garrison Gym. (Warrensburg Star-Journal)

239

Finally, after four and a half weeks in Warrensburg, under the unrelenting pressure to perform at the highest level, it was time for one last exercise. Moore asked her team to run a fast break drill to finish practice. The gym was quiet, the only sound the high-pitched squeak of sneakers on wood. The players knew what to do; Moore didn't need to shout any instructions.

Team manager Jeanne Rowlands watched in amazement as the players moved up and down the floor, running, passing, shooting, one group seamlessly giving way to the next, minute after minute, with no dribbling, no breaks, no missed shots. This was poetry in motion, and the women were confident enough to recognize it, smiling, encouraging one another, moving faster and faster still, no sign of fatigue, no errors, not wanting to stop. To Rowlands, the women were moving together in such harmony it was if they were one person. "I had never seen a team that perfect," she recalled. "I just stared." Finally, Moore called an end to practice, sending the players back to their rooms to shower before dinner.

Rowlands, Moore, Gunter, and trainer Gail Weldon stood around a small table in the gym.

Moore had developed a mental picture of what basketball perfection was supposed to look like. Her job, she believed, was to push her players to the point they could bring that vision to life. And she'd just seen it happen.

"Do you think," she asked the others, "they have any idea how good they really are?"[11]

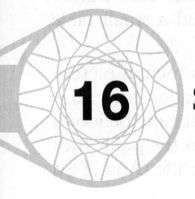

16

YOUNG, SCRAPPY, AND HUNGRY

Nine teams arrived in Hamilton, Ontario, for the final Olympic qualifying tournament, but only the top two finishers would advance to Montreal to join the four teams that had already qualified. Outside the small circle of US players and coaches, nobody seemed too optimistic the Americans would move on.

Juliene Simpson bristled at the news reports claiming the American women should be satisfied just to participate in the Hamilton tournament and took motivation from the friends whose expectations were so low they sent her off with the über-inspiring words "Just do your best."

Moore was privy to information that would have devastated her players if they found out, so she hid it from them for years after the Olympics, only confiding in Sue Gunter and Jeanne Rowlands. USA Basketball executive director Bill Wall had such little faith in the American women's chances that the organization had not prepared for the team to stay or train during the weeks between the qualifying tournament and the start of the Olympics. It had only made plans to send the players home after losing in Hamilton. Wall had booked plane tickets for each woman — not to Montreal, but back to where they came from.

In Hamilton, the US was assigned to Group A along with Mexico, France, and Poland.[1] Group B included Cuba, Bulgaria, South Korea, Great Britain, and Italy. Teams in each group would play each other once, and then the top two finishers from each side would meet. Collecting two points for each victory, whichever two teams emerged with the most points would earn the final invitations to the Olympics.

All games in Hamilton, a city of 530,000 about an hour southwest of Toronto, were played in a small gymnasium at Mc-Master University. While the American players had been sequestered from their families in Warrensburg, several families made the trek to Ontario. Juliene Simpson's husband drove 1,700 straight miles from their home in Albuquerque, relying on a supply of NoDoz to stay awake at the wheel. Pat Head's parents and her brothers Kenneth and Tommy drove up from Tennessee in Tommy's big yellow Cadillac, a surprise to Head since it was tobacco season back on the farm. Ann Meyers's brother Dave came up, along with their father, Bob. And midway through the tournament, a group of boosters from Old Dominion University in Virginia flew up to watch Nancy Lieberman, who had announced during the Warrensburg trials that she would be attending college there, concluding a highly competitive recruiting battle during which some schools offered her cars, cash, and other illegal inducements.

For Meyers, her father's presence was a mixed blessing. A year earlier, both of her parents had come to Mexico City for the Pan Am Games, but their marriage was in shambles and the tension was hard to tune out on the court. Now, a year later, her father had left her mother for good. Annie had taken her mother's side in the dispute, and she felt disloyal to her mom for even being cordial to her dad. "Family baggage," she later wrote, "had flung itself into the backseat during this crucial trip."

Trish Roberts was a phenomenal basketball player, a natural on the court with elite skills on both ends of the floor. But in the opening round game against Mexico, she could not have been more confused. Up in the wooden bleachers, an unfamiliar white man took an unusually strong interest in her performance, constantly yelling at her to shoot the ball — even when she didn't have it. *Especially* when she didn't have it.

As she ran up and down the court, Roberts asked herself who this man was and why he kept yelling at her. She didn't know him. She didn't know anybody in the stands. But it was a small gym with only a handful of fans in the bleachers, and she could hear this guy's every word.

Finally, during a timeout, she turned to one of her teammates. "I don't know who this man is," she said. "He keeps yelling at me, 'Shoot it, Trish!'"

Her teammates laughed. While everyone on the team called Patricia Head "Pat," her family back home in Tennessee called her "Trish." The man was Head's father, and he was yelling at his daughter to get more involved in the offense. With Roberts's question answered, the US cruised to an easy 80–57 win over Mexico. Ann Meyers sat out the game with a calf injury, and starting in her place, Sue Rojcewicz led the Americans with 14 points.[2]

For Meyers, who felt the need to prove herself to her father and brother, missing the game was excruciating. And her absence allowed Rojcewicz to lobby Moore for the permanent starting job, which she felt she deserved over Meyers. Moore listened, but when Meyers returned to action in the game against France, she was back in the starting lineup.

France took an early lead in the first quarter, but eventually the US players' size became too much for the French to handle. Lusia Harris led all scorers with 21 points as the Americans collected 48 rebounds and shot 52 percent from the field. Returning from injury, Meyers was second on the team with 13 points. The win put the US in great position to advance from their pool, but for Lieberman, who never got off the bench, it was a painfully embarrassing night. The group from Old Dominion had flown to Canada to see their prize recruit, and she didn't play a minute. After the game, when the visitors wanted to at least say hello, Lieberman refused to come out of the locker room. "I told somebody, 'Tell them I'm busy doing interviews,'" she recalled. "It wasn't one of my better moments, but it happened."[3]

Next up was Poland, which had also started the tournament winning its first two games. This time it was Nancy Dunkle's turn to shine, leading the US with 23 points and nine rebounds. Head (12 points), Harris (11), and Meyers (10) also scored in double figures as the Americans dominated in an 84–66 victory that secured them a spot in the final round, where they'd play the top two finishers from Group B: Cuba and Bulgaria.

Heading into the tournament, Meyers had considered these next two opponents the Americans' toughest competition. A loss to either team now would make an Olympic berth nearly impossible to achieve. The first game, against Cuba, would be the biggest any of these women had ever played.

Watching the Cubans in pregame warm-ups, Gail Marquis of Queens College said they reminded her of some of the tough high school teams she'd faced back in New York. "I was impressed," she said. "They looked like they were from Jamaica High School, looked like the sisters I played against back home. They were so quick and energetic." She wasn't the only one who was impressed. Before the game, Simpson had read sportswriters' predictions that the Cubans would win. "Everybody picked Cuba," she said. "They were taller, they could outjump us, they could shoot from downtown."

But right from the opening tip, the Americans played beautiful basketball. Everyone, Trish Roberts said later, truly understood their role. Their cuts were

Sue Rojcewicz dribbles up the court against Cuba on July 2, 1976. The tournament at McMaster University in Hamilton, Ontario, determined the final two qualifiers for the Montreal Olympics. (Women's Basketball Hall of Fame)

sharp, their passes were crisp, their shots were on target. In the first half, the US made six of every ten shots they attempted, playing at such a high level that Moore dreaded seeing the clock ticking down toward halftime, believing the break could only interrupt their momentum. "The first half of that game against Cuba," she said later, "our team played as perfect [a game] of basketball that I've ever witnessed."

At the half, the US led by the whopping margin of 60–34. But Moore took nothing for granted, pulling Simpson aside in the locker room and telling her to be more aggressive in the second half. She expected the Cubans to clamp down on Meyers and the other shooters, leaving Simpson open at the top of the key. Moore's intuition was right about one thing — Cuba's defense tightened significantly in the opening minutes of the second half, with the US missing its first eleven shots and Cuba cutting the deficit to 14 points. But then Simpson started launching the shots Moore had asked her to take. When she made her third, she looked over at the US bench and Moore shot her back a look as if to say, "See?!"

Cuba never came closer than 14 points, and the US held on for an 89–73 win, with Head and Roberts leading the way with 14 points apiece. From a phone outside the US locker room, Head called a sportswriter back in Nashville. "This team has been getting better every game," she said. "You can just see it going up the ladder. We all feel now that the pressure is off, but you don't have to worry about a mental letdown. We're psyched to the hilt. We want to go to Montreal."

The reporter asked Head how it felt to be playing such an important role on the team after languishing on the bench the previous summer. "My knee is completely well, I've lost weight, and I have a completely new attitude," Head said. "I really feel like I'm playing the best basketball of my life right now. And I attribute it to hard work, a lot of hard work."

But proud as she was of her own accomplishments, Head understood how much her team's success meant to younger girls with basketball dreams. This was about more than any individual. "We really do feel like playing on the first women's team to be in the Olympic Games is going to be great for women's basketball in the future," she said. "In the beginning, a girl could play high school ball and that was it. Then they could play college, and now the Olympics and international basketball. That's sure to carry over into the future and provide extra incentive to young girls to try their hand at basketball."

In her exuberance, Head had gotten a little ahead of herself. While the victory over Cuba put the US in a great position to secure a bid to Montreal, it wasn't quite guaranteed. With a win over Bulgaria, they were in. But if they lost to Bulgaria and Cuba beat Poland, there would be a four-way tie and it would come down to point differential.

Swish. Swish. Swish.

In the tournament's final game, the Americans came out in a 1-3-1 zone defense against Bulgaria, and it wasn't working. Ann Meyers and Sue Rojcewicz couldn't keep up with a Bulgarian guard who was draining shot after shot from the baseline.

Nancy Lieberman sat on the bench, barely paying attention, pouting over her lack of playing time. But then Moore called her name. Lieberman didn't hear it. A teammate tapped her on the shoulder. "Coach wants you!" Lieberman got up and ran over to Moore. "I want you to get in the 1-3-1 and I want you to go really hard," Moore said. "When they pass the ball to that girl, I want you to run hard at her and jump as high as you can and contest the shot. But make sure you step to the side so you don't foul."

"OK, coach, got it."

Lieberman, with all her pent-up energy, ran onto the court. Sure enough, the ball went in the Bulgarian sharpshooter's direction. As instructed, Lieberman ran toward her as hard as she could. "I left my feet as I was running toward her and my knees hit her square in the chest and sent her sprawling into the bleachers," Lieberman recalled. "As I stepped over her, I saw Billie motioning to me. 'To the side of her! To the side of her! I told you to get out of the way!'"

Imperfect execution, perhaps, but a game-changing moment. The Bulgarian player never returned, and the US took the lead. Lusia Harris blocked shots and dominated the boards, and the American fans started chanting: "Lucy! Lucy! Lucy!" When Cindy Brogdon hit two free throws with twenty-eight seconds remaining, the victory was clinched: 76–75 USA, and a ticket to the Olympic Games.

Ever so slightly, Meyers could feel a piece of herself moving out of her brother's shadow and earning respect from her father. "Dad told me he was proud that I'd played well against Bulgaria," she recalled in her autobiography. "However I may have felt about him for hurting Mom, his opinions on how well I played still mattered to me. There was a hidden part of me that was still a small child, wanting his approval."

After the game, the Americans returned to their hotel to pack their bags and check out. Harris taught Meyers a trick: roll up your clothes, don't fold them, and they won't wrinkle so much. As Moore and Gunter carried their suitcases to the elevator, Moore turned to her assistant. They'd gotten their team to peak at just the right time, playing well enough to qualify for the Olympics, which had been their goal from the start. But now another huge challenge — and opportunity — lay before them. "You know," Moore said, "I feel like two tons have just been lifted off our backs — and ten tons put back on us."

Gunter smiled. "We can only take one step at a time," she said. "And the most important one we just took. Now we can look forward to Montreal."

First, however, the coaches believed their players had earned a celebration, so they took them to Niagara Falls, about an hour away. It was July 3, 1976, a day before the US would celebrate its two hundredth birthday. Meyers was wrapped up in the patriotism of the moment. Here she was, visiting one of the country's most beautiful sites, about to represent the country as it took aim at its Cold War rival, the USSR.

"I was reminded that believing in oneself, having that winning attitude against all odds, wasn't just part of being a Meyers, or an athlete — it was part of the American spirit," she later wrote. "And I decided that no Soviet team, no matter how great, could ever eclipse that."

As the Americans took one final look at the majestic falls, a rainbow appeared over the water.

"I saw it," Meyers said, "as a prophetic sign that the pot of gold was within reach."

Maybe so.

But first Billie Moore had to find a place for her team to sleep.

TWO HUNDRED CANDLES

17

In New York City, tall ships sailed past the Statue of Liberty. In Philadelphia, legendary singer and civil rights activist Marian Anderson recited the Declaration of Independence and President Ford addressed the nation outside of Independence Hall, declaring liberty an equal and inalienable right for all American men and women. In St. Louis, nearly one million people gathered beneath the Gateway Arch in what one reporter described as a "kaleidoscopic display of sound and color."

In Warrensburg, Missouri, everyone showed up at the Central Missouri football stadium for one of the most anticipated events of the year: the annual lawn mower race that preceded the fireworks show. Warrensburg resident Max Swisher had invented the riding lawn mower, a claim to fame that inspired townspeople to soup up their mowers and speed around the cinder track, leaning through corners on two wheels.

On July 4, 1976, from Portland, Maine, to Portland, Oregon, Americans dressed in red, white, and blue, gathered for picnics and fireworks, marched in parades, listened to speeches, and grilled hot dogs as they celebrated the nation's two hundredth birthday. At a time when American self-esteem had been battered by the war in Vietnam, President Nixon's impeachment, and a turbulent economy, for many people the patriotic revelry of the bicentennial celebration provided a welcome opportunity to relax and reflect.

But not for Billie Moore. She spent her holiday on the phone, desperately trying to find a place for her team to stay, rental cars to get them there, and money for food. The US Olympic Committee had created a staging area in Plattsburgh, New York, for Olympians to live and train in before departing for Montreal. But nobody had anticipated that the women's basketball team would qualify for the Olympics, and at least for the next ten days, there wasn't any room for them.

Moore's predicament illustrated a larger truth, not just about the disparities between men's and women's sports (men's basketball coach Dean Smith wasn't scrambling for accommodations), but also throughout American society. As they observed the bicentennial, Americans questioned whether the country was living up to its founding ideals of justice and equality when it came to women.

Some people noted that American feminism was as old as the colonies themselves. In 1776, Abigail Adams wrote a letter to her husband, John, excoriating the founders' hypocritical treatment of white women (yet ignoring their infinitely greater crimes against Native American and Black women). "I cannot say that I think you very generous to the ladies," she wrote, "for whilst you are proclaiming peace and good will to men, emancipating all nations, you insist upon retaining an absolute power over wives."

Newspaper columnists recalled the Seneca Falls Convention of 1848, the young nation's first conference for women's rights. At that seminal event, Elizabeth Cady Stanton — again centering white women's concerns — proclaimed that "the history of mankind is a history of repeated injuries and usurpations on the part of man toward woman," with man "endeavor[ing], in every way that he could, to destroy her confidence in her own powers, to lessen her self-respect, and to make her willing to lead a dependent and abject life."

Taking stock of the status of women in 1976, other writers noted that women continued to face the same issues as their forebears. "In this, our 200th year as a nation based on life, liberty, [and] the pursuit of happiness," wrote a Salem, Oregon, columnist, "the female portion of our society still does not have those basic rights under the law. The incongruity is inescapably obvious."

An obvious problem in need of a solution for some, but not all. On July 4, 1976, the General Association of Regular Baptist Churches marked the occasion by condemning women's liberation, calling out women "rejecting the husband's authority in the home," and the ERA itself, which they said "belittles woman's highest and noblest calling of housewife and mother."

The anti-ERA movement was gaining steam at the time of the bicentennial, led by Missouri activist Phyllis Schlafly and supported by ever more politically powerful Christian conservatives.[1] Schlafly argued that obtaining equal rights meant giving up certain social advantages. "Of all the classes of people who ever lived, the American woman is the most privileged," she claimed. "We have the most rights and rewards, and the fewest duties . . . Why should we lower ourselves to equal rights when we already have the status of special privilege?" While Betty Friedan and other feminists had argued that women could do more than give birth and run a home, Schlafly contended it was their highest calling. While a man might work his entire career to achieve satisfaction in his profession, Schlafly said, a woman could achieve happiness merely "by having a baby." American women, she claimed, were also privileged because advancement in consumer goods and technology had made housework easier.

"The great heroes of women's liberation are not the straggly-haired women on television talk shows and picket lines, but Thomas Edison, who brought the miracle of electricity to our homes to give light and to run all those labor-saving devices," she claimed. "Or Elias Howe who gave us the sewing machine that resulted in such an abundance of readymade clothing. Or Clarence Birdseye, who invented the process for freezing foods. Or Henry Ford, who mass-produced the automobile so it was within the price range of every American . . . Our American free enterprise system has given us the gigantic food and packaging industry and beautiful supermarkets, which provide an endless variety of foods, prepackaged for easy carrying and a minimum of waiting. In America, women have freedom from the slavery of standing in line for daily food."[2]

Schlafly's arguments, as demeaning and centered in white privilege as they may have been, took hold in conservative legislatures around the country, injecting new life into the anti-ERA cause. But even as many feminists fretted over the

262

Phyllis Schlafly of St. Louis, Missouri, emerged as the most vocal and effective opponent of the women's rights movement, mobilizing conservative Christians against the Equal Rights Amendment and other social issues. (Picryl.com)

dimming prospects for ratification of the ERA, change was slowly occurring in the realm of women's sports. "If when Title IX was passed in 1972, opportunities for women were terrible," said women's sports advocate Margaret Dunkle, "now they've improved to bad — and that's certainly progress."

While university athletic departments had allocated just 1 percent of their budgets to women's sports in 1971, athletic directors could boast that their spending on the women had doubled by 1976 — to a pathetic 2 percent. The University of Georgia added a women's golf team where there wasn't one before. But female golfers received one golf ball; men got as many as they wanted. At the University of Texas, the budget for women's sports increased from $27,500 to $128,000 by 1976. But while assistant football coaches averaged $20,000 in salary, head women's coaches were paid just $2,100. Men's scholarships included housing and dining. Women's did not. At the University of Pittsburgh, women's assistant athletic director Sandra Bullman touted her program as one of the most aggressive in the country. "We want to win. We will do what has to be done to win. That is what we are here for," she said. Her budget? Just $130,000 of the university's $1.9 million overall outlay for athletics.

In environments like this, women athletic administrators and coaches had to be resourceful, striving for excellence even under less-than-ideal circumstances and searching for allies to help them creatively solve problems. Stranded in upstate New York, Billie Moore called the one person in the area who was certain to understand her predicament and do what he could to help. His name was Hunter Low, a tall, middle-aged marketing executive at Kodak, the Rochester, New York–based company that sold millions of rolls of film to American consumers each year.

A veteran of the army and graduate of Syracuse University, Low was the best kind of salesman, the type of guy who understood his clients' problems so well and worked so hard to solve them that he came to be seen as part of their team, not a vendor at all. One of his responsibilities at Kodak was selling movie film to the sports industry. He focused on the underserved market of women's basketball, getting to know coaches so well that it was Low who helped them organize their first coaches' association, and Kodak that sponsored the first All-American women's basketball teams. When the nation's top basketball players arrived in various host cities to be recognized as Kodak All-Americans, it was Low who personally picked them up at the airport.[3]

When Moore called, Low figured out a plan, working his contacts to find the team a place to stay in a dormitory at the University of Rochester. But there were a few problems. The building was under construction. There was no air-conditioning. And the beds were just small plastic mattresses.

Grateful for even these less-than-ideal accommodations, Moore, Gunter, and Rowlands rented cars and drove the team to Rochester. USA Basketball executive director Bill Wall — who hadn't booked accommodations in the first place — helped, too, handing Moore five hundred dollars in cash and his personal American Express card to cover expenses. Low looked for ways to make the women feel special even under these threadbare circumstances, convincing his supervisor at Kodak to host an impromptu cookout for the team at his spacious home on the banks of sparkling Lake Canandaigua. For the players, the chance to eat some burgers, drink lemonade, relax by the pool, and pose for photos in the colorful gardens was a welcome relief from the stress they'd en-

Hunter Low of Kodak (far right) found a place for the US women's basketball team to stay in Rochester, New York, prior to the Olympics, and helped organize a party in the team's honor at the home of another Kodak executive. (Valerie Low)

dured for so long and that would return in Montreal.

As unexpected guests in town, the team was a curiosity to locals who turned out to watch their practices. Rochester sportswriter Rudy Martzke asked Moore about her team's outlook in Montreal.[4] "There's no question the Soviet Union should be favored," Moore told him. "They haven't lost a game in six years. But I think we're next. We're capable of giving them their toughest battle. We're going there with the idea of winning the gold medal."

And then, finally, after more than a week in Rochester, Moore received the call she'd been waiting for.

It was time to move on to Plattsburgh, her team's last stop on its long and improbable journey to the Olympics.

READY
OR NOT

18

While Billie Moore and her players lived uncomfortably in the oppressively hot and under-construction dormitory at the University of Rochester, American Olympians in other sports moved into dormitories at Plattsburgh State University, three hundred miles to the northeast.

Nestled along the shores of Lake Champlain just an hour's drive from Montreal, Plattsburgh was an ideal staging area, a gathering place for American athletes to conduct their final training sessions, measure for their ceremonial uniforms, and ultimately board buses for the short drive across the border to Quebec.

On July 1, officials hoisted Olympic banners up the flagpoles at city hall and the Plattsburgh State Field House, and members of the US track team held a late afternoon workout in front of two hundred onlookers at the college. Athletes continued to pour into town on the Fourth of July as members of the local American Legion post grilled five hundred pounds of beef at a community cookout, sixty-eight groups marched in a parade, and five thousand people gathered at Plattsburgh Air Force Base for an elaborate fireworks show.

But the big news in this town of 19,000 was an upcoming visit by President Gerald Ford on July 11, an appearance meant to inspire the Olympians before they left for Montreal. Plattsburgh wasn't the kind of place many presidents deigned to come — none had bothered to visit the area since Franklin Roosevelt in 1939.

"The scheduling of the Olympic staging area in Plattsburgh is fortunate in that it provides nationally flavored icing on our bicentennial cake," gushed the editors of the *Press-Republican*. "The spotlight is already on because of the Olympics. The President's arrival can only intensify the glow."

The Plattsburgh State campus was a

sea of comings and goings, athletes in one sport arriving just as others left for Montreal. By the time Ford arrived on Saturday, July 11, nearly half the delegation had already left for Canada, but the women's basketball team was still in Rochester.

The day of Ford's visit, ten thousand citizens jammed the streets hoping to catch a glimpse of the thirty-eighth president. Standing shoulder to shoulder on Broad, New York, and Rugar streets, people waved small American flags as the president's black limousine cruised by at speeds of up to thirty-five miles per hour. Two busloads of reporters and photographers followed, and a security helicopter hovered overhead as Secret Service agents wearing dark sunglasses and carrying small radios surveyed the scene. When Ford stopped to shake hands, one woman turned to her husband. "That was exciting. That was so exciting. I mean, that was really exciting. I mean, really, really exciting. I mean really exciting."

Finally, Ford made his way to the track at Plattsburgh State, where he posed for photos, chatted with athletes, threw a discus, and signed a cast covering the broken wrist of an injured runner. Then, standing outside the field house, he addressed hundreds of Olympians and more than eight thousand citizens, some of whom had been camped out with coolers of beer for more than five hours waiting for his arrival. Deep into a presidential campaign against Democratic challenger Jimmy Carter, presiding over a country shaken by Republican scandal, racial division, and economic uncertainty, Ford called upon the bicentennial and the Olympic spirit to buoy American patriotism.

"For a variety of reasons, we weren't unified for the past four or eight years," he said. "The bicentennial clearly demonstrates now how we all feel. It's a real new rebirth of American unity and determination . . . a great way to enter our third century."

Sitting among the throng of athletes, swimmer Tauna Vandeweghe felt a jolt of inspiration. "His speech was so phenomenal," she recalled. "He put a lot of patriotism in it and made it clear we were representing not just ourselves but the

President Gerald Ford (in suit and tie at left) visited the US Olympic team's staging area in Plattsburgh, New York, on July 10, 1976. (Picryl.com)

United States. That was the first time that really hit home for me."

Whatever inspiration was to be gained from Ford's remarks was lost on Billie Moore and her players. As the president spoke, they were still crammed into rental cars, making their way through upstate New York on the drive from Rochester to Plattsburgh. It was not until the evening of July 11, after Ford's remarks, that the

USOC made room for them in the staging area.

Susan Jean Smith had never lived anywhere other than the rural, southern part of Illinois, and now here she was staying in New York's Greenwich Village and working on Park Avenue as an editorial intern at *Redbook* magazine. It was a thrilling three months for a twenty-one-year-old college student, employed in publishing and experiencing the parties and parades that came with a bicentennial summer in the city. Smith was a feminist, believing her dream of pursuing a career in the male-dominated field of journalism should not be denied simply because she was a woman.

A student at Southern Illinois University, Smith had applied for an internship program that placed college students at magazines in New York. Smith had hoped to be assigned to a news magazine like *Time* or *Newsweek,* but was given a spot at *Redbook,* a women's lifestyle publication. One of her tasks was to write an article about the joy of picking apples — not too hard-hitting, but at least it was a real writing project, making her the envy of some of the other interns. And then came the plum assignment: a chance to ride in a limousine to the airport and fly to Plattsburgh to write about a *Redbook*-sponsored makeover session for female Olympians.

Along with a photographer, a team of makeup experts, and two popular New York City hair stylists, Smith helped assemble a makeshift beauty salon in a Plattsburgh dormitory. Over the course of eight days, they invited women athletes to walk in and receive "easy-care hair shapes, skin care and make-up advice, or both." Smith stood in the salon and took notes while the photographer snapped before and after pictures. Smith's article and a photo spread appeared in the November issue of the magazine under the headline GOLD MEDAL BEAUTY.

Among the 120 women who accepted the invitation for makeovers were three members of the women's basketball team: Mary Anne O'Connor, Gail Marquis, and Lusia Harris. All three women had been living out of suitcases and showering in gyms and dormitories ever since they had arrived in Warrensburg, without the benefit of a haircut, let alone any sort of pampering. When they walked in the salon, the *Redbook* stylists noted their "dry, overheated, out-of-shape hair," and "oily skin aggravated by perspiration." For O'Connor, the experts recommended mild shampoo and protein treatments, pale-pink and green eye shadow, and clear-pink lip gloss. For Marquis, twice-daily cleaning plus toner, bronze eye-shadow, red lip gloss, and black mascara. For Harris, a grainy cleanser twice a week, charcoal eyeshadow, red-brown cheek color, and brick-red lipstick.

"The first thing I noticed was just how outstanding, frankly, their bodies were," Smith recalled. "They were walking examples of health and vitality and they looked like Greek goddesses, some of them. I suppose I envied that. I was not very sporty myself, so I couldn't relate to them on that level, but I was about their age, so I could relate to their youth. I was somewhat wowed by them."

Sensitive to the dueling stereotypes at play — that women must look beautiful to be valued on one hand, and that fe-

BEFORE   **AFTER**

Mary Anne O'Connor, Gail Marquis, and Lusia Harris visited the temporary hair and makeup salon created by Redbook magazine at the Plattsburgh staging area. Redbook intern Susan Jean Smith wrote an article about the salon for the November issue of the magazine. (Redbook)

BEFORE   **AFTER**

BEFORE   **AFTER**

male athletes were inherently unfeminine on the other — Smith was careful to accurately describe the purpose of the salon in her article. The point, she wrote, was not to make the athletes "more beautiful." Rather, "we gave them make-up and skin care advice, flattering easy-care hair shapes and wished them best of luck in the games. The myth that female athletes don't care about their appearance, which we had heard but didn't know whether to believe, left with them, too."

For Marquis, the whole experience was a welcome indulgence in a summer that had been so physically demanding. "I was not used to getting my hair done, and I never wore makeup. I let them do all that," she recalled. "It had been a while since I'd had a haircut, so I didn't look myself by the time we got to Plattsburgh. We'd been sweating so much and tying bandanas around our heads. So I really appreciated it."

The first day the shop was open, only a slow trickle of women showed up. But as word spread, athletes came flooding in. On the busiest day, forty-two women came in for hair styling. "This was important work, and the stylists put so much care into it," Smith recalled. "These people were stars. They were going to be at the Olympics and on television, and some of them did go on to win medals. We all took it seriously."

One thing Smith hadn't anticipated was how many male athletes became jealous, begging for haircuts. The *Redbook* salon was intended only for women. "So, despite their cries of discrimination, muscle flexing, monetary offers, pleas and threats, we managed to tell them all no for several days," Smith wrote. When one athlete who wanted his beard trimmed complained to Smith that she was discriminating against him, she was ready with a quick reply: "How does it feel?!"

But some of the men persisted so relentlessly, she said, that the stylists eventually gave in, giving "token haircuts" to high jumpers Bill Jankunis and Dwight Stones.

And before she flew back to New York City, Smith, the summer intern from Edwardsville, Illinois, had her hair done, too.

■ ■ ■ ■

The US Olympic Committee had commandeered the Saranac Dining Hall at Plattsburgh State, turning it into a distribution point for parade, leisure, and travel uniforms. For hours on end, athletes stood in line to collect socks, shoes, jockstraps, shorts, sweatsuits, and suitcases. They stood in line to be fitted by a tailor, to take ID photos, to get a physical exam, and to have their teeth checked. For some athletes, it was all an irritating ordeal, a mountain of inconvenience at a critical moment. For other Olympians, the same routine was a thrill, a sign that their Olympic dream was real and close at hand.

Staffers were prepared to outfit everyone from the four-foot-ten, ninety-pound rowing coxswain Irene Moreno to the six-foot-four, 330-pound weightlifter Bruce Wilhelm, with shoes ranging in size from women's 4AAA to men's 17EEE. Official clothing supplier Montgomery Ward, a national department store chain, brought belts ranging from 28 to 52 inches, dresses from 4 petite to 26 extra tall, men's suits from 14 boys to 58 XL.

Athletes queued in long lines to collect their gear, beginning in a lower-level lounge where they received red suitcases and bag tags, then ascending through the building to collect everything from underwear to raincoats, stow it in their suitcases, and take measurements. "I've never had this many pair of underpants at one time!" shouted one athlete.

Women received a navy-blue pantsuit, two red T-shirts, casual blue suede shoes, blue leather wedges, a white nylon warm-up jacket with an Olympic emblem, a navy windbreaker, a navy nylon raincoat and hat, a navy button-front dress, two Olympic T-shirts, a red, white, and blue scarf, and a red leather handbag. And that wasn't all. They also stuffed their suitcases with three pairs of pantyhose, three pairs of knee-high hose, three bras, six pairs of bikini underwear, a girdle, a slip, pink pajamas, and a long blue robe. For members of the women's basketball team, who had played for underfunded teams their entire lives, the contrast in treatment was remarkable. Marquis said the near endless supply of gear "was a wonderful thing." O'Connor had never experienced anything like it in all her years in basketball. "We got so much cool swag," she recalled. "There was an Adidas rep there to take our shoe sizes. It was amazing."

With hundreds of athletes standing in line and meeting competitors from other sports, gossip spread quickly. Some American athletes had already made it to Montreal, and word was trickling back to Plattsburgh about the conditions there. There was much talk about the cramped conditions in the Olympic Village, with reports that athletes were stacked six to a room in some apartments. There was talk of heavy security, including uniformed troops carrying submachine guns through the Village and a fleet of military aircraft on standby at a nearby air base. There was talk of a potential boycott by African nations, protesting New Zealand's presence in the Games after a rugby team from New Zealand toured apartheid South Africa.[1]

For the basketball players, who had been so intensely focused on their sport and their prospects of qualifying for Montreal, these real-world controversies were startling, like emerging from a dark tunnel into blinding sunlight. And Moore was concerned that her players, who had trained so vigorously, would go cold at just the wrong moment during this idle time before leaving for Montreal. So she rustled up a game against some local high school and college boys who could challenge her players with their size and strength.

Tom Lacey, soon to begin his senior year at Plattsburgh High, was home on July 12 when he got a call from a friend. *We're scrimmaging the women's Olympic basketball team. Do you want to play?* Lacey said sure, and walked over to the gym the next evening, expecting nothing more than a pickup game. But when he arrived, the women were dressed in their USA uniforms and the bleachers were overflowing with two thousand people. "I'd never seen Memorial Hall so crowded in all my life," he recalled. "We got booed when we came in, and they got cheered by everyone. We didn't know it was a real game with referees and a scoreboard and everything. We had no clue. We looked at one another and said, 'Is this really happening?'"

Huddled up before tip-off, the boys got a pep talk from Mitch Kupchak, one of the stars of the US men's basketball team. "Do not lose this game," he said. The idea was to give the American women as tough a game as possible, which, for some of the boys, who were taller and stronger than their competition, did not come naturally.

"We were all just excited and shocked to be playing against them," said Leo Ryan, a recent high school graduate. "These were young women who were representing our country. We didn't know if we should be aggressive, and all of a sudden, they started to bang us around a little bit. Eventually, Mike Flynn, our head coach, said, 'You guys need to play! They want to play!'"

The boys listened. One of them blocked Lusia Harris's shots on two straight possessions, drawing oohs and aahs from the crowd. Another found himself guarded closely by Pat Head, unable to get open. Lacey went up for a layup and Head swatted it out of bounds. "Everyone was cheering, and I was embarrassed and put my head down because I had my shot blocked," he recalled. "I had a little smile on my face, though, and I looked at her, and she had a smile on her face, too, like she was saying, 'Be careful what you do next time.'"

The game was full of similar competitive moments, with the boys jumping out to an early lead only to have the women come storming back. The lead continued to change hands, with Cindy Brogdon and Trish Roberts pacing the Olympians with 13 points apiece and Plattsburgh High junior Joe Cardanay leading the boys with 20. "They wanted a tough game to prepare, and we gave it to them," Lacey said of his team's 84–79 victory. Kevin Daugherty, a college player at the time, said he and his teammates didn't quite know what to expect from a team of women, but they came away impressed. "They were very fundamental and disciplined. They'd been practicing for quite a while together and they didn't make mistakes," he said. "They could really play."

The next morning, July 14, the basketball players joined 270 cyclists, divers, wrestlers, team handball players, and track and field participants for an 11:45

a.m. send-off ceremony. The athletes stood shoulder to shoulder in front of the residence halls, where they listened to letters of good luck from all fifty governors, delivered by four couriers who had run all the way from Washington, DC. New York secretary of state (and future governor) Mario Cuomo addressed the athletes. "I know what the Olympic competition means to you, but let me tell you what it means to us," he said. "Your personal success is what we yearn for when we flail around the YMCA pool or run a race in our battered sneakers or bounce a basketball around a church courtyard. You represent the best our nation is able to achieve. And it's great to see such a generation of champions, just two hundred years after our humble beginnings."

With that, the athletes climbed into white cars, vans, and buses, following the Air Force Band for one final parade through town, the caravan heading east on Broad Street and then north on Margaret Street before it was joined by a phalanx of state police vehicles for an escort to the Canadian border, police helicopters hovering overhead. When they reached the border, the American police peeled away and Canadian officers took over, leading the caravan into the Village, where each piece of luggage was manually inspected for weapons and explosives.

Two adjacent apartment buildings, each resembling a half pyramid, served as the living quarters for the athletes of the world. And the rumors of cramped conditions were true — the entire women's basketball contingent of sixteen people was given one two-bedroom, one-bathroom apartment.

As they surveyed their living quarters — bunk beds tucked into every nook and cranny — a startling message arrived:

Don't unpack your bags.

You might not be here long.

The US might back out of the Olympics.

19

SO FRENCH
AND SO
CLEAN

For two long days after they arrived in Montreal, the players lived in a state of uncertainty, worried that all the sacrifices they'd made to arrive at this moment were for nothing. At any minute, they believed, they could all be sent home.

The issue was a dispute involving the International Olympic Committee, Taiwan, and the host country of Canada. Taiwan, an island nation off the coast of China, called itself the Republic of China. Communist mainland China refused to acknowledge that name or the legitimacy of the island's government. The IOC did. But because mainland China was a major trading partner with Canada, Canadian officials bowed to pressure and refused to recognize the delegation from Taiwan as the "Republic of China." American officials objected to Canada's stance, taking Taiwan's side and threatening to boycott the Games if Taiwan wasn't allowed to compete under its preferred name.

But on the evening of July 16, the US Olympic Committee relented, calling for a compromise: let the athletes from Taiwan march under their preferred flag and play their own anthem but just not call themselves the Republic of China. Regardless of how the matter was resolved, American officials said, the US would take part in the Games. The American athletes could finally unpack their bags. They were in Montreal to stay, even after Taiwan rejected the proposed compromise and boycotted the Games.

A city of 1.4 million people located along the St. Lawrence River in the French-speaking province of Quebec, Montreal was the second-largest French-speaking city in the world. Canada's most dynamic and cosmopolitan metropolis, Montreal boasted six thousand restaurants serving cuisine from thirty nations; the world's most modern, clean, and quiet subway system; an underground labyrinth of hotels, grocery stores, shops, and restaurants protected from the Canadian winter; an Old Montreal district with cobblestone streets, museums, and cathedrals; and a reputation for unrivaled hospitality. "Montrealers are friendlier than New Yorkers and they keep their city so clean that newspapers tumbling along their gusty streets are invariably today's editions," marveled one visiting sportswriter.

Mayor Jean Drapeau was the city's ultimate booster, a small and flamboyant character determined to make Montreal "the first city of the world." To achieve his dream, he'd pursued a series of high-profile projects: hosting the World's Fair in 1967, bringing Major League Baseball — the Montreal Expos — to town in 1969, and almost single-handedly putting a winning proposal together in 1970 to land the '76 Olympics.

Whether these big-ticket events were healthy for the city was debatable. Critics pointed to financial troubles and economic disparities, arguing that the money spent on hosting a two-week international sporting event would have been better spent addressing the basic needs of the city's own citizens. But Drapeau insisted the Olympics wouldn't cost a dime — at least when the psychic value of capturing the world spotlight was considered. "The Montreal Olympics can no more have a deficit," he infamously claimed, "than a man can have a baby."

While others fretted, Drapeau understood a sad but true maxim of the modern world. The "good news that drives out the bad," wrote author Jack Ludwig, is "*spectacle* . . . Opponents who can beat up on poor urban services like sewer systems, trash collection, hospital care, the teaching of children, the care of the elderly, etc., can't usually cope with an imminent world spectacular. A mayor who sells his city's 'image' knows you can't invite tourists in to inspect an improved, and needed, sewer system. Nobody can make a prime tourist attraction out of day care centers or the raised nutritional intake of a city's children. Conventions don't ask if cities do well by their infirm. Jean Drapeau and his fellow mayors know that in the 1970s a city . . . must have its panoramic bar and restaurant at least 50 stories above its streets. From that height even slums look picturesque."

At the 1970 presentation in Amsterdam where Montreal won the Olympics over Moscow and Los Angeles, one of Drapeau's most intriguing selling points to the IOC was the promise of free accommodations for athletes in the Olympic Village, something no city had offered before. No matter that it would require displacing low-income families from their homes to build the Village. And these would be no ordinary dormitories. Drapeau intended to make a statement. Fascinated by a pair of half-pyramid-shaped condominiums on the French Riviera, Drapeau commissioned architects to mimic the buildings.

"As French Canadians, the only way we're going to survive is to make our mark not only on this country, but on the entire continent," Drapeau said. "We must never be poor copies of others. We can only survive if we accept the challenge of quality. That's why I chose [French architect] Roger Taillibert to build these Olympics," including the futuristic Olympic stadium. "He is the kind

The half-pyramid-shaped dormitories of the Olympic Village were modeled after condominiums on the French Riviera. The domed Olympic Stadium is in the distance. (Associated Press)

of man who once built the pyramids, who constructed the great cathedrals of Europe. He did not give me a building. He gave me a creation which will last long after we are gone. It will last for centuries."

Drapeau's romantic vision was continually undercut by scandal and misfortune, some of his own doing, some beyond his control. Costs skyrocketed by obscene degrees — from an estimated $310 million to more than $1.5 billion. Building projects were beset with months-long workers' strikes, bribery revelations, and kickback schemes. And the idyllic scenes he hoped to create — athletic dorms mimicking the South of France, an Olympic stadium rivaling the marvels of antiquity — were tarnished by the most intrusive of interlopers: thousands of soldiers and police patrolling the streets with submachine guns, snipers perched atop buildings, crude chain-link fences and security tents blocking entrances to the newly constructed palaces. This was the first Olympic Games since the massacre in Munich; IOC and Canadian officials were determined to prevent acts of terrorism.

Even before the American basketball team arrived in Montreal, some journalists described the Olympic Village as an "armed camp," with thousands of police officers and soldiers patrolling the city on land, in the air, and from the St. Lawrence River. "Change the scenery a bit," wrote a New York Times reporter, "and the

Olympic Village could be a concentration camp, a fortress under siege or a Wild West frontier town waiting to face the bad guys." The $100 million security plan included a task force prepared to deal with the threat of nuclear blackmail, hostage negotiators, and an elite unit of twenty-four plainclothes officers on standby in case of a terrorist attack. When these men began training for their assignment, they were greeted with an ominous warning by their instructors. "There's every chance you may not leave the Olympic Games alive."

Fears of terrorism created moments of hysteria throughout Quebec. Forty-five miles from Montreal in the tiny town of Bromont, site of the equestrian events, residents complained that they felt like prisoners in their homes, required to produce identification to walk down their own streets. An Olympic courier delivering a message to the Argentinian team there was unable to explain his presence in French to police, who proceeded to assault him. When questioned about the incident, a police spokesperson would only say that the innocent man was lucky he hadn't been shot. Rumors spread throughout Montreal that a mysterious twenty-six-year-old Latin American terrorist known only as "Carlos" had arrived in town, with police fielding a barrage of frantic calls from citizens claiming to have seen him in numerous locations around the city. They all turned out to be false alarms based on racial profiling. Carlos, admitted an Olympic security official, "can easily be mistaken for some members of Canada's numerous ethnic groups."[1]

The basketball players noticed the heavy security presence from the moment they arrived at the Village. One day, a group of players put on their swimsuits in hopes of sunbathing in the grassy area outside the dormitories. They were supposed to wear ID credentials around their necks, simple green badges held by thick strings, but they removed them for tanning purposes. A member of the Canadian air force on security detail interrupted their tanning session. "The players complained that they didn't want a white square in the middle of their chests, but [the guard] was not listening," US team manager

Jeanne Rowlands recalled. "Wear the credential or stay in your room."

Security demands aside, it was easy to understand why players looked for any opportunity to avoid their cramped apartment in the Village. Wooden bunk beds covered every inch of the place, two in each bedroom and four in the living room. Bedside tables, each topped with a yellow plastic lamp, yellow paper drinking cup, and a box of Kleenex, doubled as clothes drawers. The bathroom was so busy players resorted to brushing their teeth in the kitchen sink; hot water was in such short supply that most players chose to shower at the gym. The women took for granted a luxury that was nearly not provided: cotton sheets. To save money, Montreal officials had initially planned to cover the foam rubber mattresses with paper sheets before relenting and providing cotton bedding.

But despite these spartan living conditions, none of the players complained. This was better than Rochester, where they'd spent a week without air conditioning in a building still under construction, and there was the sheen of the Olympics, which covered any blemish. "We were just happy to have beds," said Meyers. "As I recall, we were so excited at what we had accomplished just to get there and be the first US women's team that it wouldn't have mattered how we lived," said Cindy Brogdon. "It was a dream come true from the moment we walked through security," said Juliene Simpson. "You wanted to pinch yourself." Simpson yearned to make every minute of her Olympic experience last as long as possible, choosing to walk up the exterior stairs to the apartment rather than take the elevator so she could soak up the sights and sounds of the Village.

Outside their rooms, there was plenty to enjoy before curfew. A three-thousand-seat cafeteria served international cuisine that earned rave reviews from the athletes of all nations. It was so popular that "some athletes have eaten themselves right out of the Olympics," observed a reporter from Philadelphia. "If you're looking for a place to get fat, this is it," said American hurdler Willie Davenport. Canadian water polo player John MacLeod said that each night before his team's eleven p.m. curfew, he and his teammates would each grab steak sandwiches from the cafeteria and bring them back to their room. A cafeteria manager noted that weight lifters, wrestlers, and basketball players ate "two or three" twelve-ounce steaks at a time, then carried out armloads of apples, berries, and bananas. MacLeod was fascinated by the eating styles of athletes from different countries. "I was at a table one day with some athletes from South Korea, and I would marvel at the massive bites these guys would take," he said. "They looked like they had chewing tobacco in their cheeks because there was so much food in their mouths. Then I started watching how the other countries ate — some were slow and meticulous and some powered through it."[2]

While the world's premier athletes gorged on an endless supply of food — including an estimated 100,000 pounds of ground meat, 300,000 pounds of fresh vegetables, 50,000 pounds of ham and bacon, 70,000 loaves of bread, and 100,000 gallons of juice and soft drinks — some Montrealers were disgusted by

Soviet basketball star Uljana Semjonova (center) joined other athletes to trade pins in the Olympic Village. Semjonova was known to collect teddy bears, books, and records on international trips. (Getty Images)

the gluttony.[3] Families had been evicted from their apartments by landlords who wanted to rent their places at higher prices to Olympic visitors. Others had been displaced by Olympic construction projects. These homeless and hungry families were forced to live in abandoned buildings, drawing the attention of community organizers who showed up at the Olympic Village one day to collect uneaten food they heard was being thrown out by the kitchen staff. "We are trying to demonstrate . . . the stark contrast between poor people who are starving and the $2 billion that have been sunk in the Olympic organizations," said one advocate. "They are throwing out 30 percent of the food in there."

Besides the cafeteria, another popular spot for athletes was the International Center, located across an undulating, tree-lined field from the dormitories in a school building retrofitted to serve as a social gathering place. Here athletes could mail letters and make calls, shop for gear emblazoned with the Olympic rings, browse magazines, put on headphones, listen to records in ten comfortable lounges, and drink beer under yellow umbrellas in an outdoor patio. They could trade Olympic pins with athletes from other countries, play horseshoes and miniature golf, and watch concerts and ballet performances. A theater showed new movies, and a disco pulsed with music late into the night. "I was in awe of everything," said Trish Roberts. "I mean everything." Pat Head loved visiting the disco, telling a reporter back home in Tennessee, "It's fun meeting so many different people and trying to understand what so many people are saying in so many different languages."

Head wasn't alone in enjoying the social aspect of the Village. American rower Jim Dietz called the Village the world's greatest pickup scene. "There's more talk than action," he said, "but the Olympic ideal is to try." John MacLeod, the Canadian water polo player, said one of his teammates posted up at one of the outdoor patio tables each day, taking a spot near the path that led to a beer stand. Whenever a woman walked by, he'd offer a "Hey, how are you doing?" "He was playing the odds," MacLeod said. "All he needed was one." Another teammate had a girlfriend already living in Montreal. Each night after curfew, he'd climb out his bedroom window and escape to her apartment in town, climbing back in at 6:30 a.m. "They are married to this day,"

MacLeod said decades later. "It was true love."

As much action as was taking place inside the Olympic Village, there was just as much revelry in the bars, restaurants, and clubs of Montreal. Jets carrying the rich and famous from Europe, Asia, South America, and the United States arrived at the airport daily, with celebrities checking into hotels under assumed names to avoid the paparazzi. Others wanted nothing more than to be seen — Rolling Stones front man Mick Jagger and his wife Bianca, a model, arrived in two long black limousines, Mick standing out in a purple jean jacket and red running shoes, Bianca in a white dress and dark sunglasses. Princes from Sweden, Switzerland, and Saudi Arabia checked into the Ritz Carlton, while Canadian prime minister Pierre Trudeau and members of the IOC headquartered at the posh Queen Elizabeth Hotel. Shoe companies Adidas, Puma, Pony, and a newcomer to the scene, Nike, lavished free products on athletes and media members, and companies hosted swanky parties and hospitality suites for their clients and top sales agents. Actor Paul Newman rented a mansion near downtown, and visitors spotted the likes of US secretary of state Henry Kissinger, ABC Sports commentator Howard Cosell, and the Duke and Duchess of Exeter.

"Montreal for a fortnight," wrote the author Jack Ludwig, "was a succession of New Year's Eves, South American *carnivale,* days of misrule trying hard to equal the bull run at Pamplona, the Oktoberfest, the World Series, Super Bowl, World Cup soccer finals." Not everyone enjoyed the special attention paid to the visiting VIPs. Montreal cab drivers resented the fact that army officers had been assigned to drive IOC officials and other bigwigs around town, robbing them of a significant source of income. In response, angry cabbies intentionally caused accidents and blocked traffic, creating a web of gridlock. All told, Montreal was a sunny city abuzz with life, teeming with color, energy, excitement, and protest, with visitors from around the world discovering the city and one another.[4]

But Billie Moore understood she was

in Montreal for a reason, and it wasn't to party. There would be only one "first American women's basketball team," one opportunity to supercharge the game in America and around the world. She believed her team had peaked in Hamilton, as it should have. They wouldn't have even made it to the Olympics if they hadn't played their best ball there. But now it was time to get ready for their first Olympic opponent: Japan, a team that had outperformed the US at the World Championships in 1974 and the Asian tour in April. To the dismay of Moore and her players, the game was scheduled to tip off at the absurdly early hour of nine a.m. on July 19.

Moore thought it was important to get her team acclimated to the early start time, asking Rowlands to walk around the apartment banging pots and pans to wake everyone up at five a.m. in the days prior to the game. ("Some of the girls don't realize there is such a time," quipped Moore.) The players understood why Moore was doing this but didn't like it. Nancy Dunkle said the early morning wake-up calls backfired, leaving the players exhausted rather than well adjusted. And one morning, Mary Anne O'Connor, Sue Rojcewicz, and Dunkle decided to mock their coach by showing up at the early morning workout still wearing pajamas.

Moore made them practice in their flannels.

PEAKS AND VALLEYS

20

All Juliene Simpson needed to do to gain a dose of inspiration was to dip her chin and look down at the pendant dangling around her neck, a gold star she'd worn ever since the day she'd learned that women's basketball would be an Olympic sport.

"It's the star in my impossible dream," she told anyone who asked. "It comes off after the Games."

As they prepared to play Japan, there was an air of confidence in the team's apartment. Yes, in some ways their journey still felt like an impossible dream. Their eighth-place finish in the World Championships, the general lack of respect for women's basketball in the US, and the dominance of the Soviet team were hard to ignore.

But success in Hamilton boosted the players' spirits. Nancy Dunkle admitted that coming out of Warrensburg, she had questioned whether she made the team just because she played for Moore at Cal State Fullerton. But now, playing a big role on a team that was clicking, she knew she deserved her spot. But even this newfound confidence brought its own challenges. "Psychologically," American basketball executive Bill Wall wrote in a pre-Olympics press release, "the big problem will be maintaining the peak they needed just to get into the Games."

If anything, the players had climbed to higher emotional ground during the Games' opening ceremony on July 17. For Gail Marquis, it was when she walked into Roger Taillibert's creation with 470 other American athletes that she finally understood the significance of it all. The Olympians had congregated outside the stadium, moving closer and closer, waiting their turn to join the parade of ninety-four nations at around 3:30 p.m. Peering through a gate, Marquis could see throngs of people in the upper decks, hear the anticipatory chants of "USA!

Pat Head and fellow co-captain Juliene Simpson are dressed and ready to go to the opening ceremony at Montreal's Olympic Stadium. (Women's Basketball Hall of Fame)

USA!" When she entered the stadium, "it was like an explosion went off" as Americans in the crowd went "berserk" at the site of their fellow citizens. Then Marquis looked to her right and saw the queen of England, dressed in pink gloves and a matching pillbox hat, waving right back at her. "I realized what I had done and what we had done as a team," she recalled. "During training camp, everything hurt; it was painful. And we all thought at some time, 'What the hell are we doing this for?' But at that moment after I saw her, during those ceremonies, it hit me that we were the US Olympic basketball team, not just a team. I had no complaints after that."

For Ann Meyers, who had grown up reading about the exploits of Babe Didrikson and dreaming of competing in the Olympics as a high jumper, the ceremony was a childhood wish come true. She looked around the stadium, taking pictures in her mind, hoping to capture mental images that would last a lifetime.

Walking alongside Nancy Dunkle and Sue Rojcewicz, Mary Anne O'Connor scanned the crowd looking for her family — a needle-in-a-haystack proposition. A Volkswagen dealership in their hometown of Fairfield, Connecticut, had donated a VW bus so her parents, siblings, and eighty-six-year-old grandmother could make the drive to Montreal, and a Campbell Soup executive had donated a room for them at the Sheraton. O'Connor's mother had recently injured her back, so when O'Connor saw a woman looking her way and shaking a crutch high in the air, she knew who it was. "Nancy! Sue! Look!" she yelled. "It's my mom!"

Spectacular as the event was, with a colorful cast of three thousand dancers, musicians, and other performers, the ceremony was equally notable for what was missing. Taiwan had boycotted the Games, as had nearly seven hundred athletes from African nations, protesting the presence of New Zealand. And nowhere to be seen were the long navy-blue dresses and stockings the American women were supposed to wear. After a meeting of representatives from each sport, the American women deemed the outfit simply too ugly, old-fashioned, and uncomfortable. Instead, they chose to wear blue pants, red blouses, and puffy white windbreakers along with red purses and red, white, and blue scarves. Sitting on the stadium's infield grass for more than two hours as the ceremony dragged on after the parade, American swimmer Tauna Vandeweghe, daughter of a former Miss America, had just one thought. *Thank goodness,* she

311

told herself, *we didn't have to wear those dresses.*

Most important for the fortunes of the American basketball team, assistant coach Sue Gunter was missing, too. Shortly before leaving Plattsburgh for Montreal, she'd received a call from home. Her father had died of a heart attack. Moore insisted that Gunter fly home to be with her mom and to stay as long as she needed, even if that meant missing the entire Olympics. Trainer Gail Weldon and manager Jeanne Rowlands drove Gunter to the airport in the middle of the night, singing to each other all the way back to try to stay awake.

Gunter's departure was devastating for two reasons. One, the coaches and players had built strong emotional bonds. "You're part of this family and then you have a member who's distraught because they've lost a parent," said Meyers. "To see someone in such pain — our emotions were with her." Second, Gunter was the only assistant coach, and Moore had come to rely on her advice, especially Gunter's ability to make mid-game adjustments based on an opponent's tendencies. It was Gunter who had led the team of American women to Japan when Moore couldn't make the trip. No coach in America knew more about the Japanese players than Gunter. Moore was counting on her counsel for the entire tournament, but especially against their first opponent.

In the moments before the nine a.m. tip-off, Moore and her players thought not only about the game at hand but also about the long-term implications of it. Moore had noticed how young girls began taking gymnastics lessons after Olga Korbut of the Soviet Union charmed the world with her magnificent performance in Munich in 1972. She believed that with a strong performance in Montreal, her players would have a similar impact, inspiring a new generation of basketball players. Her players, meanwhile, had a more immediate goal. They wanted to be the first team to score. Not just to get off to a good start against Japan, but to make history. There would only be one first women's Olympic basketball game. Would they rather go down as the first team ever to score, or the first team to give up a basket?

When Japan controlled the opening tip and began driving down the court, Juliene Simpson was determined not to allow a shot. She lunged at the dribbler near the free throw line, practically tackling her, drawing a quick foul. When a few of Simpson's teammates gave her a look as if to say, "What was that all about?" Simpson reminded them of the plan. "She can't score!" After the US gained possession, Simpson pushed the ball down the lane and passed to Lusia Harris under the hoop. The woman who taught herself to play on a rickety backyard hoop in Mississippi scored the historic basket.

It was a brief but important sequence that went according to plan in a game where everything else seemed out of sorts for the Americans. Despite outrebounding the Japanese team, committing fewer turnovers, collecting more assists, and making more field goals, the US struggled to turn any of those advantages into an edge on the scoreboard. Referees whistled the Americans for 28 fouls to

Cindy Brogdon, a sharpshooter from Mercer College in Georgia, lets a jumper fly over Keiko Namai in the United States' opening-game loss to Japan (84–71). Namai was the tournament's leading scorer with 20.4 points per game. (Getty Images)

Japan's 21, and Japanese shooters made the US pay, making 26 of 30 free throws. Harris led the US with 17 points, while Dunkle and Meyers added 14 apiece, but it wasn't enough to keep pace with Japan, which shot 53 percent from the field and turned a 49–42 halftime lead into an 84–71 victory. "It took the American men 36 years to lose their first Olympic basketball game," wrote one sportswriter covering the game. "It took the American women just one day."

There were excuses aplenty for the defeat. Ann Meyers said she and her teammates were distracted by the Japanese players' constant chatter on the court. Nancy Dunkle said the early morning wake-up calls left the players with no energy. Simpson believed the Japanese players were flopping — repeatedly pretending to be fouled — and blamed the officiating, which resulted in Japan shooting twice as many free throws as the US. Pat Head blamed shoelaces, believing five-foot-four Japanese guard Keiko Namai stopped the game to unnecessarily tie her shoes on two separate occasions, delays in the game that gave the Japanese time to rest (four players played all forty minutes) and interrupted US momentum in a second-half comeback attempt. Meyers and Moore said Gunter's absence was a major factor.

All the excuses may have sounded like whining — with a strong dose of xenophobia — from a team that had lost three of its previous four games against Japan anyway. And the American press corps validated many of the players' depictions of the game. Lawrie Mifflin of the *New York Daily News,* one of the few women covering the Olympics, reported that the Japanese team not only led the game in points but also in "theatrics." Gary Stein of the Gannett News Service called the pigtailed Namai "the real Shakespearean expert in the group, who somehow found time to score 35 points when she wasn't falling backwards onto the floor every time an American girl took a deep breath." He credited her with putting on an "Academy Award performance."

But the game was over, and making excuses wasn't Moore's style. "They used every technique, and it worked," she told reporters. "The things that happened today are the things that you have to be able to put up with . . . I guess we just weren't able to put up with it. We just didn't do a good job of controlling the tempo of the game."[1]

With a near-certain loss to the Soviet Union still on the horizon, there was no more room for error if the US hoped to medal. As they showered and dressed, the players wanted nothing more than to get back to their apartment, get some rest, and begin preparing for their game against Bulgaria. But they couldn't leave the Étienne Desmarteau Center yet.

At halftime, an Olympic official had tapped Jeanne Rowlands on the shoulder, telling her that Nancy Dunkle and Ann Meyers had been randomly selected for drug testing after the game, a routine part of the Olympics' anti-doping policies. Rowlands had alerted all the players back in Warrensburg that this was going to happen. They'd just need to pee in a cup and turn over their urine sample. Each venue had a refrigerator in the drug-testing area stocked with water, beer, and other liquids. A technician told Meyers and Dunkle they could drink as much of whatever they wanted, and when they were ready, the technician would watch them pee, just to make sure the sample was legitimate.

As they drank beers, the technician explained to Dunkle and Meyers that they were to take two plastic receptacles, collect a urine sample, and bring the jars to the lab room. There, the technician and a manager would watch them pour half the sample into the other receptacle. Then the tech would place lids on the containers and seal them with an official stamp. "He explained that one container would be sent to the laboratory in the Olympic complex for analysis and the other would be placed in a vault in the basement of a Montreal bank," Dunkle recalled.

Shocked and slightly buzzed, Dunkle blurted out, "Are you telling me that there is a Montreal bank that has a basement full of pee?"

"Absolutely," the tech replied, explaining that if the first sample tested positive, they would test the other half.

Dunkle left for the toilet area but came back to the waiting room just a few minutes later, leaning over and whispering in Rowlands's ear.

"Jeanne, that lady is watching me!"

"Nancy, I explained to all of you that this would be a witnessed sample collection and modesty would get you nowhere," Rowlands replied.

"I can't do this if she's watching me. I'll never do it if she's watching me!"

"Nancy, have two more beers and you won't care who is watching. Go ahead and sit down and drink."

She did, and that took care of the problem.

WOMAN'S WORLD

21

Twelve unhappy players walked back into their apartment at the Olympic Village. Losing to Japan wasn't in the script they'd imagined. Nancy Lieberman considered the outcome a costly reminder that the Soviets weren't the only stiff competition in Montreal. Pat Head phoned a reporter in Tennessee and told him the loss made her feel sick to her stomach. Billie Moore assured an American sportswriter that the team hadn't come this far to give up. But their next game, to be televised in prime time in the US, would be a tough one against Bulgaria, a team they'd only managed to beat by two points at the qualifying tournament in Hamilton.

Just one game into the Olympics, the heat was officially on the American women.

"I think we had a lot of pressure on us to prove what we could do," Cindy Brogdon later told team historian Kathryn Lee Kemp. "I felt that. Women's basketball had not been on TV very often and now we were going to be internationally exposed. We had a lot to prove to the US, but we also had a lot to prove to each other and to our individual selves."

The pressure was magnified by the responsibility Moore and many of the players felt to popularize their sport and to prove the worth of women's athletics in general. "We understood what the next step needed to be," Meyers said. "The intensity, the focus, the camaraderie we had, and really the understanding of how historical it was to be a part of the first Olympics, that drove us. That really drove us. I never believed we were going to lose."

But now they had.

All the skepticism and taunts these women had endured, all the stereotypes and limitations they'd overcome, all the chauvinists they'd proven wrong — all of it was in question now. A loss to Bulgaria followed later in the tournament by what was sure to be a loss to the USSR wouldn't just be an embarrassment for themselves and their team, wouldn't just dash all hopes for a medal — it would also be a brutal blow to women's sports in America and a terrible setback, from an American perspective, on the long journey toward equality for women in the Olympic movement.

Discrimination against female athletes was an Olympic tradition as old as any other. In the ancient Greek Games, women were banned from competing in or even watching the events. Those who tried anyway could be sentenced to death. The founder of the modern Olympics in 1896, French aristocrat Pierre de Coubertin, strongly opposed women's sports, believing "womanhood" and strenuous activity were contradictory notions and that it was immoral for men to watch women sweat. "I do not approve of the participation of women in public competitions," he once said. "In the Olympic Games, their primary role should be to crown the victors."

When a handful of female athletes first

participated in the 1900 Olympics in Paris, it was more of an accident than by design. American socialite Margaret Abbott happened to be in Paris studying art that summer when she learned of a women's golf tournament taking place in town. She entered, won, and received a porcelain bowl for her efforts, never realizing — even at her death fifty-five years later — that she had competed in the Olympics.

With the all-male members of the International Olympic Committee continuing to oppose the opportunities for women in the first two decades of the twentieth century, one determined woman decided female athletes didn't need the IOC, anyway. Alice Milliat of France organized an Olympics for women under the auspices of her International Women's Sports Federation, drawing tens of thousands of spectators and hundreds of athletes from Europe and the United States to attend elaborate, well-organized events throughout the 1920s and early 1930s. By the late '20s, the IOC had grown envious and pledged to add more women's events if she stopped calling her event the Women's Olympics.

For Milliat, success in forcing the Olympics to admit more women was bittersweet. There was less need for, and interest in, a separate affair for women, and her event folded after 1936.

In 1932, Mildred "Babe" Didrikson of Beaumont, Texas, became the first female American Olympian to capture the national spotlight, winning five events and setting two world records at the Olympic trials and then becoming the first woman to win medals in three different track and field events at the Los Angeles Games. When she returned to Texas, ten thousand admirers showed up at the Dallas airport to greet her, and thousands more lined the streets for a tickertape parade. Sportswriter Grantland Rice called her "the most flawless section of muscle harmony, of complete mental and physical coordination, the world of sport has ever known."[1]

But Didrikson was also the subject of intense ridicule, criticized for her "manly" appearance and personality. Joe Williams of the *New York World-Telegram* wrote that instead of competing on the track, it would be "much better if she and her ilk stayed at home, got themselves prettied up and waited for the phone to ring." Avery Brundage, president of the American Olympic Committee at the time, felt the same way. "I am fed up to the ears with women as track and field competitors," he said. "[Their] charms sink to something less than zero." And it wasn't just men who objected to the presence of women at the Olympics. After watching Didrikson and other women compete at the 1932 Olympics, one female columnist wrote that women were "awkward, ugly to watch, in many cases thoroughly ridiculous. Cavorting around on the same field with the flower of male champions, they made you ashamed and embarrassed for them."

Nearly forty years later, the rhetoric had hardly changed. Heading into the 1968 Olympics in Mexico City, *San Francisco Examiner* columnist Prescott Sullivan wrote that sex tests were necessary in women's athletics to prevent "farcical mismatches between mannish types who shave twice a day and fluffy types who, bless 'em, are what girls should be — all girl . . . . Track and field is a man's game.

Women weren't meant to be his equal at it."

"Femininity tests" had first been implemented at the 1966 European track championships, with 243 participants forced to parade naked in front of three gynecologists to prove their gender. At the Commonwealth Games in Jamaica that year, the international track governing body mandated a more invasive test, one that English athlete Mary Peters described as "the most crude and degrading experience" of her life. "I was ordered to lie on the couch and pull my knees up," she said. "The doctors then proceeded to undertake an examination which, in modern parlance, amounted to a grope. Presumably they were searching for hidden testes. They found none and I left."

By 1976, gender exams still existed, but in a new form. Female athletes in Montreal had to report to the "Feminine Control Centre" to have genetic samples scraped from inside their mouths.[2] And antiquated policies persisted in other areas. Women still weren't permitted to run the marathon, and there were no female members of the IOC. Many male sportswriters, including those considered the best in the business, still wrote about female athletes in terms they'd never apply to men. In a *Sports Illustrated* roundup of the gymnastics competition, a writer described various gymnasts as a "wide-eyed strawberry blonde ingenue," a "peanut," "pixieish," "hauntingly beautiful," and an "innocent little chimney sweep" with "dusky, soulful eyes."

The condescending characterization of female athletes belied the fact that it was an eighty-six-pound, fourteen-year-old girl who emerged as the record-breaking sensation of the '76 Games and one of the most popular Olympians in history.

Nadia Comaneci had grown up playing on her grandmother's farm in Romania, climbing fruit trees and swinging from limb to limb, playing soccer with boys, fishing, and digging carrots. One time she climbed to the top of her family's Christmas tree, sending it — and herself — toppling to the ground. A young gymnastics coach named Bela Karolyi discovered Nadia one day scampering around a school playground and was intrigued by her courage and aggression. "The small

Fourteen-year-old Romanian gymnast Nadia Comaneci was the star of the 1976 Olympics, earning seven perfect 10s and three gold medals. She defected to the United States in 1989 and now lives in Norman, Oklahoma. (Wikimedia Commons)

girl was naturally fearless and would try anything," he recalled.[3]

As a kid, Nadia had no female athletic role models and she'd never heard of the Olympics. By 1976, she'd performed well in European gymnastics meets but was largely unknown in the US and Canada.

Arriving in Montreal, she figured the Olympics were just another event. But when she checked into the Olympic Village, she was immediately "blown away" by the sights, sounds, and smells, the movies, the soft drinks, the bags, hats, and pins. She'd never seen pizza, peanut butter, or breakfast cereal in Romania. "To me, it was so high-tech, so strange and exciting and absolutely wonderful," she recalled. "That first day, I was afraid to close my eyes because I didn't want to miss anything."

With the gymnastics competition starting the day after the opening ceremony, Nadia skipped the parade to conserve energy. The first time the world saw her was on the uneven bars. Dressed in a white leotard with red, yellow, and blue stripes down the arms, her goal was to perform better than anyone in the competition. Instead, she performed better than anyone in history, earning the first-ever perfect 10 score from the judges. And she'd go on to earn six more 10s in other events, an astounding performance that captured the attention of television viewers all over the world. "It was the purest, most joyous theater that the Olympic Games can offer," wrote one American magazine reporter, "and every twist, leap and smile proved that the star was worthy of her role."[4]

Comaneci achieved perfection through grace. But grace wasn't going to help the US women's basketball team beat Bulgaria. And thankfully for Billie Moore, her trusted confidant, Sue Gunter, was now back in Montreal to help her develop a game plan. Team manager Jeanne Rowlands and trainer Gail Weldon had called Gunter after her father's funeral and begged her to come back to Montreal. "[Sue] said the look on my face when she came back told more than words could express," Moore recalled.

Moore and Gunter's defensive strategy was to alternate between Simpson and Lieberman at the back of a 1-3-1 zone, asking them to run hard at the Bulgarian shooters. Between Simpson's army-tank toughness and Lieberman's teenage fearlessness, Moore counted on the pair to disrupt the Bulgarians' offensive timing. Lieberman had made an impact—literally

— in the game against Bulgaria in Hamilton, launching herself squarely into the chest of a jump-shooting guard. Though Simpson started the game in Montreal, Moore brought Lieberman into the game earlier than usual, instructing her, just like the last time, to harass Bulgaria's top scorer with a physical brand of defense. "She remembered me from Hamilton," Lieberman wrote later. "Every time I would look her way, she would get rid of the ball in a hurry."

With four thousand fans jammed into the Desmarteau Center, most of them waving American flags and cheering wildly for the red, white, and blue, the game was tight throughout the first half and in the early minutes of the second. But with the US leading 60–56, Trish Roberts took control, scoring one basket, then another, and then feeding Harris and Rojcewicz for baskets on the next two possessions. The American lead ballooned to 12, and from that point on the Bulgarians never threatened to catch up. Nancy Dunkle got hot in the second half, too, scoring 11 of her team-high 17 points in the final two quarters. With Roberts,

Charlotte Lewis pulls down a rebound in the United States' 95–79 win over Bulgaria. (Getty Images)

Meyers, Harris, and Brogdon also scoring in double figures, Meyers adding nine assists, Simpson bringing the crowd to its feet with hustling defensive plays, and the US outrebounding Bulgaria 43–28, it was a thorough team effort, and a 95–79 victory, one that Moore considered "one of our best games ever."

Writing for the Gannett News Service,

Bob Kenney described the American women's performance as "a dazzling display for their sport."

Pat Head agreed. "We felt an obligation," she said. "Just being here, as one of the six best teams in the world, has to help women's basketball in the United States. Playing well, as we did today, is a great boost. It has to create a lot more interest."

But to really grow the game, the US would need to medal. And to keep those hopes alive, they'd need to beat the local heroes with the home-court advantage.

Canada, which had beaten the US at the World Championships in Colombia a year earlier, was up next.

NATIONAL PASTIME  **22**

Before coaching basketball at the University of Kansas, before serving in the United States Army, before meeting his wife in Springfield, Massachusetts, and before inventing the game of basketball there, all the significant moments in James Naismith's life took place in Canada. He was born and grew up in Almonte, Ontario, and attended both McGill University and Presbyterian College in Montreal.

When men's basketball made its first appearance at the 1936 Games in Berlin, the Canadian team advanced all the way to the finals, losing to the Americans in a game played outside in a driving rainstorm, with Naismith there to witness what he called the greatest moment of his life. It was fitting, Canadian sports officials believed, that women's basketball made its Olympic debut in the inventor's native land.

Naismith had been dead for twenty-seven years by the time of the 1976 Olympics, but the Montreal Games were still an opportunity for the Canadian women's basketball team to do the inventor proud. As host nation, Canada didn't have to qualify for events as other countries did; it received automatic invitations in every discipline. With this unprecedented opportunity and TV exposure, the Montreal Olympics had the potential to elevate basketball and other sports in Canada like nothing before.

Preparations for the 1976 Olympics took place within the context of two important developments in Canadian society. First was the establishment of the Royal Commission on the Status of Women in 1967, a national initiative to study inequities and issue recommendations to ensure equal opportunities for women in all aspects of Canadian life, including sports. Second was another federal program designed to support elite athletes and teams across Canada, with the goal of improving the country's medal chances in Montreal by investing more heavily in training, coaching, development, nutrition, and international travel.

But in a development that shocked the players and coaches who had been preparing for the Olympics, less than a year before the opening ceremony, some Canadians began to question the country's approach to Olympic competition. Critics said the national effort was too large, suggesting that certain team sports, including men's soccer, men's volleyball, and men's and women's basketball, should decline their automatic berths. "Quality over quantity" was their focus, and they argued that Canadians should not compete in every event but only in sports where they had a strong chance to medal. Even some of the people who had supported the prior investments had reason to consider this proposal; poor team performances in Montreal would make their efforts appear unsuccessful.

The threat to women's hoops in the lead-up to the Games shocked Canadian Amateur Basketball Association executive director John Restivo. "Look, we've spent $400,000 on women's basketball pointing towards the Olympics," he told reporters. "Our team is currently on tour in China, and now they seem to be trying to suggest we pull out of the Games gracefully. I can't believe it. All of our girls have sacrificed almost everything to be with this team."

And those sacrifices were paying off. The Canadian women had already beaten the Americans at the World Championships in Colombia. And just a few months after the calls to disband the program, they traveled to Czechoslovakia and beat the mighty Soviet team by 15 points in an exhibition game (Semjonova did not play). Critics eventually backed off and Canada competed in each of the sports that had been on the chopping block, but an air of uncertainty and distrust continued to hover around the basketball team at the Olympics.

One of the unintended consequences of the increased investment in women's sports in the 1970s was the sudden interest of male coaches. Back when there was little funding for women's programs, men stayed away. But now that there was money flowing toward women's athletics, men found coaching jobs attractive. And they often had a head start on female candidates, having gained experience at high levels of men's competition when those opportunities simply hadn't existed on the women's side. When the Canadian Amateur Basketball Association went looking for a coach for the women's team at the '76 Olympics, one of the men who applied for the job was Brian Heaney, a twenty-nine-year-old American who had never coached women before and had no international experience.

An outstanding basketball player at Brooklyn's Bishop Laughlin Memorial High School, Heaney played college ball at Acadia University in Nova Scotia, winning a national championship, setting a record by scoring 74 points in one game, and earning All-Canadian honors. When the NBA's Baltimore Bullets drafted him in 1969, he became the first Canadian Intercollegiate Athletic Union player to appear in an NBA game. After a brief pro career, he returned to Canada in 1970 at the age of twenty-five to become head coach of men's basketball at St. Mary's University in Halifax, Nova Scotia, winning a national championship in 1973. In 1975, he interviewed for the women's national team job, and to his surprise, he got it. And while he knew the Soviets were the team to beat in Montreal, he always kept a close eye on the Americans.

The American and Canadian basketball players gravitated toward each other at international tournaments, their shared language and similar cultures making friendships easy to form. Sylvia Sweeney, a Black Canadian player from Montreal, developed a bond with Nancy Lieberman, appreciating the young New Yorker's openness to new experiences. "Nancy was always effervescent, the type of person who embraced everything that was going on," Sweeney recalled. "She was always the one to say, 'Hey, how are you doing?' When other people were walking around like they had a stick up their butt, she was a bridge-builder between countries and teams." Sweeney and Lieberman shared a common background in that their love for basketball made them outsiders in their families. Sweeney's mother was a highly regarded musician and popular piano teacher in Montreal, and her mom's brother, Oscar Peterson, was a famous jazz pianist who performed with Black American jazz greats including Duke Ellington, Louis Armstrong, Ella Fitzgerald, and Dizzy Gillespie. "Our family's formation was in the arts," Sweeney recalled. "I was the outlier when I decided to pick up a basketball."[1]

Sweeney joined the Canadian national team in 1974 and would go on to star on the team for a decade, earning a reputation as "Canada's First Lady of Basketball." Along with another supremely talented Black player from Montreal, guard Liz Silcott, she gave the Canadian women a fighting chance in international play. In the lead-up to Montreal, the team had played extremely well at both the World Championships and in several European tournaments. One Canadian sportswriter praised the team's accomplishments as "almost inconceivable," comparing them to Canada's most legendary women's basketball powerhouse, the Edmonton Grads, who had compiled an astonishing 502–20 record between 1915 and 1940, including a 114–6 record against teams from the United States.[2]

But even with their success, tensions within the team were building to feverish levels in the month leading up to the Olympics, especially between Heaney and the team's only two Black players: Silcott and Sweeney.

A high-scoring five-foot-six guard, Silcott's on-court excellence had partially masked her ongoing battles with mental illness, but her coaches had shown little patience for her struggles. Jack Donohue, who coached both the Canadian men's and women's national teams before Heaney took over the women's team, had accused Silcott of insubordination and laziness — the most transparent of racially coded criticisms of Black players — and kicked her off the national team during a trip to Cuba. "They say that I have to get my head screwed in right," Silcott said at the time. "Maybe they're right."

But Silcott was a fan favorite, a player with uncommon individual skills and explosive scoring ability who once collected 77 points in a two-game span and earned numerous MVP and all-tournament honors. She accomplished all this while operating under the restrictive "white gaze" of coaches, teammates, and fans in a country that was only about 3 percent Black, and while battling internal demons and anxieties that very few people around her attempted to understand.

So when Silcott butted heads with Heaney, prompting him to boot her from the national team just two weeks before the Olympics, both Silcott and Sweeney believed there were underlying prejudices working against her. First, they believed Heaney was insensitive to Silcott's mental illness and resented her freewheeling style of play because she was Black; both players publicly accused Heaney of racism. Second, they believed Heaney was biased against players from French-speaking Canada. Silcott told reporters that Heaney had once told her the national team would include no "frogs from Quebec," an incendiary slur in a country where tensions between French and English speakers were at a boiling point.

Whatever Heaney's motivation for dropping his best player from the Olympic team, the move didn't sit well with Sweeney. "We rolled into the '76 Olympics a very divided team," she said. "I remember sitting by the fence in the Olympic Village before the first game, not wanting to get on the bus to the arena. I remember just playing extremely passively and not caring anymore. That was my Olympic experience."

By the time the US and Canada met at the Étienne Desmarteau Center for their game on July 22, the Canadians had lost their first two games, blown out by the Soviet Union 115–51 and Japan 121–89. Even so, had they not been a team in such disarray, the game against the US could have been winnable.

Sweeney knew the key to beating the Americans was slowing down their fast break, and the conditions at the Desmarteau Center made that goal achievable. One sportswriter described the building's unusually small court as "pocket-sized," a full eight feet shorter than the typical ninety-four-foot-long playing surface. Without as much room to run, the Americans' speed advantage was muted. Heaney's scouting report told him that Dunkle and Harris had the potential to dominate in the paint

Tickets for the basketball events at the Desmarteau Center and Montreal Forum. (Ed Markey)

and that Simpson would control the ball and distribute to shooters like Brogdon and Meyers. "It would be hard to zero in on any one or two of them," he said. "You had to play their whole team — well beyond the starting five. They were balanced offensively, and defensively they hustled and closed off the driving and passing lanes. They rebounded well and then they were off on the fast break."

Beating the Americans would be a tough task under any circumstances; without Silcott, it was nearly impossible. But Heaney believed his team still had a chance. "It was a tough decision to make," he said, nearly fifty years later, of his decision to cut a star player. "But it's a team game, and when we beat the US in the World Championships, we didn't have her on the team then, either. The players we did have played good team basketball. All of our players were talented. We still felt we could win."

In the first half of the game, it appeared Heaney might have been right. To the delight of their fans, Canada took the lead midway through the half. With Carol Turney and Bev Bland leading the way with hot outside shooting, the hosts held a two-point advantage at halftime. But Gunter and Moore made a critical adjustment at halftime, telling their players to abandon their man-to-man defense in favor of a zone, forcing the Canadians to shoot from farther away from the basket. The strategy worked, and as Canada struggled to find open shots, the US capitalized by forcing turnovers, inducing guard Joanne Sargent to commit five miscues in the second half alone. In one stretch beginning with thirteen minutes remaining in the game, Sue Rojcewicz ignited an American rally with an inspired run of stellar defense, forcing Canada to turn the ball over repeatedly, either scoring herself or dishing out assists on four straight possessions. This sparked a 14–0 run that gave the US the lead for good. With Dunkle scoring 15 points, Simpson adding 14, and Harris and Roberts scoring 11, the US won easily, 89–75.

The loss dropped Canada to 0–3 and out of the running even for a bronze. "[We] really thought [we] could come into this tournament and win a medal," Heaney said after the game. "But we're out of it now. Our only goal now is to try and win a game so we will at least have something to show for all the work we've put in." That didn't happen; Canada lost its next three games and finished the tournament winless in six attempts. Canadian athletes in other sports fared little better; Canada finished twenty-seventh in the medal count with five silver and six bronze medals, becoming the only host nation in the history of the modern Olympics not to earn a single gold.

Meanwhile, the victory left the Americans in solid medal contention and gave Moore reason for optimism heading into the much-anticipated game against the mighty Soviets.

"We're still thinking about the gold," she told reporters. "We have the best chance to beat them. Hopefully this is what we've been waiting for."

CERTAIN DOOM

23

The first time Ann Meyers played against the Soviets, in a series of 1974 exhibition games, she marveled at the size and maturity of the Russian women — women in their thirties, women with children. A friend had told her Communist countries injected female athletes with "pregnancy hormones" to boost performance, a Cold War rumor that Meyers was tempted to believe. "Whether that was true or not," she recalled, "there was no doubt these ladies had something extra."

Something extra? More like several things. Height. Talent. Confidence. Tradition. And motivation. Though they hadn't lost a major international competition in nearly two decades, the Soviets felt a continual measure of disrespect from the American players and coaches.

One night during the series of 1974 exhibition games, the Soviet and US teams joined each other for dinner, Russians on one side of the table and Americans on the other.

Meyers found herself seated next to the Jersey girl with no filter, Juliene Simpson, and across from Soviet captain Tatyana Ovechkina and the towering center, Uljana Semjonova.[1] Semjonova's fingers were so big one sportswriter had harshly compared them to "sausages with nail polish," her hands so huge Pat Head thought apples looked like golf balls in her grasp. Given the language barrier, Meyers held out her palms and motioned for Semjonova to do the same. "Your hands are very large," Meyers said slowly. Simpson took off her wedding ring, motioning for Semjonova to do the same so they could compare sizes — the Russian's ring was big enough to fit a fifty-cent piece through with room to spare. Ovechkina said something in Russian to Semjonova and both women laughed. Simpson pretended to understand.

"That's what I'm saying," she said loudly. "You've got really huge hands! I'll bet you have big Bozo feet too." In her autobiography, Meyers recalled that "Juliene snickered at the thought she could be so rude and get away with it," continuing to joke at the Russians' expense until it was time to leave. "Well adios, ladies, see you tomorrow."

To Simpson's shock, Semjonova didn't miss a beat. "See you tomorrow."

Stunned, Simpson turned to an interpreter. "I thought they didn't speak any English?"

"Not much," the interpreter replied. "But they *understand* everything."

The next night, Semjonova, Ovechkina, and the Soviets showed no mercy, beating the Americans by more than 30 points.

Billie Moore told reporters after the Canada game that her team had as good a chance as any to knock off the Soviets in Montreal. It would have been hard to find anyone outside her own locker room who believed her, including USA Basketball chief Bill Wall. The Soviets were "awe-inspiring and tougher than hell," he told the *Boston Globe*. "They have devastated everybody . . . They have to be the overwhelming favorite."

But Simpson said Moore "always got us to believe in things other people didn't believe in. If you had a good game plan and everybody did what they were supposed to do, you could win." And as she walked out onto the court for the opening tip, Meyers, too, brimmed with confidence. "I've never doubted going into a game that we're going to win," she said. "No matter what the numbers say or who the opponent is, I believe in our ability."

Optimism before the game was one thing; after tip-off, it was something else altogether. The Soviets, Meyers quickly understood, didn't intend to give the US "even a glimmer of hope."

Again and again, the Soviets scored. Again and again, the Americans missed a shot or turned the ball over. Only four and a half minutes had run off the clock and the game was already over, the Soviets leading 17–0.

From the bench, all Moore could summon was gallows humor.

"Please promise me we're going to score," she said to Gunter.

"Billie," her assistant replied, "there are no assurances here."

Semjonova was unstoppable. On the defensive end, she'd plant her feet under the basket and nonchalantly grab rebounds "as if picking cherries," wrote *New York Times* reporter James Tuite. On offense, she'd camp in the lane, catch passes high above her head, and simply turn and drop the ball in the hoop. "The United States players . . . leaped about her like puppies yelping for their lunchtime snack," Tuite wrote. "It was almost ludicrous."

Moore's defensive strategy was technically sound. The plan was to have one defender stand in front of Semjonova, forcing the Soviet guards to throw the ball over the top, and then have another player slide in behind her as she caught the ball and turned toward the basket. The problem was the frontside defender barely registered in Semjonova's consciousness — a "petrified" Pat Head tried to front her and realized she only came up to the Russian's armpit —

and the backside defender faced certain doom.

During one timeout, Moore repeated the defensive strategy to her players. "We're going to front her and then the weakside defender will come over and take the charge," she said. "When she swings, she'll hit you and they've got to call it." Sure enough, the Soviets lobbed the ball over Lusia Harris's head to Semjonova — but nobody took the charge, and the Russian center scored easily. Upset by her team's lack of execution, Moore sent Trish Roberts into the game. "And here I'm thinking, 'Do what the coach says,'" Roberts recalled years later. The next time the Russians threw the ball into Semjonova, Roberts slid over behind her and was instantly knocked to the floor. The collision threw the 280-pound Semjonova off-balance. "All I could see was this big seven-foot-two body falling toward me," Roberts recalled. "I crawled out of that lane like a baby as fast as I could. I knew if she fell on me, it was over."

Watching the scene from the bench, team manager Jeanne Rowlands winced in sympathy. "I'm sure Trish was trying to figure out what truck that was that hit her."

And with that, Roberts changed her mind about following her coach's orders.

"I did not go over and help on the weak side again," she said.

Semjonova was a dominant force, "a woman made for a larger world," in the words of AP reporter Victoria Graham. She scored 20 points in the first half alone, but the problem for the Americans was that her team was much more than a one-woman show. With talented players at every position, the Soviets could run the fast break, catch and shoot, create shots without dribbling, or take the ball to the hole.

Ever since she had seen them for the first time in Moscow in 1973, Moore had admired the Soviets' skills in every facet of the game. "The best machine I saw in the Soviet Union wasn't a car, it wasn't a tank, it was the women's basketball team." Now that machine was running over her players, shifting into reverse, and backing over them for good measure, a

Trish Roberts shoots over the outstretched arms of Tamara Dauniene (14) and Uljana Semjonova of the Soviet Union during the USSR's 112–77 win over the US. (Getty Images)

"punitive expedition," in the words of Coach Lidia Alexeeva, in retaliation for the Americans' boasts that they would win the game. At halftime, the Soviets led 54–34. They scored even more efficiently in the second half, winning by a whopping margin of 112–77.

"I've never seen anyone dominate a women's basketball game like [Semjonova] did tonight," Moore said afterward.

Semjonova was clearly the star of the game, a player to be admired. But her jaw-dropping size and strength, qualities that drew male athletes' admiration, brought out the worst in some people. Fans in the Desmarteau Center mocked her size, yelling cruel jokes in her direction. A female journalist said watching Semjonova trudge up and down the court was "sad and freakish." Another reporter dismissed the Russian as "a Jolly Red Giant." Still another compared her to the monster-like character Lurch from *The Addams Family.*

"She is the absolute flip side to Nadia Comaneci," wrote Leigh Montville in the *Boston Globe.* "If Comaneci, the Romanian gymnastic pixie, is everyone's kid sister, [Semjonova] is the relative placed in a closet and discussed only in whispers at the closest of family gatherings . . . She probably is the most dominating athlete in the 21st Olympiad, but no *Newsweek* magazines or ABC Sports crews ever will rush to make her the object of their affections . . . She never is going to be anyone's darling. She always is going to have to settle for being the most awesome women's basketball player anyone could ever imagine . . . She killed the American women's basketball team. She pulverized it."

Even so, the Americans who had attempted to get to know Semjonova felt a strong empathy for her. Though none of them were nearly as tall, in most cases, they, too, had endured bullying for their size and physique. Semjonova, they learned, was a soft-spoken, kind, and gentle soul. On trips to America, she shopped for teddy bears, once buying one that was so big it required its own seat on the flight back to Russia. Self-conscious of her height, she chose not to march in the opening ceremony. "I hate when people yell things at her," said Pat Head. "She must hear so much of it every day of her life. It's sad, really. She seems like a nice person, but no one ever is going to think about that."[2]

For the Americans players, Semjonova's dominance made losing palatable; it was far easier to bounce back from a blowout against an unstoppable player than to lose a close game to a team they should have beaten. And the way the Olympic tournament was unfolding, they still had a chance to make history.

One game remained.

If they could beat Czechoslovakia, they'd win a silver medal.

24 SWEET AS SILVER

Lusia Harris sat in the basketball team's crowded Olympic Village apartment, handwriting a letter to her coach at Delta State, Margaret Wade. It was the night before the game against Czechoslovakia, and Harris thanked her coach for the lessons she'd taught her, for putting her in position to make history on the first American women's Olympic basketball team.

Wade's life in basketball spanned the arc of the game's history in the US. She'd loved playing as a young woman in the 1920s and early '30s, was brought to tears and burned her jersey in frustration when her college dropped the sport after her junior year, and reemerged four decades later to revive the program as head coach at her alma mater in the era of women's liberation. Wade's reputation in the game was so strong the national player of the year award would be named in her honor two years after the Olympics. And now, on the eve of the biggest game of her life, Harris wanted to let her coach know she'd been paying attention to the lessons she'd shared.

Sportswriters had latched on to what they considered the most intriguing individual stories on the team — the little sister of an NBA star, the outspoken redheaded teenager from Queens, the farmer's daughter who was already a collegiate head coach back home. But Harris understood the outcome of the next day's game wouldn't come down to any one individual's performance.

"Coach," she wrote. "If we don't play as a team tomorrow, we won't win."

Pat Head called a reporter in Clarksville, Tennessee, from one of the Village's telephone banks. Her hometown newspaper had kept tabs on her throughout the tournament, printing her comments after each game. Now, Head was in a reflective mood. The mental and physical pressure had taken a toll; she was the oldest player on the team. This would be the last competitive game she'd ever play. It was time, she said, to move on to a new stage of her life and focus on coaching. "As far as I'm concerned, Monday is it. I'm hanging my shoes up," she said. "I have received an awful lot through my participation, but it is time for me to look toward a job and the future and something other than just playing all the time. If we win [the game against Czechoslovakia], we can leave here very satisfied."

With one game left for each team to play, four countries — the US, Czechoslovakia, Japan, and Bulgaria — shared identical 2–2 records. If the Americans beat Czechoslovakia, they'd be in a prime position to win a silver medal. That was because Japan was almost certain to lose to the undefeated USSR, which had already clinched the gold, and even if Bulgaria beat winless Canada, the US held a tie-breaking advantage over the Bulgarians, having beaten them earlier in the tournament. Because of the round-robin format of the Olympic tournament, the Americans were in the unusual but enviable position of having a chance to *win* a game to earn a silver medal. More commonly, tournaments conclude with championship games where the winner takes gold and the loser accepts silver as consolation.

"We're going to try to do what we do best — run hard and play pressure defense," Moore told reporters. "The one thing we haven't done well here is shoot, but we have good shooters and we hope to bring that around tomorrow."

In the final minutes before tip-off, Nancy Lieberman looked around the locker room and felt only pride, strength, and confidence. The music was loud, players were singing, talking, yelling, and laughing. "Our leaders — Lusia Harris, Pat Head, Juliene Simpson — had a look in their eyes that said they wouldn't be denied," she recalled. "We knew the Czech team was bigger and strong, but we were big and quick and had great athletes."

The room grew quiet as Moore delivered what Lieberman recalled as "one of the greatest locker room speeches ever."

Moore talked about the team's game

plan, but her most important message had nothing to do with the specifics of the forty-minute game and everything to do with the sport of basketball itself, the history these women would make, and the young people they would inspire. More than anything, she wanted the women seated around her, several of whom would be playing the final game of their lives, to understand that there would be other basketball Olympians in the years ahead, but only they, forever, would be the first.

"I understood the history, understood the opportunity and the doors opening," Lieberman said. "Back then there weren't really any pro sports for women, so the top of the mountain was the Olympics." This team had the potential to help women and girls envision higher mountains to climb.

Lieberman looked Moore squarely in the eyes as her coach sent the team on the court. "This is about more than just a win; this is about more than just a medal," she said. "Ladies, this will change women's basketball for the next twenty-five years."

■ ■ ■ ■

The final-round games had been moved from the tiny Desmarteau Center to the cavernous Montreal Forum, home of the NHL's Canadiens and the site of Nadia Comaneci's perfect performances — and a full-sized basketball court. Nearly twenty thousand fans packed the arena, the vast majority cheering for the Americans, chanting, "USA, all the way! USA, all the way!"

After tip-off, the teams traded baskets for much of the first half, both squads hungry for a silver medal, neither team able to distance itself from the other. When the Americans returned to their locker room at halftime, the score was deadlocked at 37–37.

Moore and Gunter huddled to discuss strategy. Without the benefit of film, scouting reports, or advanced analytics, the most important decisions came at halftime, when the coaches had a chance to talk about what they'd seen from the opponent in the first half. "So much of what we had to do was by the seat of our britches," Moore recalled. "We used halftime to make adjustments from a technical standpoint."

With no time for another motivational speech, Moore explained a change in defensive strategy. They would switch from man-to-man to a 1-3-1 zone. The lack of advance scouting went both ways. Moore kept the zone in her back pocket, breaking it out in key moments, knowing that opponents weren't well prepared for it. "We were primarily a man-to-man team, so I just thought it was different and gave us an element of surprise," Moore said. "We had some athletic players on the wings, so I thought it would work."

Initially, the move made little difference and the teams continued to trade baskets. With ten minutes and fifteen seconds remaining in the game, the Czechs led 53–52.

Once again, just as she had in the win over Canada, Sue Rojcewicz caught fire and changed the momentum of the game. After scoring a basket to put the US ahead by one point, she drew a crucial charging foul on the six-foot-four Czech center Dana Ptackova, fouling her out of the game.

Without Ptackova's shot-blocking and rebounding presence in the lane, the Americans turned their offense into a higher gear, summoning one final burst of energy. They had played basketball practically every day, sometimes three times a day, for the last two and a half months. Every single player was on the verge of collapsing from mental and physical fatigue. Moore and Gunter had lost fifteen pounds apiece since the start of training camp, the demands of the job wearing their bodies down.

But for four straight minutes, the American crowd roared and the players could do no wrong. It was a cascading wave of steals, layups, fast breaks, blocked shots, and isolation plays for Dunkle and Harris — a run of fifteen consecutive points for the US and a 67–53 lead. "During that streak, it just felt like you were sitting on a cloud that kept getting higher and higher and higher," said Dunkle. "We got hungry," O'Connor said. "Hungry for the ball."

Even after the Czechs finally scored again, the Americans continued to pour on the gas. Moore had believed her play-

Nancy Dunkle scored 14 points in the US's 83–67 silver-medal-clinching win over Czechoslovakia. Dunkle was the Americans' second-leading scorer in the tournament, averaging 13 points per game. (Getty Images)

ers had peaked in Hamilton and suffered a letdown in the early games in Montreal. But now they were back in top form, playing like the finely tuned machine she had seen that last day of camp in Warrensburg. Rojcewicz tugged up her shorts in her trademark style, daring the Czech guards to come at her. Roberts and Lieberman flew around in the back of the 1-3-1 harassing Czech shooters, and Dunkle and Harris went to work in the paint.

Sitting on press row, Lawrie Mifflin of the *New York Daily News,* who had started a women's field hockey team as a student at Yale and covered her own games for the school newspaper because no one else would do it, channeled the passion of millions of American women who had pushed so hard to create opportunities for themselves and others.[1]

"The American women played like they had never wanted anything more intensely in their lives," she wrote. "They scrambled all over the floor, pressing the taller Czechs unmercifully, stealing the ball repeatedly, and drawing fouls and sinking points on quick, flashy moves under the basket."

As the game entered its final minute with the US comfortably ahead, players on the bench clasped hands, rocking back and forth, sneaking glances at the seconds on the clock and the smiles on the faces of their coaches. Nancy Lieberman looked up in the crowd and spotted her mother in a sea of red, white, and blue as a deafening chant of "USA! USA!" filled the arena.

The final buzzer sounded, the USA winning 83–67, and players on the bench ran toward their teammates on the court, smiling, hugging, cheering, giddily flopping over one another in what reminded Mary Anne O'Connor of a pile of puppies. The crowd was on its feet now, chanting, "USA, all the way! USA, all the way!" in unison with the players as they clustered together at center court.

"For all of us, this was the biggest game in our lives," O'Connor recalled. "I wanted to go right through the roof when it was over."

Meeting with the press after the game, Moore continued to hammer away at the themes that had guided her throughout the journey: the US may have overcome

American players and coaches celebrate their victory over Czechoslovakia. (Associated Press)

incredible odds this time around, but because of the success of this team, American women would not be underdogs in the future.

"I think there was a lot of doubt in the States that we could win a medal here. Remember, we hadn't done much in the past two years in international competition," she said. "But it never dawned on us that we wouldn't win a medal here. We came here hoping to win the gold, but I, personally, would have been very disappointed had we not won at least the silver medal. I think what we did will

371

have a tremendous effect on girls' basketball."

Someone asked if it was realistic to expect the US to compete with the Soviets.

"I would say that the gap between the
United States team and the Russian team
is about ten inches," she quipped, refer-
ring to Semjonova's height advantage.
"Really, I think we've closed the gap between us and them. If we keep making
the same strides in the next four years as
we have in the past three, I really think
we'll go into the 1980 Olympics as the
team favorite."

As Moore spoke to the media, Nancy
Lieberman struggled to fulfill the obligations of the post-game drug test.

She went into the stall with an observer.

"I can't pee with you in here."

Teammates came by.

"Nancy, they won't give us medals until
you pee."

The pressure didn't help. Someone
brought her some apple juice, then some
water.

Pat Head came in and yelled for Nancy to drink a beer.

"I don't drink beer!" Lieberman replied. "I just turned eighteen!"

"Drink. The. Beer!" Head shot back.

"I don't like beer!"

More teammates came in.

"What the hell is taking so long? We'd like to get our medals!"

"Then make another Olympic team!" Lieberman shouted back.

Several gallons of water later, Lieberman was able to produce her sample. "I was finally able to go to the bathroom," she said, "and America has not been the same since."

With a few hours to wait until the medal ceremony, Moore begged her players not to celebrate too wildly in the meantime. "You've earned this," she told them. "We deserve a party. But do me a favor and wait until after the medal ceremony to celebrate too much so you will remember standing on that platform." The players broke up into smaller groups, planning to meet up again at the ceremony.

Mary Anne O'Connor and Sue Rojcewicz, friends and teammates from their
days at Southern Connecticut State, es-
caped the Olympic Village and drove
out into the country, joining a group of
Rojcewicz's family members partying at
a campground. Two silver medalists in
the woods, exhausted and ecstatic, feeling the weightless buzz of a job well done.

When the team reunited at the Montreal Forum, they gathered off to the side
of the court, preparing to walk out to the
podium. Sue Gunter zipped from player
to player, straightening collars, flattening
wrinkles. "We can dress you up, but we
can't take you out!" she joked. Olympic
officials told the players to walk out to
receive their medals. Juliene Simpson saw
Gunter and Moore leaving to take a seat
in the stands.

"Where are you guys going?"

"We don't get a medal, only the players," Moore replied.

"I'm not going out there if you don't get
a medal," Simpson said.

"Go," Moore said, looking straight into
Simpson's eyes. "Go."

One by one, the twelve American players dipped their heads as silver medals were draped around their necks. Then, in unison, they all turned toward the corner of the arena, pointed, and raised their medals toward their coaches as a sign of respect and love. Gunter immediately knew it was a moment she would never forget. Moore felt the ultimate satisfaction of a coach, content that she had played a part in molding a diverse group of women into a team, proud that they were able to experience this joy when there had never been any guarantee of reward.

She suspected that at this moment, her players believed that all the sprints they had run in a sweltering gym in Missouri, every night they had crawled into bed with aching muscles, every sacrifice they had made was insignificant in comparison to what they had gained.

Then the flags were raised: the hammer and sickle of the Soviet Union, the Stars and Stripes of the United States, and the white, green, and red bars of third-place Bulgaria.

US basketball players receive a standing ovation from fans at the Montreal Forum after receiving their silver medals. (Associated Press)

Head stared at the American flag, marveling at all the stereotypes and limitations she'd overcome. No longer would she allow anyone to call her poor, backward, country, or inferior, to demean her because she was a woman.

Meyers looked up at the flag, too, her heart swelling with pride.

Silver, she believed, was sweet.

HOOKED ON A FEELING

Ann Meyers and her mom boarded a plane from Montreal to Los Angeles. Somewhere over the American Midwest, the pilot came on the intercom to share an important piece of news: an Olympic silver medalist was on board. The passengers erupted in cheers.

Soon after they arrived home in Southern California, Meyers walked into a popular restaurant. Patrons stood and applauded.

In New York City, Gail Marquis's mom and dad met her at the airport holding a WELCOME BACK poster. As they drove up to her parents' house, Marquis saw dozens of kids lined up outside. She assumed they were waiting to greet her and was surprised when none of them paid any attention as she stepped out of the car. "I thought they were there for me," she recalled. "But they were there for lunch." During the time Gail had been away at training camp, the Hamilton tournament, and the Olympics, her mother had set up a free lunch program for low-income children in the neighborhood. The arrival of the silver medalist on this day just meant lunch would be served late.

Marquis's accomplishment didn't go completely unnoticed. In September, New York officials would honor her and Nancy Lieberman at a banquet celebrating the Olympic medalists from New York City and Long Island.

All over the country, politicians, civic clubs, athletic officials, and school administrators rushed to shower the basketball players with gifts and praise, complimenting them for bringing honor to their country, hometowns, and universities. It was welcome recognition, but not without irony and hypocrisy: these were the same people and places that provided little funding or support for women's athletics or, in many cases, broader women's issues.

Town leaders in Fairfield, Connecticut, declared August 19 "Mary Anne O'Connor Day," presenting her with the key to the city, plaques from the Lions Club and chamber of commerce, and a bouquet of roses, as a high school drum line entertained onlookers.

At Paramus Catholic High School in New Jersey, Sue Rojcewicz visited a basketball day camp for girls. The camp had attracted just twenty-two girls when it opened nine years earlier, but now more than 120 young women turned out for six and a half hours of drills every day. Wearing her blue Olympic warm-up suit, Rojcewicz told the girls to take advantage of the opportunities coming their way. Growing up, she said, there had been no competitive basketball leagues for girls until she reached junior high. And her high school didn't offer basketball until her junior year. "By the time I got to college, I was ashamed to tell a guy I was a phys ed major," she said. "So I used to make up all kinds of weird majors. Girls have come a long way since then. You've proved that by your turnout today." The campers gave her a standing ovation.

Pat Head had flown directly from Montreal to California with Billie Moore to help lead a series of basketball camps for girls the entire month of August, so it wasn't until the evening of September 3 that she finally arrived back in Tennessee. More than one hundred residents of Ashland City met her at the Nashville airport, where a representative of the governor met her in the terminal to present a plaque commemorating "Pat Head Day" in Tennessee. The Ashland City crew then led her back home in a motorcade straight to a celebration hosted by the Lions Club. One after another, local officials, former coaches and teammates, and friends lauded her with words of praise and gifts, including a color television, wristwatch, and stereo. "I knew my family would be at the airport to meet me," she told the crowd, wiping away tears. "But I didn't know there were this many people in Ashland City."

Her father, Richard, the stern disciplinarian who rarely uttered a word, let alone a kind one, told reporters how proud he was of the way his daughter had come back from a knee injury that

When Pat Head returned to Tennessee after the 1976 Olympics, residents of her hometown met her at the Nashville airport and escorted her back to Ashland City for a celebratory banquet. (UT Martin Athletics)

would have ended the careers of most people. "Patricia sure worked hard for this medal," he said. "I've never seen anyone who loves basketball the way Patricia loves it."

In California, proud students and staff at Cal State Fullerton organized a lighthearted roast for the school's two returning heroes, Nancy Dunkle and Billie Moore, selling banquet tickets for four dollars apiece and inviting friends and former players to join in the good-natured ridicule of the guests of honor.

Former player Donna Connally mocked the coach's famous intensity. "As a coach, Billie is sound; a constant nerve-racking sound," she said. "When she puts her foot down, one of her players is usually under it."

Seated at a head table decorated with flowers, Moore and Dunkle smiled through all the ribbing. And before the evening ended with a screening of highlights from Montreal, there were words of genuine appreciation, too. Men's basketball coach Bob Dye told the crowd that "the only thing better than Billie as a coach is Billie as a person." University president Donald Shields said he was proud the school could boast the "most outstanding women's basketball coach and also the most outstanding women's basketball center in the country."

■ ■ ■ ■

The most socially significant celebrations took place in Monroe, Georgia, and Cleveland, Mississippi, homes of Trish Roberts and Lusia Harris. Both were Deep South towns dripping with patriarchy and ugly histories of racist violence — not the kinds of places where white citizens held up Black women as heroes. But now, Roberts and Harris had brought home rare international glory.

Roberts's hometown of Monroe, Georgia, owed its existence to the two original sins of white supremacy in America: the forced removal of Native Americans by white colonizers and the institution of slavery. Home to numerous cotton-producing slave-labor plantations after the removal of the Cherokees, and to exploitative sharecropping farms after the Civil War, Monroe counted among its prominent citizens men such as Clifford Walker, a Georgia governor in the 1920s who was a member of the Ku Klux Klan, and Prince Hulon Preston Jr., a US congressman in the 1950s who adamantly opposed school desegregation. In

1946, just nine years before Roberts was born, Monroe had been the site of one of the most notorious lynchings in postwar history, when two Black couples were murdered by a mob of white vigilantes who had been encouraged by Georgia governor and KKK member Eugene Talmadge.

When Roberts's flight arrived at Atlanta's Hartsfield Airport, her mom, brother, niece, and nephew were there to greet her. They drove Trish to her sister's house nearby, where her mom insisted that she put on her blue sweatsuit and silver medal. Trish refused. She was tired. Couldn't they just do this when they got home to Monroe? When her mom started crying, Trish relented, digging through her suitcase and putting everything on. Exhausted, Roberts was relieved when her brother-in-law offered to drive everyone to Monroe, an hour east of Atlanta. But just as they arrived on the outskirts of town, the flashing blue lights of a police car appeared behind them. How embarrassing, Roberts thought, to be pulled over in her Olympic sweatsuit.

But that's when her mom let her in on

the secret — it was "Patricia Roberts Day" in Monroe, and the police officer was there to lead them into town for a parade. The whole crying "put on your sweatsuit" routine was a setup. All the stores in Monroe had closed for the day, and people lined the streets, waving as Roberts drove into town. A big stage had been set up in front of the county courthouse, where the mayor presented Roberts the key to the city and a bouquet of roses. That would have been enough of a surprise, but just then Roberts's high school basketball teammates came riding up in a pickup truck and Roberts was escorted to a convertible for a parade through downtown and out to the school, where the gymnasium was packed with admirers. Roberts walked down a red carpet to an oversized chair, her family seated in a special section in front of her. A procession of former teammates, coaches, friends, and even Roberts's pastor offered their congratulations and told stories about her life. Roberts hadn't realized anyone was following her career so closely. "It was unreal," she recalled. "I was crying through the whole thing."

Trish Roberts said the reception she received back home in Monroe, Georgia, after returning from the Olympics, including a parade and citywide cookout, was "the most wonderful event" in her life. (Walton Tribune)

After the remarks, everyone went outside for a cookout, Black and white residents of a town with a troubled history grabbing paper plates, sitting down to eat together, and celebrating one of their own. "Imagine," Roberts said. "A whole town having a party. To this day, it was the most wonderful event in my life."

A similar scene unfolded in the Mississippi Delta when Lusia Harris returned home. Governor Cliff Finch kicked off "Lusia Harris Day" at Delta State in Cleveland, Mississippi, by telling Harris, in front of two thousand well-wishers, that all Mississippians were proud of her: "Proud of your accomplishments, proud of the examples you have set as a student-athlete and a person." Harris, the governor said, was a goodwill ambassador for the state of Mississippi. After the Delta State marching band played the Olympic theme, the mayor of Cleveland presented Harris a gift and said, "Except for you, I don't know how we could have gotten Cleveland mentioned on three national networks."

Wearing her silver medal around her neck, Harris thanked everyone for all the encouraging letters they'd sent her in Canada, admitting she was a bit embarrassed by all the attention. "If I knew that I was going to have such a crowd when I got back," she said, "I think that I would keep going." Members of Harris's Delta Sigma Theta sorority presented her with red and white carnations, and the Delta State student government association gave her green and white carnations.

Seated beside Harris in metal folding chairs on stage were her parents, one of her sisters, and a cousin. Harris was touched by her aging parents' presence and proud they were able to be treated like royalty for the first time in their lives. "I think it's real nice," her father said. "It couldn't have been done any better."

Decades later, Harris said she believed the affection and appreciation shown to her that day by the politicians and university leaders was genuine, that the events had been meaningful and heartwarming. And it was certainly well deserved. To this day, Nancy Lieberman maintains that "the most important thing going for our team was Lucy Harris," calling her one of the greatest post players in the history of the sport.

Still, the scene in Cleveland illustrated an enduring hypocrisy.

Students, school administrators, and civic leaders in Cleveland, Mississippi, honored their Olympic hero with Lusia Harris Day. "It's easy to boost a winner," one alum told her. (Delta State University)

The best-known Black woman living in the Mississippi Delta at the time was Fannie Lou Hamer, the courageous civil rights leader who had grown up the twentieth child of sharecroppers in Sunflower County. Hamer's fearless advocacy for voting rights and economic opportunities for Black citizens in the South would earn her international respect as a heroic figure in the civil rights movement, but she was not the kind of Black woman most white Mississippians chose to celebrate. They threw her no parades. Instead, they subjected her to a vicious cruelty: a wealthy landowner fired her for attempting to vote, a doctor performed a hysterectomy without her consent, and jailers beat her brutally after she attempted to desegregate a bus station.

Lusia Harris's rise to basketball prominence was a living refutation of the same white supremacist system that inspired Fannie Lou Hamer's activism. But Harris's basketball success could be more easily appropriated by white civic boosters than Hamer's righteousness. Everyone was eager to claim this Black woman, a silver medalist, as one of their own. And one speaker that day in 1976 admitted as much. After the chamber of commerce presented Harris with an engraved silver bracelet and the Delta State alumni association gave her a jewelry case to display her medal, the president of the Delta State booster club took the microphone.

"It's easy to boost a winner," he told the sharecropper's daughter. "We're behind you all the way."

26   LEGACY

Pat Head and her teammates stayed up all night in the Olympic Village celebrating their silver medal on July 26, 1976, laughing and telling stories about their shared experience.

For Head, it was a moment to reflect on all they'd accomplished and all she'd learned along the way, wisdom she never would have gained without the opportunity to play basketball.

"I remember the understanding that came with it; when you set a goal of such distant possibility and reach it, you gain an insight into what it takes that lasts the rest of your life," she wrote. "It felt utterly life-altering. To summon the competitiveness to work every single day for a goal that was months and even years ahead was the most invaluable lesson I'd ever learn. I thought I could accomplish anything. And I thought I could teach it to others."

After marrying Ross Summitt in 1980, Head was known for the rest of her professional life as Pat Summitt. As the head women's basketball coach at the University of Tennessee from 1974 to 2012, she would mentor young women who came streaming through the doors opened by the pioneers, elevating the game in larger numbers and with greater skills than previous generations. Summitt won more games (1,098) than any basketball coach in history, including eight NCAA national championships. The basketball court at the University of Tennessee, where both the men's and women's teams play their home games, is now known as "the Summitt."

But change didn't happen just in Knoxville.

In the minutes before the 1976 team's silver medal game against Czechoslovakia, Billie Moore told her team that what they did on the court that day would influence the course of women's athletics in the United States for the next twenty-five years. Little girls would be watching; their parents would be watching; coaches and athletic directors, just beginning to understand how to meet the demands of Title IX, would be watching. Win the game, and they'd all take pride in the accomplishments of American women. They'd all see what was possible.

All over the country in the summer and fall of 1976, girls' lives were changed by that silver medal, whether they understood it yet or not. "It's indisputable that the country has finally noticed women's basketball," wrote one observer at the time, "and towns and cities everywhere are catching the fever." In 1973, only eight states sponsored girls' high school state basketball tournaments; by 1977, only one state did not. From 1972 to 1981, the number of girls' high school basketball players grew by tenfold, from 400,000 to 4.5 million.

In South Georgia and Southern California, two twelve-year-old girls who watched the 1976 Olympics became the stars of the next American women's basketball team (after the US boycotted the

1980 Games), leading the US to its first gold medal in 1984. Teresa Edwards, the kid from Cairo, Georgia, grew up to win five Olympic medals in all — four of them gold; some say Cheryl Miller of Riverside, California, the six-foot-two sister of NBA star Reggie Miller, became the greatest player of all time. In Philadelphia, a six-year-old girl named Dawn Staley played around with a small basketball during the '76 Games. She'd grow up to carry the American flag at the 2004 Olympics in Athens, win three basketball gold medals as a player, become the second Black coach to win an NCAA women's basketball tournament title, and coach the US national team to its seventh consecutive gold medal at the 2020 Olympics in Tokyo.

The women of '76 inspired girls to play other sports, too. At the time of the Montreal Olympics, there was no women's World Cup, and women's soccer wasn't yet an Olympic sport. But the new acceptance and emphasis on women's team sports in the late 1970s and '80s inspired legions of young soccer players. Mia Hamm was four years old in the summer of '76; Julie Foudy, five; Brandi Chastain, eight. When the inaugural women's World's Cup came in 1991 and the first women's Olympic soccer tournament in 1996, Hamm, Foudy, and Chastain were ready, leading the US to championships in both historic events. Until 2013, Hamm had scored more international goals than any player, man or woman, ever. Foudy became president of the Women's Sports Foundation. When Chastain scored the World Cup–winning goal in a penalty kick shootout against China in 1999, she celebrated by ripping off her jersey and sliding to her knees in her sports bra with her fists clenched above her head, an iconic and norm-destroying scene that signaled the arrival of another new era in women's sports, one of confidence and self-determination.

In the years following Montreal, as the Association for Intercollegiate Athletics for Women gave way to the NCAA and big-time college athletic departments invested in women's sports, the quaint stories of nun-powered juggernauts and West Texas flying queens disappeared. A girl in Tennessee wouldn't go to UT Martin to play basketball anymore; she'd go to an SEC school like Vanderbilt or the University of Tennessee. A talented player in Connecticut wouldn't choose Southern Connecticut State; she'd go to UConn.[1] It was Mississippi State over Delta State, Stanford over Fullerton, the University of Texas or Baylor over Wayland Baptist. Gone were the bake sales and car washes; in came full scholarships and chartered planes. Most of these changes are considered positive developments. But some of the old PE teachers' reluctance to embrace change was also proven prescient. Many of these women feared that women would lose control over their own programs when the NCAA took on women's sports and that male administrators and coaches would be among the biggest beneficiaries. And they were right about that. As of 2020, nearly 40 percent of NCAA Division I women's basketball coaches were men.

At the Olympic level, the American women were never again an underdog, just as Billie Moore had predicted. When the US boycotted the 1980 Olympics in Moscow and the USSR returned the favor by boycotting the 1984 Games in Los Angeles — where the gold-medal-winning US team was coached by Pat Head — it meant the two powers didn't play in the same Olympic tournament again until the '88 Games in Seoul, where the US won 102–88 en route to a second gold medal. After the fall of communism and the breakup of the Soviet Union, athletes from the former Soviet states competed as the "Unified Team" at the 1992 Games in Barcelona. There, coached by former Immaculata star Theresa Shank Grentz, the US lost to the former Soviets, 79–73, settling for a bronze medal. As of 2022, it was the last time the US women lost even a single game in the Olympics. At the 1996 Summer Games in Atlanta, the US went undefeated and won gold. They repeated the feat in 2000 in Sydney, 2004 in Athens, 2008 in Beijing, 2012 in London, 2016 in Rio de Janeiro, and 2020 in Tokyo (played in August 2021 due to COVID-19), an astonishing seven straight undefeated gold medal runs, one of the most dominant streaks in the history of international sports.

In Montreal, the US women slept on uncomfortable bunk beds, all twelve players, two coaches, a manager, and a trainer stuffed into one apartment where they shared a single bathroom. At the 2016 Olympics in Rio, the US women's basketball players shared a massive, 16,000-ton, 296-room cruise ship with the men's team. While Olympic organizers in Montreal boasted that the dorms came stocked with wastebaskets and paper cups, the luxurious *Silver Cloud* docked in Rio featured a pool, lounge areas with panoramic views of the city, a fitness center, a library with comfortable leather chairs, a beauty salon, an onboard casino, a bar, a cigar lounge, and multiple dining areas. White-gloved porters carried the Olympians' bags on board.

Which is not to say that significant systemic inequities do not still exist, in basketball and other sports. During the 2021 NCAA basketball tournament, blatant discrepancies in how men's teams were treated compared to women's went viral on social media. The exposure of glaring disparities in food, gear, and workout facilities forced the NCAA to commission a study on broader inequities in the sport. The report found that the NCAA had underfunded and undervalued the women's basketball tournament for years, "perpetuating a mistaken narrative that women's basketball is destined to be a 'money loser' year after year. Nothing," the report concluded, "could be further from the truth."

At the time of the '76 Olympics, professional basketball opportunities for women were nonexistent in the US, forcing players to head overseas if they wanted to continue to play ball. Three American pro leagues — the Women's Professional Basketball League, Women's Basketball Association, and American Basketball League — failed to gain traction before the NBA launched its counterpart for women, the WNBA, in 1997. But even with this measure of progress, the inequalities are clear — there are only twelve teams in the WNBA, compared to thirty in the NBA, meaning there are fewer jobs and opportunities for women at the highest level. Differences in pay are so stark that many WNBA players have historically supplemented their incomes by playing in Europe in the off-season, taking them far away from their friends, family, and support networks in the States.

In 1976, a women's basketball team was a novelty. Today, there are female coaches in the NFL earning Super Bowl rings, women scoring points in major college football games, women athletic directors and conference commissioners, women broadcasting nationally televised sporting events and hosting sports radio shows, women athletes with multimillion-dollar endorsement deals. Boys wear the jerseys of their favorite women's soccer players, NBA stars buy front row seats for WNBA games and cheer the loudest for their female counterparts. There are Black, Latina, Asian, and Indigenous women in powerful positions in sports, gay women presented as the faces of their franchises, courageous women challenging sexual abuse and harassment by powerful men in their sports. But we know these gains are not enough.

Outrageous disparities in media coverage persist — studies show that about 95 percent of annual televised live sports and highlights are of men's sports. That said, television coverage of the Summer Olympics has trended in an entirely different, and positive, direction. During the Tokyo Olympics of August 2021, women's sports received 60 percent of prime-time coverage on NBC, compared to just 40 percent for men, and researchers from the Representation Project found "no gender gaps in discussions of romantic partners, marital status, parenting, appearance, or body shaming." But even in coverage of the Olympics, some sexist norms of previous generations remain. The same researchers reported that Olympic "commentators are overwhelmingly men, women athletes are shown in more revealing clothing than male athletes overall, and camera angles are more likely to sexualize women athletes. Also, women athletes are more likely to be referred to as 'female athletes' instead of just 'athletes,' and they continue to be described with gender diminutive terms, such as 'girls.'"

While it was basketball that first raised the nation's consciousness of women's team sports, other sports have since become more popular for girls and women to play and for viewers to watch. Girls' volleyball and soccer have steadily added participants at the high school level, while basketball participation has declined. Many reasonable explanations are given — soccer is easier for young kids to play, volleyball requires less running, knee injuries are more common in basketball — but some observers point to a more pernicious subtext of the shift in popularity: race and sexual orientation. Soccer, especially, and volleyball to a lesser extent, are for "cute white girls in ponytails," the perception goes. Basketball, then, must be for Black and gay women, two "untouchables" in a white, cisgender, male-dominated culture.

Sue Bird, the WNBA star and five-time Olympic gold medalist married to soccer star Megan Rapinoe, spoke of the tendency for Americans to fall in love with US national women's soccer teams while ignoring women's basketball at elite levels. "To be completely blunt, but also kind of simple, soccer players generally are cute little white girls. And I think basketball players, we're all shapes and sizes," Bird told a CNN interview. "It's

70 to 80 percent Black women, a lot of gay women. We're tall; we're big. And I think there's just maybe this intimidation factor with that . . . What I feel like I've learned throughout that process is you have to . . . be true to who you are and authentic."

Perhaps not surprisingly, then, it is women's basketball that leads the entire sports world in the areas of social awareness and action. Entire WNBA teams took a knee during the national anthem to protest police brutality as far back as 2016, and the league dedicated its 2020 season to Breonna Taylor, the Louisville EMT killed by police who broke into her apartment during a botched raid. Members of the WNBA's Atlanta Dream organized massive support for underdog Raphael Warnock's successful run for a US Senate seat in Georgia after Dream owner and incumbent senator Kelly Loeffler condemned the Black Lives Matter movement. WNBA MVP and two-time Olympic gold medalist Maya Moore quit the game at the height of her career to work to free an innocent man from prison.

"The WNBA is a league that is gritty by necessity," Black sports scholar Amira Rose Davis told National Public Radio. "It catches so much hate because it's 'too Black, too queer' . . . And I think it draws the ire of a lot of people. And so they as a league have always been fairly outspoken, because it's the only way to be. Their very presence on a court, their very insistence that they have the right to play and make a living playing, is a political act in and of itself. So I think they were already kind of primed towards action."

In some ways, the summer of 1976 seems so far away — the bicentennial celebrations, the disco tunes, the polyester suits and wide collars, the striped socks and ringer T-shirts all a distant memory, recalled in a faded tint.

But we inherited the progress made that summer. And the key characters are almost all still living. Trainer Gail Weldon passed away in 1991, Sue Gunter in 2005, Charlotte Lewis in 2007, Jeanne Rowlands in 2008, and Pat Head Summitt in 2016. And before her death in 2022, Lusia Harris — in her home in the Mississippi Delta — occasionally brought out her scrapbook, scanning the newspaper articles she chose not to let distract her during her playing days. But the other women associated with the historic basketball team are still with us. Mildred Barnes, in her nineties, still plays pickleball and goes out to lunch with friends. On her wall in Missouri is a reminder of her contribution to American sports history: a framed photo of the '76 Olympic basketball team.

In East Tennessee, Carolyn Bush Roddy, one of the last players cut in Warrensburg, still considers some of her teammates her "most precious" friends in life. She asked Lusia Harris to be the maid of honor in her wedding; every year, she exchanges Christmas cards with Ann Meyers. "It's an indescribable bond and friendship we three ladies have had," she says.

Mary Anne O'Connor owns an IT company in San Francisco; Juliene Simpson is a retired athletic director in New Jersey. In Southern California, Billie Moore watches college sports and the Anaheim Angels, and still plays golf regularly. Like Barnes, she keeps an unassuming reminder of her past in her home: a photo collage from Montreal. To those who ask, she'll say her players deserve all the attention and praise they can get. They paid a price. They were first. They got things rolling, and look at the national team now.

Every year, when USA Basketball brings a new group of elite players to Colorado Springs, team director Carol Callan tasks the women with learning the history of the program, believing the exercise to be an important part of building a team culture. And although FIBA allows national teams to use whatever jersey numbers they want, USA Basketball has chosen to continue using only the numbers that Billie Moore's team wore in Montreal. New players learn that Lusia Harris's number 7 jersey was also worn by Sheryl Swoopes and Maya Moore; Ann Meyers's number 6 by Lynette Woodard and Sue Bird; Charlotte Lewis's number 9 by Cheryl Miller, Lisa Leslie, and A'ja Wilson.

Women who weren't on that team in Montreal, who were just kids in '76, remember that summer, too. In Wisconsin, Jane

Burns considers herself a child of Title IX, a member of the generation coached by women who never got a fair chance to pursue their own athletic dreams. Burns had to start a petition as an elementary school student just for girls to gain equal access to the school gym. She ended up playing high school basketball and becoming a sportswriter, covering the women's Final Four. She looks around now and sees girls playing multiple varsity sports as if it had always been that way, shopping for basketball shoes and wearing sweats without censure.

"I have never in my life heard women of different generations covet what girls and women have now or complain about it," she says. "It's always more pride and amazement. Things like, 'Can you believe what the girls are doing now?' or 'Can you believe what the girls have now?'"

Truth be told, such grace wasn't always the case for Gail Marquis. There were times in the past, she admits, when she resented the scholarships and the pampering a new generation of women athletes took for granted. But eventually, Marquis let go of what she called "a slow burn" and found peace and acceptance. There is always progress to be made. Every generation has its call. Everyone plays their part. As members of a pioneering generation of athletes, she and her contemporaries did the best they could with what they had so that others could continue the march forward.

"I helped pass the baton to the great players and coaches we have now," she says. "I accept my role in history."

When she's in her car and sees a group of girls outside playing basketball or soccer or softball, she'll pull over, get out, lean against the fence, and just watch for a while.

The girls don't know who the woman is watching them, or why she has a smile on her face.

But if they looked a bit closer, they might understand.

That pendant dangling from Gail Marquis's neck?

It's her silver medal from 1976.

And a piece of it belongs to each of them.

The 2020 US Olympic women's basketball team won the program's seventh consecutive gold medal in Tokyo in a Summer Games delayed until

2021 due to COVID. Players still wear the same
jersey numbers worn by members of the 1976
Olympic team. (USA Basketball)

NOTES

CHAPTER 1

1. Nine of the twelve players, along with head coach Billie Moore and assistant Sue Gunter, have been inducted into the Women's Basketball Hall of Fame, as have Mildred Barnes, the administrator who put the team together, and Bill Wall of USA Basketball.

CHAPTER 2

1. The site of the gymnasium in Springfield, Massachusetts, where James Naismith invented basketball is now a McDonald's. The sport of volleyball was also invented at the same location.

CHAPTER 3

1. The Amateur Athletic Union was founded in 1888 to create national standards for youth sports. It sanctioned national championships and, until the 1970s, hosted the US Olympic trials for many sports. The AAU began sanctioning women's basketball in 1923 and held a national women's basketball tournament from 1926 to 1970.

2. Another perspective of American wartime basketball emerged in the internment camps, where Japanese American parents created leagues for basketball and other sports to provide their children a sense of normalcy in the midst of the inhumanity. Following the war, Japanese American leagues continued on the West Coast. While the early leagues were mostly for boys, girls did play.

3. Margie Hunt of Wayland Baptist once took a charge against Nera White and never forgot what White whispered to her as they ran back down the court. "Do that again," she said, "and I'll kill you." Hunt said that White in-

vented some of the moves popularized by NBA players. "They think some man came up with the first finger-roll layup," she said. "Not true. Nera White did that forever."

4. White audiences similarly demanded "clowning" from Black basketball teams such as the Harlem Globetrotters and baseball teams such as the Indianapolis Clowns.

CHAPTER 4

1. Miss America winner Judith Ford was a college athlete — a gymnast at what is now the University of Louisiana at Lafayette — at a time when that was rare for women. A straight-A student, she was the first woman at the school to earn a varsity athletic letter. She had also overcome tragedy. A year before the pageant, a tornado killed twenty-three people in her hometown, injured more than three hundred, and destroyed two hundred homes, including her own. After her yearlong reign as Miss America, she transferred to the University of Illinois, where she earned a degree in physical

education. She later earned a master's in the same subject from Western Illinois University, taught PE at the elementary school level, served on the President's Council on Physical Fitness and Sports, and coached golf and basketball.

2. White feminists' failures on race were especially alarming on three counts. First was the mix of hypocrisy and appropriation at the heart of it: many feminist strategies and tactics were straight out of the civil rights playbook. Second was their historic willingness to embrace racism when convenient: white suffragists such as Elizabeth Cady Stanton had once argued that if Black and immigrant men could vote, surely white women should be able to as well, appealing to their whiteness and ability to cancel out Black men's votes. Third, they failed to acknowledge and learn from a long lineage of Black feminists, from Sojourner Truth (who famously asked, "Ain't I a woman?") to Anna Julia Cooper (the "mother of Black feminism") to Mary Church Terrell (the suffragist who

made it clear that Black women faced the "two heavy handicaps" of race and sex) to Pauli Murray (the NOW cofounder who fought racism and sexism and even called out chauvinism within the civil rights movement).

CHAPTER 5

1. Friedan cited a 1960 *Ladies' Home Journal* article about a Texas housewife as a prime illustration of the image promoted by media and advertisers. "An honor student at high school, [Janice was] married at eighteen, remarried and pregnant at twenty." "By 8:30 a.m., when my youngest goes to school," she said, "my whole house is clean and neat and I am dressed for the day," meaning "rouge, powder and lipstick," and a freshly pressed cotton dress. "I am free to play bridge, attend club meetings, or stay home and read, listen to Beethoven, and just plain loaf." Janice raved about her "four-poster spool bed with a pink taffeta canopy" ("I feel just like Queen Elizabeth sleeping in that bed"), while noting that her husband slept in a separate

room because he snored. "I'm so grateful for my blessings," Janice went on. "Wonderful husband, handsome sons with dispositions to match, big comfortable house . . . I'm thankful for my good health and faith in God and such material possessions as two cars, two TVs and two fireplaces."

Friedan's problems with the article were numerous. First, it presented an ideal that many women could not achieve even if they wanted to, unrepresentative as it was of the fact that half of all American women worked outside the home. Further, for most women who did stay home, real life was far less idyllic than Janice's. The relentlessness of homemaking was so well known there was an old saying for it: "Man must toil from sun to sun, but a woman's work is never done." Not only that, but women also got no credit for their efforts, as if it were all ordained by nature. "Performed for love, not money," wrote Estelle Freedman of the hypocrisy, "domestic work does not count in the same way that men's labor does."

2. In addition to founding NOW, Betty Friedan also helped create the National Women's Political Caucus and the National Association for the Repeal of Abortion Laws (now called NARAL Pro-Choice America).

3. There was no denying the difficulty of the feminists' cause, as journalist Gail Collins points out: "Sociologist Alice Rossi said [sexism was] the only instance in which people being discriminated against lived in much more intimate association with the 'enemy' than with other members of their own group. Women's interests were bound up with those of their fathers, husbands, brothers, and sons in every aspect of their lives." Journalist Diane Monk further claimed that the women's liberation movement was perhaps the most sweeping of all movements because it called for change not only in the country's political, economic, and social structure, but also in the way men and women viewed their very identities. And in questioning such long-held assumptions, feminists faced another immense challenge: the

warped idea that their advocacy for personal freedom and collective justice was inherently anti-American. Cold War politics, Friedan observed, stigmatized the unconventional, especially as it related to family, sex, and gender. Women's roles in domestic life and consumerism were linked to Americans' "better way of life" in comparison to communism, and thus to national security. As in movements against white supremacy, resisting the unjust-but-traditional could be portrayed by right-wing critics as un-American.

CHAPTER 6

1. Sharon Shields went on to work for Indiana Senator Birch Bayh when he was shepherding Title IX legislation through the US Senate and later became a professor at Peabody College in Nashville, where Sue Gunter and Nera White studied while playing for the AAU team sponsored by Nashville Business College.

2. In Bunny Sandler's 2019 obituary in the *New York Times,* Katharine Seelye

writes that as a young girl in the 1930s and '40s, Sandler "was annoyed that she was not allowed to do things that boys could do, like be a crossing guard, fill the inkwells or operate the slide projector."

3. Billie Jean King and her husband, Larry, launched a magazine called *womenSports* in 1974. "There had to be some way to let young women know that there was indeed a way to make a living playing sports, that their desire to compete and excel wasn't abnormal," King said. She wasn't the first with the idea. In 1973, a twenty-six-year-old former ad copywriter, model, and go-go dancer named Marlene Jensen launched a magazine called *The Sportswoman*. Readers could subscribe to receive six issues a year for $4.50. "This is a wide-open field that needs a voice," she said.

4. "The female athlete must learn to see herself as a pioneer," said Cal State Long Beach professor Betty Brooks. "She must prove herself on male turf and be aware that she will uncover hostility because of the tremendous

fear that most men have that women will somehow pass them."

CHAPTER 7

1. Pat Head won numerous ribbons competing in barrel racing events in local rodeos as a high school student. She considered her horse, Trigger, her "most beloved friend."

2. There is a difference between the World University Games the US competed in in Moscow in 1973 and the World Championships in Colombia in 1975. The World University Games event welcomed college-age athletes in multiple sports and was not an Olympic qualifier. The World Championships, administered by the international basketball governing body known as FIBA, was a basketball tournament only and was a qualifying event for the Olympics.

CHAPTER 8

1. Marsha Mann attended North Carolina before the school offered athletic scholarships for women. She had four coaches in four years, saying that the

job of coaching the women's basketball team fell to the PE instructor who "drew the short straw." Mann's daughter, Shea Ralph, became an outstanding player in her own right in a new age of women's sports, one of the most highly recruited high school players in the country as a senior in 1996. She attended several basketball camps run by Pat Summitt at the University of Tennessee, but ultimately decided to play at powerhouse UConn, where she was part of a national championship team in 2000. Ralph was named head coach at Vanderbilt, where I work, while I was writing this book. I watched her introductory press conference while sitting next to Marsha, who was holding Shea's young daughter.

2. John F. Kennedy College in Wahoo, Nebraska, existed for just a decade, from 1965 to 1975. In addition to sponsoring a highly successful women's basketball team, the college's women's softball team also gained national acclaim, winning the first three Women's College World Series championships from 1969 to 1971.

3. Antisemitic tensions that had flared during the opening ceremonies continued to mar the event and cast an embarrassing light on the hosts. During each of the Israeli men's basketball team's games, a hundred Soviet police dressed in blue track suits formed a ring around the court. They whistled, stomped their feet, and chanted antisemitic slurs at the Israeli players. When Russian Jews showed up to support the Israeli team in their game against Puerto Rico, the officers accosted the Jewish fans, knocking men and women to the ground, twisting arms, and breaking one man's eyeglasses. A French player, standing in the arena awaiting his team's game against Great Britain, was disgusted by the authoritarian scene. "It made me want to vomit," he told an American reporter.

Violence interrupted the American men's game against Cuba, as well, but the Russian police had nothing to do with it. With just a minute and thirty seconds remaining and the Americans leading by an insurmountable margin, two American players and one Cuban went diving for a loose ball. Frustrated by the impending loss, Cuban coaches and players objected to the way the two Americans charged after the ball. Cuban coach Ernesto Diaz sprinted from his bench and chased after American coach Ed Badger, while several Cuban players began swinging folding chairs at American players. One Cuban player threw a glass Coke bottle, gashing an American player's arm, while another Cuban found a starter's pistol on press row and fired it into the air, sending everyone in the arena ducking for cover. Someone kicked Badger so hard in the gut a footprint was plainly visible on his white shirt. The melee lasted several minutes before Soviet police scrambled onto the court and pushed the Cubans into a corner. Badger had suspected something like this might happen — political tensions between the US and Cuba carrying over to the basketball court — and he had instructed his players not to retaliate if a fight broke out. They listened, and the Soviet fans noticed their restraint. The Russian fans had been cheering for their Communist brethren throughout the game, but after the fight they switched allegiances, cheering the American side when the game resumed, and chanting, "America, sí, Cuba, no!"

CHAPTER 9

1. The Americans' 52–51 loss to the Soviet Union was the first defeat for the US since basketball was introduced at the 1936 Olympic Games. Leading 50–49 with three seconds remaining, the US lost when confusion over timeouts and time remaining resulted in the final seconds being replayed twice, giving the Soviets an extra chance for a desperation pass and basket. American players felt they had been cheated by the referees and have refused to accept their silver medals ever since.

2. Soviet guard Nadezhda Zakharova had attended a Shipbuilding Institute before moving to the Institute of Physical Culture. "Her husband is

basketball," said Soviet coach Lidia Alexeeva.

CHAPTER 10

1. Fort Shaw starters: Belle Johnson (Piegan mother and white father), captain and center; Nettie Wirth (Assiniboine mother and German immigrant father) and Minnie Burton (West Shoshone and Lemhi Shoshone), forwards; Emma Sansaver (Métis and Chippewa-Cree) and Genie Butch (Assiniboine mother and white father), guards.

2. Indigenous women continue to excel at basketball. One notable Native American player is Natalie Diaz, who advanced to the 1997 NCAA Final Four as a member of the team at Old Dominion (the same school Olympian Nancy Lieberman attended) and played professionally in Europe and Asia. She has since become a Pulitzer Prize–winning poet. One of her poems, "Top Ten Reasons Why Indians Are Good at Basketball," mocks stereotypes of Indigenous people.

3. Phog Allen had a contact within the

Nazi government who helped him lobby German officials to include basketball in the 1936 Games. As a young man, Fritz Sieweke had attended a basketball camp at Springfield College, where Allen was an instructor. In the Hitler regime, Sieweke was an official in the Nazi Youth organization.

4. Maude Naismith was supposed to travel with her husband to the 1936 Olympics in Berlin but suffered a heart attack prior to their trip. She stayed behind with relatives in Dallas while Naismith traveled alone.

CHAPTER 11

1. Barnes's sterling reputation and expertise also earned her a committee position with the National Collegiate Athletic Association at a time when the NCAA didn't even sponsor women's sports, and a trustee role with the National Basketball Hall of Fame, the first woman to serve in that capacity.

2. Ed Rush became an NBA referee in 1966 at age twenty-four, the youngest official in league history.

3. The feel-good nature of Immaculata's story is further tarnished by elements of intolerance associated with the program and one of its most prominent former players. The first Black player on the team did not appear until the 1974–75 season, after the school's run of championships. Rene Muth Portland, a star player on the three Immaculata championship teams, later became the longtime head coach at Penn State, where she infamously told the *Chicago Tribune* that she would not allow lesbian players on her team. She was later forced to resign her job and pay an out-of-court settlement to a former lesbian player, whom she had dismissed from the team, after the university found that Muth had created a "hostile, intimidating, and offensive environment."

4. In 1976, Rush was open about her interest in leaving Immaculata. When she took her team to a road game at the University of Maryland, she used the opportunity to interview for the head coaching position there, visiting with a screening committee before the

game, which Immaculata won 77–76. "Everyone who saw me today said, 'Good luck . . . no, bad luck, in the game,'" she told a reporter from the *Baltimore Sun*. "It was . . . strange." Rush did not get the job and retired from coaching a year later.

CHAPTER 12

1. Ann may have grown up in her brother Dave's shadow, but she eventually eclipsed his basketball accolades. Dave was a two-time national champion at UCLA, where he also earned All-American honors one time. He was the second overall pick in the 1975 NBA Draft and played five professional seasons with the Milwaukee Bucks. Ann was a four-time All-American at UCLA, AIAW national champion, and number one overall pick in the WBL draft. She was inducted into the Naismith Memorial Basketball Hall of Fame, Women's Basketball Hall of Fame, and FIBA Hall of Fame. She also married former Los Angeles Dodgers star pitcher Don Drysdale.

2. Varsity competition for women was deemphasized at many Black colleges in the 1950s and '60s, just as at white schools. Tuskegee Institute, the school Bessie Stockard had attended on a basketball scholarship, dropped its varsity hoops team in the early '60s.

3. The popularity of the women's basketball team at Wayland Baptist exposes some of the contradictions and traps that female athletes still must contend with. As with other teams that "struck a balance" between on-court intensity and off-court femininity, historians Pamela Grundy and Susan Shackelford write, teams such as the Queens brought about "tenuous" achievements. "The strategy did not win support for women's athletics in and of itself. Rather, it suggested that female athletes could be acceptable if they also met all the requirements of conventional femininity. As a result, it did little to dislodge the idea that sports was properly a male endeavor or to stake a strong female claim to the virtues of strength, determination, and assertiveness. It left

athletes who did not fit feminine ideals open to attack . . . The consequences for women's sports were palpable. Athletes who were lesbians worried about exposure. Those who were not feared being tarred by suspicion. Concerns about possible connections between women's sports and lesbianism reduced enthusiasm among institutions, spectators, and sometimes players themselves."

CHAPTER 13

1. Lusia Harris was selected by the NBA's Utah Jazz in the seventh round of the 1977 NBA Draft, becoming the first woman officially drafted by the men's league. She declined to try out for the Jazz but did play professionally for the Houston Angels of the WBL in 1979–80. She later became a collegiate and high school coach. In 1992, she joined Nera White as the first women inducted into the Naismith Memorial Basketball Hall of Fame, escorted to the podium by her idol, former NBA star Oscar Robertson. When Harris returned home to Mississippi after

the trip to Asia, she was honored at her high school. Classmate Lesidia Meredith told the crowd that Harris's influence extended well beyond the basketball court. "We love you and we need you," she said. "We look to you for leadership and representation. You are the guiding light for our lives. It is said the key to success is taking a chance. You have and done well." Harris, dubbed "The Queen of Basketball" in an Oscar-winning short film, passed away as I was making copyedits on this book.

2. Charlotte Lewis said she was "definitely a kid heading in the wrong direction" before a coach named Peaches Brown showed her that sports "was a good way off the streets." Her braces came off her legs at the age of ten, and she began to run almost immediately — often from bullies who made fun of her for her good grades and skinny legs. Lewis attended Illinois State more interested in volleyball than basketball. But one day she was fooling around tipping volleyballs through a basketball hoop when members of

435

the basketball team saw her and convinced her to try out.

3. Bill Wall was the men's basketball coach at MacMurray College in Jacksonville, Illinois, from 1957 to 1975. He was elected president of the National Association of Basketball Coaches in 1972 and served as executive director of the organization from 1973 to 1975.

CHAPTER 14

1. Billie Moore began her collegiate coaching career as an assistant at Southern Illinois University. In the summer, she played softball for the famed Raybestos Brakettes in Connecticut. A teammate there, Lou Albrecht, was also head women's basketball coach at Cal State Fullerton. When Albrecht retired, she recommended Moore for her job. Moore coached eight seasons at Fullerton, winning an AIAW national championship in her first season (1970). She moved on to UCLA, where she coached from 1978 to 1993, winning a second national championship, again in her first season at the school, in 1978.

2. Sue Gunter was named head coach of the 1980 US national team, but when the US boycotted the Moscow Games, she lost her chance to coach in the Olympics. One of the most successful college coaches in history, Gunter ended her career in 2004, ranked among the leaders in several coaching categories: seasons coached (number one: 40); games coached (number three: 1,016); wins (number three: 708); and twenty-win seasons (number four: 22).

3. Bessie Stockard has lived a rich life. When she taught at Archer High School in Atlanta, Gladys Knight was a student in her homeroom. One of her basketball players was Edith McGuire, who won a gold medal (200 meters) and two silvers (100, 4x100 relay) at the 1964 Olympics in Tokyo. As a pioneering tennis player in Atlanta's club circuit, she earned a personal congratulations from Martin Luther King Jr. Stockard attended the 1976 Olympics and did television commentary for women's basketball with NBA Hall of Famer Bill Russell.

As a twenty-three-year-old writer at his first job in 1998, Ta-Nehisi Coates wrote a long feature on Stockard and her success at Federal City College (by then part of the University of the District of Columbia) for the *Washington City Paper*.

4. Referee Chuck Osborne's opportunity to travel with the women's national team came in part due to his friendship with ABAUSA director Bill Wall; Wall had been Osborne's basketball coach in high school and college. Osborne met his wife, the captain of the English team, on another trip to Taipei. "The night I worked her first game, I went out for cocktails with the team afterward. I got back to the hotel and got a telegram my mother had died that day. I was up that night getting ready to go home and sat in a quiet bar with the English team. I was shedding a tear and she came over and said, 'What's your problem?' I explained my mother died today, so she sat up all night with me in the hotel. I said, 'Lady, I'm coming back to see you one day.' I flew home and buried

my mother in Pennsylvania and was back in Taipei in three days."

CHAPTER 15

1. One of Warrensburg's claims to fame is as the place where the term "man's best friend" was first used to describe a dog. Attorney George Vest coined the phrase in a trial over the killing of a dog named Old Drum.

2. There was the tiniest hint of danger in Warrensburg. With an air force base just eight miles east, area farms were pocked with underground silos containing nuclear missiles prepared to launch toward the Soviet Union. Schoolkids knew their town was a Soviet target, and every year they practiced hiding under their desks in the event of thermonuclear war.

3. One day in practice, Moore had the team practicing a 1-3-1 zone defense. Playing in the back of the zone, Nancy Lieberman was too slow to cover the player with the ball. "Nancy, my grandmother could have gotten there quicker!" Moore yelled. Lieberman whispered to herself, "Billie's grand-

mother doesn't know how to play the back of a 1-3-1."

4. Ann Meyers described the un-air-conditioned gymnasium in Warrensburg as "a sauna straight from the underworld . . . We'd arrive at the gym drenched from just from walking into the dorms. And we'd stay that way. But we didn't mind. We were two dozen women literally dripping with hope."

5. Billie Moore's counterpart on the 1976 US men's basketball team, University of North Carolina coach Dean Smith, was also born in Kansas (Emporia). Smith's team went 7–0 in the tournament and won the gold medal.

6. Marianne Crawford Stanley won two AIAW national championships in 1979 and 1980 as head coach at Old Dominion University (where Nancy Lieberman was her star player) and was named WNBA Coach of the Year in 2002 with the Washington Mystics.

7. While other members of the team would only later discover or publicly acknowledge that they were lesbians,

McKenzie was aware of her identity, though she was still in the closet at this stage of her life. She said she would have to "sneak out" to call her girlfriend in Manhattan with updates from Warrensburg.

8. Cardte Hicks's nephew, Aaron Hicks, is a Major League Baseball outfielder.

9. Billie Moore's rationale for keeping a young player such as Lieberman to give her experience for the next Olympics ran counter to a quote she gave the *New York Daily News* on May 9: "I just want the top fifteen players for 1976," she said. "I'm not concerned about 1980 right now."

10. However the decisions were made, only four Black players made the team in 1976. In every Olympics since then, at least half the roster has been Black, with an average of nine Black players per team.

11. To understand how good this team was, consider that four women who were cut from the team during tryouts — Carol Blazejowski, Carolyn Bush, Tara Heiss, and Marianne Crawford

Stanley — have been inducted into the Women's Basketball Hall of Fame.

CHAPTER 16

1. A night before the tournament began, a letter arrived from the North Korean delegation, informing organizers they'd no longer be participating in the Hamilton tournament. Advancing out of Group A got a little easier for the United States.

2. Following the 1976 Olympics, Trish Roberts and Cindy Brogdon both transferred to the University of Tennessee to play for Pat Head. (Roberts made history as the first Black player for the Lady Vols.) Billie Moore had declared that she would not recruit any of the USA players to transfer to her team at Cal State Fullerton, but Head saw no ethical dilemma. She took criticism from some coaches and media who saw her actions as inappropriate.

3. Things worked out quite well for Nancy Lieberman at Old Dominion despite the embarrassing night in Hamilton. Her teams won one WNIT

championship and two AIAW national championships, and Lieberman became the first woman to win the Wade Trophy as national player of the year, twice.

CHAPTER 17

1. Phyllis Schlafly opposed the Equal Rights Amendment, gay rights, and abortion, and was a major influence in the Republican Party's adoption of these positions. Following the Supreme Court's *Roe v. Wade* decision that legalized abortion nationally, Schlafly worked to link feminist support for the ERA with their support for reproductive rights and to help grow the influence of the religious right in opposition. In her book *The Republican War Against Women,* author Tanya Melich argues that Schlafly "unearthed the political gold of misogyny. It was Schlafly who translated fear of women's liberation into a political force in the Republican party and thereby extended the foundation of the Republican southern strategy. Now not only did the strategy flour-

ish on the backlash of the civil rights movement, but it was broadened to include a backlash against the women's movement too." Prior to the rise of the religious right, Republicans officially supported the ERA, and an anti-abortion plank wasn't added to the Republican platform until 1976.

2. Author Gail Collins writes that Phyllis Schlafly's effective debating drove women's rights activists crazy. "They felt like they spoke for women," Collins writes. "But here a woman was their biggest opponent." One of Schlafly's most effective arguments was the idea that under the ERA, women could be drafted into the military. Despite the fact the draft had been abolished in 1973, Friedan and her followers agreed with Schlafly that their vision of equality did include the potential for military service via the draft. Noting that only 20 percent of American approved of women being drafted, Collins writes, "It was an admirable principal, but a tactical disaster."

3. Hunter Low was inducted into the

Women's Basketball Hall of Fame in 2005, a rare honor for someone who wasn't a player or coach.

4. Rudy Martzke went on to a long career as the sports media columnist for *USA Today*.

CHAPTER 18

1. African nations boycotted the 1976 Olympics to protest the fact that New Zealand had not been expelled from the games for breaking an international ban on athletic competitions involving South Africa. Despite the ban, a New Zealand rugby team had toured South Africa immediately after South African police killed at least 176 Black citizens, mostly students, during what was known as the Soweto uprising.

CHAPTER 19

1. While ultimately not present at the Games, Venezuelan "Carlos the Jackal" is one of the most notorious terrorists of all time. Convicted of numerous murders, he is now in his seventies and serving three life sentences

in France. He is the subject of the 2010 miniseries *Carlos*.

2. John MacLeod said one of the Canadian water polo team's favorite pastimes in the Olympic Village was to pull pranks on their coach, fifty-nine-year-old Dezso Lemhenyi. "He was a wonderful man but a taskmaster," MacLeod said, "and he always would become an even harder taskmaster if there was a crowd watching. Whether in practice or games, he would put on a show. When you walked into our apartment in the Village, when you came through the front door, there was another doorway there. We unscrewed the light bulb and put a mattress in the second doorway, so he walked in in total darkness and slammed right into the mattress. Then we put Saran Wrap over the toilet bowl in his bathroom, and one of the players remade his entire bed and between the mattress and sheets put pages from the newspaper. Every time he rolled around, he could hear the crunching and not know why."

3. Even with the endless options at the

Olympic Village cafeteria, some countries shipped their own food to Montreal. The Italians sent pasta, the French their own wine and cheese, and the Germans brought their own beer.

4. Tim Wendel attended the Olympics as a twenty-year-old and considers Montreal the "last everyman Olympics." His father had simply mailed away for tickets and received them. When the Wendels wanted to attend a track and field event, they walked right up to the stadium and someone gave them some tickets. "It just seemed more accessible then," Wendel recalled. "We were just a middle-class family from Podunk upstate New York wanting to go to the Olympics, and we were able to do it. I don't think that would happen now. It has gotten so expensive and so highbrow."

CHAPTER 20

1. Japanese coach Masatoshi Ozaki said that his team's two victories over the US during the Americans' trip to Japan in April gave him confidence

heading into Montreal. Also, he said he "secretly" went to Hamilton to scout the US and Bulgarian teams during the qualifying tournament. "Let's win the first game in Montreal," he told his players. "Let's tackle the miracle in Montreal." Basketball had been introduced to Japan in 1908 by physical education teachers who had studied in the US.

CHAPTER 21

1. Babe Didrikson's legacy is diminished by her hostility and racism toward the first Black members of the US track team in 1932. On the team's train ride to Los Angeles for the Olympics, African American runners Louise Stokes and Tidye Pickett were made to eat in their bunks while the rest of the team ate at a banquet hall during a stop in Denver. Later on during the trip, Stokes and Pickett were sleeping in their shared compartment when Didrikson tossed a pitcher of ice water on them.

2. One woman was excused from having to submit to the gender test: Princess

Anne of Great Britain, who, as an equestrian competitor, became the first British royal to participate in the Olympics.

3. Bela Karolyi and his wife, Marta, defected to the United States in 1981 and continued their successful and controversial coaching careers. Bela Karolyi coached numerous US Olympic medalists, but many athletes have criticized his abusive coaching methods and the fact that Larry Nassar, the team doctor convicted of sexually assaulting young gymnasts for decades, committed many of his crimes at the Karolyis' Texas training facility.

4. While Nadia Comaneci was the undisputed sensation of the 1976 Olympics, other women also posted remarkable performances and gained media attention. The *Wall Street Journal* editorial board, which had opposed Title IX's application to athletics, changed its tune when it came to the 1976 Olympics: "Certainly the current Olympics are proving again that women's sports are just as demanding and spectacular as the men's, and that by giving them

short shrift, Americans have been missing out on a lot of excitement."

CHAPTER 22

1. Captain of the Canadian national team from 1979 to 1984, Sylvia Sweeney was part of the Canadian team at the 1984 Olympics in Los Angeles, falling just short of a bronze medal. Sweeney was inducted into the Canadian Basketball Hall of Fame in 1994 and the Canadian Olympic Hall of Fame in 1996. She has also enjoyed a successful career as a television commentator and movie producer.

2. Basketball inventor James Naismith once called the Edmonton Grads "the finest basketball team that ever stepped out on a floor." Retaining their amateur status, the Grads played exhibition games at the 1924, 1928, 1932, and 1936 Olympics — winning every game they played. The team disbanded during World War II.

CHAPTER 23

1. Tatyana Ovechkina's son, Alexander Ovechkin, is considered one of

the best ice hockey players of all time, winning a Stanley Cup with the Washington Capitals in 2018. In a *Sports Illustrated* feature on the '76 Games, Ovechkina was described as "quite possibly the dirtiest performer in the Games regardless of age, sex, race or national origin" — just what one might expect of a hockey star's mom.

2. Uljana Semjonova bought records on her trips around the world, once estimating her collection at more than six hundred. She also enjoyed reading; British novelist Charles Dickens and Russian poet Sergei Yesenin were her favorite authors.

CHAPTER 24

1. "As an athlete I was offended because the *Yale Daily News* wasn't covering our games, and originally they said it was because we were not a varsity sport," Lawrie Mifflin recalled. "We became the first varsity sport for women in the fall of 1972, so I went back to the newspaper office and said, 'Now you're going to cover the games,

right?' They sent someone who didn't know anything at all about our sport and didn't really care. I said, 'This isn't fair, because the female athletes here are putting just as much effort and care into their sport as the male athletes are, and it's not fair to get coverage in the paper that is kind of dismissive and uninformed.' So I went to the *Yale Daily News* editors and said, 'I will cover the other women's sports teams here. I would like to have someone covering the women's sports teams who understands the effort they're putting in.' I covered basketball, tennis, squash, gymnastics, lacrosse. And that was that. I went to Columbia Journalism School for [my] master's and was hired by the *New York Daily News,* which back then was the nation's largest-circulation newspaper."

CHAPTER 26

1. While the University of Connecticut's women's basketball program has become the sport's gold standard, UConn athletic officials did not al-

ways support the school's programs for women. In 1976–77, the school awarded ninety-two athletic scholarships — sixty-five for football, fifteen for basketball, and twelve for all other sports, including women's. All but $10,000 of the school's $270,000 athletics budget went toward men's sports.

INTERVIEWS

Marjorie Albohm, Linda Bales, Mildred Barnes, Joan Bonvicini, Vic Bozarth, Jane Burns, Carol Callan, Susan Smith Cornwell, Clarence Gaines, Mel Greenberg, Lloyd Grove, Althea Gwyn, Lusia Harris-Stewart, Brian Heaney, Cardte Hicks, David Israel, Bruce Kidd, Marsha Mann Lake, Marion Lay, Nancy Lieberman, John MacLeod, Bill Mallon, Ed Markey, Gail Marquis, Michelle McKenzie, Ann Meyers, Lawrie Mifflin, Brenda Moeller, Billie Moore, Maris Noviks, Mary Anne O'Connor, Chuck Osborne, Nina Partin, Cherri Rapp, Trish Roberts, Sheila Robertson, Carolyn Bush Roddy, Doris Rogers, Sharon Shields, Juliene Simpson, Bob Starkey, Bessie Stockard, Sylvia Sweeney, Wayne Swisher, Bruce Uhler, Tauna Vandeweghe, Florian Wanninger, Tim Wendel, Helen Wheelock.

BIBLIOGRAPHY

ABC Sports. *How to Watch the Olympic Games: Summer 1976. The Com-*

plete *ABC/Montreal Star/New York Times Guide.* Montreal: Optimum, 1976.

Babashoff, Shirley, with Chris Epting. *Making Waves: My Journey to Winning Olympic Gold and Defeating the East German Doping Program.* Santa Monica, CA: Santa Monica Press, 2016.

Belanger, Kelly. *Invisible Seasons: Title IX and the Fight for Equity in College Sports.* Syracuse, NY: Syracuse University Press, 2016.

Brokhin, Yuri. *The Big Red Machine: The Rise and Fall of Soviet Olympic Champions.* New York: Random House, 1977.

Byrne, Julie. *O God of Players: The Story of the Immaculata Mighty Macs.* New York: Columbia University Press, 2003.

Collins, Gail. *When Everything Changed: The Amazing Journey of American Women from 1960 to the Present.* New York: Little, Brown, 2009.

Comaneci, Nadia. *Letters to a Young Gymnast.* New York: Basic Books, 2004.

Converse, Casey. *Munich to Montreal: Women's Olympic Swimming in a Tarnished Golden Era.* Self-published, 2016.

Daniels, Stephanie, and Anita Tedder.

A Proper Spectacle: Women's Olympians, 1900–1936. Bedfordshire: ZeNaNa Press, 2000.

de Groote, Roger. *Sports Olympiques Album Officiel Montreal 1976/Olympic Sports Official Album Montreal 1976.* Boston and Toronto: Little, Brown, 1975.

Drysdale, Ann Meyers, with Joni Ravenna. *You Let Some Girl Beat You? The Story of Ann Meyers Drysdale.* Lake Forest, CA: Behler Publications, 2012.

Engdahl, Sylvia. *The Women's Liberation Movement.* Perspectives on Modern World History. Detroit: Greenhaven Press, 2012.

Freedman, Estelle B. *No Turning Back: The History of Feminism and the Future of Women.* New York: Ballantine Books, 2002.

Friedan, Betty. *The Feminine Mystique.* New York: W. W. Norton, 1963.

Grundy, Pamela, and Susan Shackelford. *Shattering the Glass: The Remarkable History of Women's Basketball.* Chapel Hill: University of North Carolina Press, 2007.

Jenner, Caitlyn, and Phillip Finch. *Decathlon Challenge: Bruce Jenner's Story*. Hoboken, NJ: Prentice Hall, 1977.

Kemp, Kathryn Lee. *Just for the Love of It: The Story of the First US Women's Olympic Basketball Team*. Kearney, NE: Morris Publishing, 1996.

Kirillyuk, Vladimir. *The Soviet Union Today and Tomorrow: Sport*. Moscow: Novosti Press Agency Publishing House, 1980.

Lieberman-Cline, Nancy, with Debby Jennings. *Lady Magic: The Autobiography of Nancy Lieberman-Cline*. Champaign, IL: Sagamore Publishing, 1991.

Ludwig, Jack. *Five Ring Circus: The Montreal Olympics*. New York: Doubleday, 1976.

Morris, Michael (Lord Killanin). *My Olympic Years*. New York: William Morrow, 1983.

Naismith, James. *Basketball: Its Origin and Development*. Lincoln: University of Nebraska Press, 1996.

Smith, Lissa, ed. *Nike Is a Goddess: The History of Women in Sports*. New York: Atlantic Monthly Press, 1998.

Summitt, Pat, with Sally Jenkins. *Reach for the Summitt: The Definite Dozen System for Succeeding at Whatever You Do.* New York: Broadway, 1998.

———. *Sum It Up: A Thousand and Ninety-Eight Victories, a Couple of Irrelevant Losses, and a Life in Perspective.* New York: Crown, 2014.

Towle, Mike. *I Remember Pat Summitt: Personal Memories, Insights and Testimonials About the Legendary Tennessee Lady Vols Basketball Coach.* Hendersonville, TN: Fitting Words, 2016.

Triumph Books. *Grace & Glory: A Century of Women in the Olympics.* Chicago: Triumph Books, 1996.

Webb, Bernice Larson. *The Basketball Man: James Naismith.* Lawrence: University Press of Kansas, 1973.

NEWSPAPERS, MAGAZINES, WEBSITES, JOURNALS, ARCHIVES

Albuquerque Journal, Associated Press, *Atlanta Constitution, Baltimore Sun, Bet-*

ter *Homes and Gardens, Boston Globe, Bridgeport Post, Cal State Fullerton Daily Titan, Chicago Defender, Chicago Tribune, Christian Science Monitor, Clarksdale Press Register, Clarksville Leaf-Chronicle,* CNN .com, *Cosmopolitan, Delta Democrat-Times, Des Moines Register, Essence,* FIBA, *Fort Lauderdale Sun-Sentinel, Fort Worth Star-Telegram,* Gannett News Service, *Globe and Mail, Harper's Magazine, Hartford Courant, Hattiesburg American, Huffington Post,* International Olympic Committee, *Jackson Clarion-Ledger, Kansas City Times, Knoxville News-Sentinel, Ladies' Home Journal, Los Angeles Sentinel, Los Angeles Times, Needles Desert Star, New York Daily News, New York Post, New York Times, New York World-Telegram, Newsday, Newsweek, Ocean City Reporter, Oneonta Daily Star, Passaic Herald-News, Philadelphia Inquirer, Philadelphia Tribune, Pittsburgh Courier, Plattsburgh Press-Republican, Redbook, Rochester Democrat and Chronicle, Rockford Morning Star, Ruston Daily Leader, Sacramento Bee, San Mateo Times, Santa Ana Register, Scott County Times, Seventeen, South Mississippi Sun, Sporting News, Sports Illus-*

trated, St. Louis Post-Dispatch, Syracuse Herald-Journal, Tennessean, TIME, United Press International, USAB.com, USA Basketball, *Wall Street Journal, Walton Tribune, Warrensburg Star-Journal, Washington City Paper, Washington Post, Washington Star, Washington Times,* Wikipedia, Women's Basketball Hall of Fame.

1973 World University Games Roster

Name	Position	Ht.	Wt.	School	Hometown
Janice Beach	G	5-6	130	Wayland Baptist	Altus, OK
Juliene Brazinski (Simpson)	G	5-6	175	J.F. Kennedy College	Roselle Park, NJ
Phyllis Cupp	C	6-1	160	Western Michigan	Mendon, MI
Nancy Dunkle	C	6-2	155	Cal State Fullerton	La Habra, CA
Dorothy Easterwood	F	5-9	130	Miss College/Women	Starkville, MS
Pat Head	F	5-10	145	UT Martin	Ashland City, TN
Marsha Mann	F	6-1	175	North Carolina	Dunn, NC
Brenda Moeller	C	5-10	150	Wayland Baptist	Indianola, IA
Cherri Rapp	F	5-11	140	Wayland Baptist	Estelline, TX
Theresa Shank	C	6-1	145	Immaculata	Springfield, PA
Marilyn Smith	G	5-8	135	Parsons College	Fairfield, IA
Barbara Wischmeier	C	6-3	160	Kennedy College	Sperry, IA

Head Coach: Jill Upton (Mississippi College for Women)
Assistant Coach: Billie Moore (Cal State Fullerton)
Manager: Jeanne Rowlands (Northeastern)

462

1975 World Championships and Pan Am Games Roster

Name	Position	Ht.	Wt.	School	Hometown
Carolyn Bush	F	6-2	145	Wayland Baptist	Kingston, TN
Nancy Dunkle	C	6-2	155	Cal State Fullerton	La Habra, CA
Rita Easterling	C	6-5	134	Miss College/Women	Morton, MS
Lusia Harris	C	6-2	180	Delta State	Minter City, MS
Pat Head	F	5-10	155	UT Martin	Ashland City, TN
Charlotte Lewis	C	6-2	180	Illinois St.	Peoria, IL
Nancy Lieberman	G	5-9	140	Far Rockaway HS	Far Rockaway, NY
Ann Meyers	G	5-8	135	UCLA	La Habra, CA
Mary Anne O'Connor	G	5-10	158	So. Connecticut St.	Fairfield, CT
Cherri Rapp	F	5-11	150	Wayland Baptist	Estelline, TX
Sue Rojcewicz	G	5-7	135	So. Connecticut St.	Worcester, MA
Juliene Simpson	G	5-6	156	Kennedy College	Roselle Park, NJ

Head Coach: Cathy Rush (Immaculata)
Assistant Coach: Billie Moore (Cal State Fullerton)
Manager: Mildred Barnes (Central Missouri)

463

1976 Olympics Roster

Name	Position	Ht.	Wt.	School	Hometown
Cindy Brogdon	F	5-10	155	Mercer	Buford, GA
Nancy Dunkle	C	6-2	155	Cal State Fullerton	La Habra, CA
Lusia Harris	C	6-2	180	Delta State	Minter City, MS
Pat Head	F	5-10	155	UT Martin	Ashland City, TN
Charlotte Lewis	C	6-2	180	Illinois St.	Peoria, IL
Nancy Lieberman	G	5-9	140	Far Rockaway HS	Far Rockaway, NY
Gail Marquis	F	5-11	165	Queens College	St. Albans, NY
Ann Meyers	G	5-8	135	UCLA	La Habra, CA
Mary Anne O'Connor	G	5-10	158	So. Connecticut St.	Fairfield, CT
Trish Roberts	F	6-1	150	Emporia St.	Monroe, GA
Sue Rojcewicz	G	5-7	135	So. Connecticut St.	Worcester, MA
Juliene Simpson	G	5-6	156	Kennedy College	Roselle Park, NJ

Head Coach: Billie Moore (Cal State Fullerton)
Assistant Coach: Sue Gunter (Stephen F. Austin)
Manager: Jeanne Rowlands (Northeastern)
Trainer: Gail Weldon (Western Illinois)

1976 US Olympic Team Cumulative Statistics

NAME	G	FGM-FGA	PCT	FTM-FTA	PCT	REB/AVG	PTS/AVG	AST
Harris	5	29-46	.630	18-28	.643	35/7.0	76/15.2	7
Dunkle	5	26-51	.510	13-18	.722	26/5.2	65/13.0	10
Roberts	5	23-44	.523	14-24	.583	19/3.8	60/12.0	3
Meyers	5	19-46	.413	10-11	.909	16/3.2	48/9.6	26
Simpson	5	12-34	.353	16-16	1.000	18/3.6	40/8.0	22
Rojcewicz	5	16-44	.364	4-6	.667	10/2.0	36/7.2	19
Brogdon	5	10-37	.270	9-10	.900	10/2.0	29/5.8	5
Head	5	12-31	.387	1-2	.500	27/5.4	25/5.0	7
O'Connor	5	7-13	.538	8-10	.800	12/2.4	22/4.4	8
Lieberman	5	4-9	.444	4-4	1.000	6/1.2	12/2.4	1
Lewis	2	1-5	.200	0-0	.000	3/1.5	2/1.0	0
Marquis	1	0-2	.000	0-0	.000	0/0.0	0/0.0	0
USA	5	159-362	.439	97-129	.752	182/36.4	415/83.0	108
OPP.	5	170-337	.504	77-96	.802	164/32.8	417/83.4	123

1976 Olympic Women's Basketball Results

Date	Score
July 19	Japan 84, USA 71
July 19	USSR 115, Canada 51
July 19	Bulgaria 67, Czechoslovakia 66
July 20	Japan 121, Canada 89
July 20	USA 95, Bulgaria 79
July 20	USSR 88, Czechoslovakia 75
July 22	USSR 91, Bulgaria 68
July 22	Czechoslovakia 76, Japan 62
July 22	USA 89, Canada 75
July 23	Bulgaria 66, Japan 63
July 23	Czechoslovakia 67, Canada 59
July 23	USSR 112, USA 77
July 25	Bulgaria 85, Canada 62
July 26	USA 83, Czechoslovakia 67
July 26	USSR 98, Japan 75

Japan 84, USA 71 (July 19)

USA

Name	FG	FT	Pts	Reb	F	A	TO	MIN
Brogdon, Cindy	0-1	2-2	2	0	1	0	0	3
Rojcewicz,Sue	1-11	0-0	2	1	1	1	1	23
Meyers, Ann	6-13	2-2	14	3	5	1	5	20
Harris, Lusia	7-8	3-6	17	7	4	3	4	26
Dunkle, Nancy	6-15	0-0	12	8	4	4	0	35
Lewis, Charlotte	0-0	0-0	0	0	0	0	0	0
Lieberman, Nancy	1-3	0-0	2	3	3	0	2	11
Marquis, Gail	0-0	0-0	0	0	0	0	0	0
Roberts, Patricia	5-12	4-4	14	5	0	0	2	25
O'Connor, Mary Anne	0-0	0-0	0	1	2	1	1	3
Head, Patricia	1-5	0-0	2	7	3	5	3	28
Simpson, Juliene	3-10	0-0	6	2	5	4	2	26
TOTAL	**30-80**	**11-14**	**71**	**37**	**28**	**19**	**20**	**200**

Japan

Name	FG	FT	Pts	Reb	F	A	TO	MIN
Hashimoto, Kimiko	0-0	0-0	0	0	0	0	0	2
Kadoya, Kazuko	0-0	0-0	0	0	0	0	0	0
Wakitashiro, Kimi	7-14	3-6	17	6	3	2	2	40
Fukui, Mieko	0-0	0-0	0	0	0	0	0	0
Otsuka, Miyako	0-0	0-0	0	1	4	0	2	8
Matsuoka, Miho	0-0	0-0	0	0	0	0	0	0
Hayashida, Kazuyo	0-0	0-0	0	0	0	0	0	0
Miyamoto, Teruko	4-10	2-2	10	4	3	5	0	30
Namai, Keiko	8-14	19-20	35	6	3	5	13	40
Aonuma, Reiko	0-0	0-0	0	0	0	0	0	0
Yamamoto, Sachiyo	0-1	2-2	2	2	4	4	2	40
Satake, Misako	10-15	0-0	20	11	4	1	5	40
TOTAL	**29-54**	**26-30**	**84**	**30**	**21**	**17**	**24**	**200**

467

USA 95, Bulgaria 79 (July 20)

USA

Name	FG	FT	Pts	Reb	F	A	TO	MIN
Brogdon, Cindy	5-11	0-0	10	4	1	0	2	13
Rojcewicz, Sue	2-7	0-0	4	2	3	5	1	15
Meyers, Ann	5-12	5-5	15	6	4	9	1	27
Harris, Lusia	5-7	3-4	13	6	3	0	3	24
Dunkle, Nancy	5-9	7-8	17	5	4	0	5	23
Lewis, Charlotte	0-2	0-0	0	1	0	0	0	6
Lieberman, Nancy	1-1	2-2	4	0	5	1	0	8
Marquis, Gail	0-2	0-0	0	0	1	0	1	5
Roberts, Patricia	5-5	6-6	16	4	2	1	3	15
O'Connor, Mary Anne	1-3	0-0	2	2	1	1	0	10
Head, Patricia	3-8	0-0	6	7	2	1	5	24
Simpson, Juliene	3-6	2-2	8	6	2	7	1	30
TOTAL	35-73	25-27	95	43	28	25	22	200

Bulgaria

Name	FG	FT	Pts	Reb	F	A	TO	MIN
Goltcheva, Nadka	0-3	0-0	0	1	3	3	1	15
Metodieva, Penka	2-8	0-0	4	2	3	7	4	23
Makaveeva, Petkana	7-16	2-2	16	2	3	1	1	19
Mikhailova, Snejana	5-9	5-8	15	2	0	2	4	22
Gyurova, Krasimira	0-0	0-0	0	0	1	0	1	13
Bogdanova, Krasimira	0-1	0-0	0	0	3	0	0	7
Yordanova, Todorka	4-6	2-2	10	2	2	0	2	16
Dilova, Diana	0-0	0-0	0	0	2	2	1	3
Shtarkelova, Margarita	1-7	1-2	3	5	2	2	2	20
Stoyanova, Maria	0-1	0-0	0	0	3	3	2	14
Skerlatova, Gergina	2-5	0-0	4	6	3	0	2	13
Stoyanova, Penka	9-12	9-10	27	8	2	2	3	25
TOTAL	30-68	19-24	79	28	30	22	23	200

468

USA 89, Canada 75 (July 22)

USA

Name	FG	FT	Pts	Reb	F	A	TO	MIN
Brogdon, Cindy	2-7	0-0	4	2	0	1	1	13
Rojcewicz, Sue	3-10	2-4	8	3	0	4	1	17
Meyers, Ann	3-6	3-4	9	7	5	10	7	23
Harris, Lusia	5-7	1-2	11	3	2	2	4	27
Dunkle, Nancy	6-10	3-4	15	5	5	2	0	22
Lewis, Charlotte	0-0	0-0	0	0	1	0	0	3
Lieberman, Nancy	0-0	0-0	2	1	0	0	1	12
Marquis, Gail	0-0	0-0	0	0	0	0	0	0
Roberts, Patricia	5-9	1-4	11	2	3	0	0	17
O'Connor, Mary Anne	2-2	1-2	5	4	4	1	0	11
Head, Patricia	5-8	0-0	10	5	0	0	4	27
Simpson, Juliene	3-7	8-8	14	3	1	4	2	28
TOTAL	**34-66**	**21-30**	**89**	**35**	**21**	**24**	**20**	**200**

Canada

Name	FG	FT	Pts	Reb	F	A	TO	MIN
Douthwright, Joyce	0-0	0-0	0	0	0	1	0	3
Sargent, Joanne	0-2	0-0	0	2	5	6	5	20
Hurley, Anne	1-2	0-0	2	0	3	5	3	20
Critelli, Christine	2-7	0-0	4	0	1	1	3	8
Bland, Beverley	6-11	2-2	14	3	5	4	2	24
Dufresne, Coleen	0-0	0-0	0	0	1	1	0	2
Strike, Sheila	6-10	2-2	14	1	2	2	1	29
Sweeney, Sylvia	3-5	0-0	6	3	5	1	1	16
Turney, Carol	11-15	2-2	24	4	2	6	3	35
Hobin, Donna	1-3	0-0	2	0	0	0	0	8
Johnson, Angela	3-7	0-0	6	0	0	2	1	11
Barnes, Beverly	1-1	1-4	3	9	5	0	2	24
Total	**34-63**	**7-10**	**75**	**22**	**29**	**29**	**21**	**200**

469

Soviet Union 112, USA 77 (July 23)

USA

Name	FG	FT	Pts	Reb	F	A	TO	MIN
Brogdon, Cindy	2-12	3-4	7	2	0	0	1	14
Rojcewicz, Sue	6-11	0-0	12	2	3	7	3	25
Meyers, Ann	1-7	0-0	2	0	3	2	4	18
Harris, Lusia	6-13	6-10	18	10	4	0	3	26
Dunkle, Nancy	3-6	1-2	7	0	5	0	1	17
Lewis, Charlotte	1-3	0-0	2	2	0	0	1	11
Lieberman, Nancy	1-4	0-0	2	1	1	0	2	10
Marquis, Gail	0-0	0-0	0	0	0	0	0	0
Roberts, Patricia	3-10	3-8	9	6	0	1	2	17
O'Connor, Mary Anne	2-3	7-8	11	4	2	3	1	16
Head, Patricia	2-6	1-2	5	4	0	1	1	25
Simpson, Juliene	1-7	0-0	2	2	2	2	0	21
TOTAL	28-82	21-34	77	33	20	16	19	200

USSR

Name	FG	FT	Pts	Reb	F	A	TO	MIN
Rupsiene, Angele	1-2	0-0	2	0	2	2	2	10
Zakharova, Tatyana	1-3	2-2	4	1	1	0	2	9
Kurvyakova, Raisa	0-5	2-2	2	2	2	0	2	9
Barisheva, Olga	3-6	2-2	8	1	3	2	1	22
Ovechkina, Tatyana	5-8	0-0	10	6	5	6	1	24
Shuvaeva, Nadezhda	7-12	2-2	16	3	3	8	5	22
Semjonova, Uljana	16-19	0-0	32	19	2	0	0	23
Zakharova, Nadezhda	1-3	1-2	3	2	1	11	2	26
Feryabnikova, Nelli	4-7	2-2	10	10	5	0	1	16
Sukharnova, Olga	0-0	0-0	0	0	0	0	0	0
Dauneine, Tamara	4-9	4-4	12	7	3	4	2	27
Klimova, Natalia	5-8	3-4	13	1	5	3	2	12
TOTAL	47-82	18-20	112	52	32	36	19	200

USA 83, Czechoslovakia 67 (July 26)

USA

Name	FG	FT	Pts	Reb	F	A	TO	MIN
Brogdon, Cindy	1-5	4-4	6	2	1	4	0	11
Rojcewicz, Sue	4-5	2-2	10	2	3	2	3	21
Meyers, Ann	4-8	0-0	8	0	4	4	3	24
Harris, Lusia	6-11	5-6	17	9	2	2	4	32
Dunkle, Nancy	6-11	2-4	14	8	3	4	2	32
Lewis, Charlotte	0-0	0-0	0	0	0	0	0	0
Lieberman, Nancy	1-1	0-0	2	1	0	0	2	7
Marquis, Gail	0-0	0-0	0	0	0	0	0	0
Roberts, Patricia	5-8	0-2	10	2	2	1	2	14
O'Connor, Mary Anne	2-4	0-0	4	1	0	2	2	13
Head, Patricia	1-4	0-0	2	4	0	0	4	18
Simpson, Juliene	2-4	6-6	10	5	2	5	2	28
TOTAL	32-61	19-24	83	34	17	24	24	200

Czechoslovakia

Name	FG	FT	Pts	Reb	F	A	TO	MIN
Kralikova, Ludmila	1-2	0-0	2	4	2	1	2	9
Ptackova, Dana	1-8	0-0	2	0	5	0	1	14
Davidova, Pavla	0-0	1-2	1	2	4	0	0	12
Chmelikova, Ludmila	0-1	0-0	0	2	0	0	3	4
Babkova, Martina	1-3	0-0	2	2	2	2	2	12
Korinkova, Ivana	6-9	2-4	14	4	3	8	5	37
Pollakova, Yvetta	1-1	0-0	2	1	2	2	2	12
Nechvatalova, Lenka	1-3	0-0	2	0	2	2	1	16
Vrbkova, Vlasta	2-3	0-0	4	3	0	1	1	8
Pechova, Marta	5-11	2-4	12	4	5	0	5	19
Dousova, Hana	5-11	2-2	12	10	4	2	3	27
Miklosovicova, Bozena	7-17	0-0	14	0	2	1	2	30
TOTAL	30-70	7-12	67	32	29	19	27	200

All-Time Olympic Women's Basketball Medal Table

Year	Location	Gold	Silver	Bronze	USA Coach
1976	Montreal	USSR	USA	Bulgaria	Billie Moore
1980*	Moscow	USSR	Bulgaria	Yugoslavia	Sue Gunter
1984**	Los Angeles	USA	South Korea	China	Pat Summitt
1988	Seoul	USA	Yugoslavia	USSR	Kay Yow
1992	Barcelona	Unified Team	China	USA	Theresa Grentz
1996	Atlanta	USA	Brazil	Australia	Tara VanDerveer
2000	Sydney	USA	Australia	Brazil	Nell Fortner
2004	Athens	USA	Australia	Russia	Van Chancellor
2008	Beijing	USA	Australia	Russia	Anne Donovan
2012	London	USA	France	Australia	Geno Auriemma
2016	Rio	USA	Spain	Serbia	Geno Auriemma
2020	Tokyo	USA	Japan	France	Dawn Staley

*USA boycotted 1980 Olympics in Moscow

*USSR boycotted 1984 Olympics in Los Angeles

ALL-TIME OLYMPIC JERSEY NUMBERS

 Cindy Brogdon (1976), Tara Heiss (1980), Teresa Edwards (1984, 1988, 1992, 1996, 2000), Shannon Johnson (2004), Cappie Pondexter (2008), Lindsay Whalen (2012, 2016), Jewell Loyd (2020)

 Sue Rojcewicz (1976), Holly Warlick (1980), Lea Henry (1984), Kamie Ethridge (1988), Daedra Charles (1992), Dawn Staley (1996, 2000, 2004), Seimone Augustus (2008, 2012, 2016), Skylar Diggins-Smith (2020)

Ann Meyers (1976), Lynette Woodard (1980, 1984), Cindy Brown (1988), Clarissa Davis (1992), Ruthie Bolton (1996, 2000), Sue Bird (2004, 2008, 2012, 2016, 2020)

Lusia Harris (1976), Anne Donovan (1980, 1984, 1988), Tammy Jackson (1992), Sheryl Swoopes (1996, 2000, 2004), Kara Lawson (2008), Maya Moore (2012, 2016), Ariel Atkins (2020)

Nancy Dunkle (1976), LaTaunya Pollard (1980), Cathy Boswell (1984), Teresa Weatherspoon (1988, 1992), Jennifer Azzi (1996), DeLisha Milton-Jones (2000, 2008), Ruth Riley (2004), Angel McCoughtry (2012, 2016), Chelsea Gray (2020)

 Charlotte Lewis (1976), Jill Rankin (1980), Cheryl Miller (1984), Bridgette Gordon (1988), Vickie Orr (1992), Lisa Leslie (1996, 2000, 2004, 2008), Asjha Jones (2012), Breanna Stewart (2016), A'ja Wilson (2020)

 Nancy Lieberman (1976), Debbie Miller (1980), Janice Lawrence (1984), Vicky Bullett (1988, 1992), Carla McGhee (1996), Chamique Holdsclaw (2000), Tamika Catchings (2004, 2008, 2012, 2016), Breanna Stewart (2020)

 Gail Marquis (1976), Cindy Noble (1980, 1984), Andrea Lloyd (1988), Carolyn Jones (1992), Katy Steding (1996), Kara Wolters (2000), Tina Thompson (2004, 2008), Swin Cash (2012), Elena Delle Donne (2016), Napheesa Collier (2020)

 Patricia Roberts (1976), Carol Blazejowski (1980), Kim Mulkey (1984), Katrina McClain (1988, 1992, 1996), Natalie Williams (2000), Diana Taurasi (2004, 2008, 2012, 2016, 2020)

 Mary Anne O'Connor (1976), Denise Curry (1980, 1984), Jennifer Gillom (1988), Medina Dixon (1992), Rebecca Lobo (1996), Yolanda Griffith (2000, 2004), Sylvia Fowles (2008, 2012, 2016, 2020)

 Pat Head (1976), Rosie Walker (1980), Pam McGee (1984), Cynthia Cooper (1988, 1992), Venus Lacey (1996), Katie Smith (2000, 2004, 2008), Tina Charles (2012, 2016, 2020)

 Juliene Simpson (1976), Kris Kirchner (1980), Carol Menken-Schaudt (1984), Suzie McConnell (1988, 1992), Nikki McCray (1996, 2000), Swin Cash (2004), Candace Parker (2008, 2012), Brittney Griner (2016, 2020)

NOTABLE MOMENTS IN US WOMEN'S SPORTS HISTORY

1892 Senda Berenson introduces basketball at Smith College

1896 First intercollegiate women's basketball game between Cal and Stanford

1900 Margaret Abbott becomes the first American to win an Olympic gold medal

1926 The Amateur Athletic Union hosts a national basketball tournament for women for the first time

1932 Babe Didrikson sets four world records in one day at the US Olympic trials

1943 All-American Girls Professional Baseball League is formed

1948 Alice Coachman becomes the first African American woman to win an Olympic gold medal

1953 Toni Stone becomes the first woman to play Negro League Baseball

1956 Althea Gibson wins the French Open, becoming the first African American woman to win a tennis Grand Slam event

1960 Wilma Rudolph of Tennessee State University wins three track gold medals at the Rome Olympics

1967 Kathrine Switzer, in disguise, becomes the first woman to run the Boston Marathon

1971 The Association for Intercollegiate Athletics for Women (AIAW) is formed

1972 President Richard Nixon signs Title IX into law

1972 New Jersey twelve-year-old Maria Pepe becomes the first woman to play Little League baseball

1973 Billie Jean King beats Bobby Riggs in the Battle of the Sexes tennis match

1974 The Women's Sports Foundation is created

1976 US wins a silver medal at the first Olympic women's basketball tournament

1977 Janet Guthrie becomes the first woman to drive in the Indy 500 and Daytona 500

1984 Women are allowed to compete in the Olympic marathon for the first time, and Joan Benoit of the US wins gold

1991 US beats Norway in the first women's soccer World Cup

1993 Julie Krone becomes the first female jockey to win a Triple Crown event, riding Colonial Affair at the Belmont Stakes

1996 At the Atlanta Olympics, American women win gold medals in the team sports of basketball, soccer, softball, and gymnastics

1997 WNBA launches

1998 US women's hockey team wins the sport's inaugural gold medal at the Nagano Olympics

1999 US women's soccer team beats China to win the World Cup in front of the largest crowd ever to witness a women's sporting event (90,185 fans)

2002 University of New Mexico kicker Katie Hnida becomes the first woman to appear in a Division I-A football game

2003 Serena Williams wins the Australian Open tennis tournament, making her the defending champion in all four Grand Slam events

2008 Danica Patrick becomes the first woman to win an IndyCar race

2010 UConn women's basketball team wins its ninetieth consecutive game, a streak that included two national championships

2014 Becky Hammon of the San Antonio Spurs becomes the first full-time female NBA assistant coach

2017 Burn It All Down, a feminist sports podcast, is launched

2020 Vanderbilt's Sarah Fuller becomes the first woman to score points in a Power 5 college football game

2021 Women's sports receive 60 percent of prime-time Tokyo Olympic television coverage on NBC, an all-time high

2022 For the first time, U.S. Soccer Federation guarantees equal pay for members of the men's and women's national teams.

ACKNOWLEDGMENTS

Though my parents say I was fascinated by the ski jumpers during the 1972 Winter Olympics, the first Olympics I actually remember watching on TV were the Montreal Games of 1976. I was six years old, and our family had recently moved to Lawrenceville, New Jersey. A few weeks after Revolutionary War reenactors marched down our street to celebrate the bicentennial, my parents and sister and I huddled around a small black-and-white television to watch Nadia Comaneci.

It wasn't until high school in the mid-1980s that I began paying attention to women's basketball. Our family had moved from Washington, DC, to Austin, Texas, where Jody Conradt led the University of Texas to a national championship our first year in town. A few summers later, while interning in the sports department at the *Austin American-Statesman,* I had a chance to interview Sheryl Swoopes, who was a high school phenom at the time and later became an Olympic gold medalist.

As a college student at Vanderbilt University in Nashville and later as the publicist for the men's basketball team there, I got to know the coaches and players on the women's team at a time when women's basketball was biggest thing in town (and state). I'll always remember the game against Pat Summitt's Lady Vols in 1993 when Memorial Gym was sold out, with thousands of fans outside clamoring to get in. In the Vandy sports information office, I was fortunate to work alongside June Stewart and Tammy Boclair, two legendary trailblazers in the field. Thank you to Tammy for vouching for me with several interview subjects in this book.

Now, having returned to Vanderbilt after nearly twenty years away, I'm incredibly fortunate to work for athletic director Candice Lee, a former Commodores basketball team captain, and to know Shea Ralph, the former UConn star now coaching at VU. My son even played for a youth team coached by Stephanie White, the former collegiate Player of the Year.

The idea for this book came after visits to Lexington Trails Middle School in De Soto, Kansas, and East McDowell Middle School in Marion, North Carolina. I traveled to both schools to talk about my book *Games of Deception,* the story of the first US men's Olympic basketball team. At both schools, students asked what I knew about the first women's team. I didn't know anything other than that the year was 1976, so I decided to write a book to learn more. Thank you to my friends Nikki Leisten and Vickie Blankenship, librarians at those schools, for the invitations to visit, and to their students for providing the inspiration to tell this story.

A huge thank you to Josh Sullivan at the Women's Basketball Hall of Fame in Knoxville, whose advance work made my research at the museum incredibly productive, and who provided several photos for the book. Caroline Williams at USA Basketball arranged interviews with members of the '76 Olympic team and provided archival documents and photos, while Florian Wanninger and Miguel Font at FIBA provided details on the process that led to women's basketball's inclusion in the Olympics. Linda Bales in Warrensburg, Missouri, visited with Mildred Barnes and sent along documents from Barnes's collections, while Debby Jennings, the longtime Lady Vols media director, helped connect me with several key subjects in the book. Bob Starkey was kind enough to send me a basketball autographed by members of the '76 team as inspiration. Vic Bozarth went above and beyond to describe life in Warrensburg in 1976, while Maris Noviks in Latvia provided a primer on Soviet basketball and Yutaka Mizutani did the same for Japan, even translating an interview with the Japanese coach from 1976. Thank you also to Bill Mallon and Steve Dittmore for their Olympics expertise, Valerie Low for helping me understand her father, and Vanderbilt librarian Pam Morgan for her expert guidance. Everything these people did to help was made more difficult due to the limitations imposed by COVID-19, and my gratitude is even deeper because of it.

It was a joy to interview players and coaches not only from the '76 team but also from the US national teams that preceded it. A special thank you to Coach Billie Moore for always responding to texts with answers to random questions, and to Ann Meyers, Gail Marquis, Cherri Rapp, and Carolyn Bush Roddy for their extra efforts to connect me with people to interview, share photos, and confirm various facts or details.

I feel fortunate to work with good, solid, smart, and funny people in the publishing industry. Thank you to my agent, Alec Shane of Writers House, for his wisdom, guidance, and straight-shooting perspective, and to my editor, Kelsey Murphy at Viking. It is a joy working with you, Kelsey, and I so appreciate your ability to help me craft a stronger narrative with the best interests of young readers in mind.

Thank you to Monique Sterling, who designed the interior; Maria Fazio and Kristin Boyle, who designed the cover; Deborah Kaplan; and Rob Zilla III, the cover artist. Thank you to Krista

Ahlberg, Sola Akinlana, Gaby Corzo, and Gerard Mancini in managing editorial and production editorial, as well as all the copyeditors and proofreaders who worked on this book, Lauren O'Neal, Vivian Kirklin, and Kate Frentzel. Thank you to Lisa Schwartz in production. And thank you to everyone at Viking and PYR, including Ken Wright and Tamar Brazis, Lathea Mondesir in publicity, Bri Lockhart, Christina Colangelo, Emily Romero, Shanta Newlin, Elyse Marshall, Felicity Vallence, Shannon Spann, James Akinaka, Alex Garber, Carmela Iaria, Trevor Ingerson, Summer Ogata, Rachel Wease, Danielle Presley, Felicia Frazier, Debra Polansky, everyone in sales, Jen Loja, Jocelyn Schmidt, and Robyn Bender.

Thank you to all the librarians, teachers, parents, and students standing up to the legislatures, school boards, and other zealots who seek to keep the truth out of schools by banning or restricting access to books dealing honestly with American history.

Writing books while working a regular job and helping to raise two kids is not possible without everyone else in my life making sacrifices. I am grateful for the support of my entire family. Thank you to my amazing in-laws, Doug and Cathy Williams, for doing so much to help us function! I haven't gotten to see my parents, David and Linda, much over the last couple of years due to COVID, but the few visits have been sweet, and their constant encouragement has mattered more than they know.

It's awkward writing about the sacrifices one's wife has made to make a book on feminism possible. So let me instead point out that Alison won the top award in her professional field this year, almost always wins our family March Madness pool, has an uncanny sense for determining which TV shows or movies are worth watching, knows her bourbon, reads more than anyone I know, and is our rock when the rest of the family is careening out of control. I love you, Ali!

Our kids, Eliza and Charlie, are finally getting old enough to read my books, and I can't wait for them to read this one and to learn about some strong and courageous women. It hasn't been easy being a kid in the age of COVID, but Eliza and Charlie have made the best of it and will be more resilient for the experience. They make Alison and me smile, and make us so proud, every day.

INDEX

Page numbers in *italics* indicate photos.

Channels, Izzy, 20
Chastain, Brandi, 398
civil rights movement, 145–46, 391–92
Clarenbach, Kathryn, 56
Cleveland, Mississippi, 389–90, *391*
coaching, 338–39, 399
Collins, Gail, 53
Comaneci, Nadia, 328–31, *329*, 357
Connally, Donna, 384
Court, Margaret, 59
Cox, Alberta, 224–25, 234
Crawford Stanley, Marianne, 154, 207,
    214, 232, 234
Cuomo, Mario, 286

D
Daugherty, Kevin, 285
Dauniene, Tamara, *356*
Davis, Amira Rose, 407
de Coubertin, Pierre, 323
Delta State University, 21, 173–76, *175*,
    389–90, *391*, 392–93
Didrikson, Mildred ("Babe"), 310
Drapeau, Jean, 290–94

Miss America Pageant protest, 30–36, *31, 32, 35*

Mississippi Delta, 167–76, *171, 175*

Mississippi State College for Women ("The W"), 81–82

Moeller, Brenda, 80–81, 93, 104–5, 207, 234

Monroe, Georgia, 385–89, *388*

Montreal, Quebec, 289–94, *293,* 303–4

Montville, Leigh, 357–58

Moore, Billie (Billie Jean's father), 210–11

Moore, Billie Jean, 8–10, 81–85, 94–95, 97–98, 132, 134, 184–88, *185,* 200–203, 208–14, *215,* 230–31, 238–41, 250, 258–59, 267–68, 304–6, 316–17, 348, 363–69, 370–72, 373–78, 384, 408–9

Moscow State University, 77–78

N

Naismith, James, 11–14, 108, 110, 335–36

Namai, Keiko, *315,* 316–17

Nashville Business College, 24, *25*

133, 156, 157, 205–6, 217, 232, 244, 298, 307, *309,* 314, 332, 350–51, 408

ABOUT THE AUTHOR

New York Times bestselling author **Andrew Maraniss** writes sports and history-related nonfiction, telling stories with a larger social message. His first book, *Strong Inside,* received the Lillian Smith Book Award for civil rights and the RFK Book Awards' Special Recognition Prize for social justice, becoming the first sports-related book ever to win either award. His young readers adaptation of *Strong Inside* was named one of the Top Biographies for Youth by the American Library Association and was named a Notable Social Studies Book by the Children's Book Council. His acclaimed second book for kids *Games of Deception* was a Sydney Taylor Book Award Middle Grade Honor Recipient, a Junior Library Guild selection, and was praised by authors Steve Sheinkin and Susan Campbell Bartoletti. He is also the author of *Singled Out: The True Story of Glenn Burke.* Andrew is a contributor to ESPN's sports and race website, TheUndefeated.com, and is a visiting author at the Vanderbilt University Athletic Department.

The employees of Thorndike Press hope you have enjoyed this Large Print book. All our Thorndike, Wheeler, and Kennebec Large Print titles are designed for easy reading, and all our books are made to last. Other Thorndike Press Large Print books are available at your library, through selected bookstores, or directly from us.

For information about titles, please call:
  (800) 223-1244

or visit our website at:
  http://gale.cengage.com/thorndike

To share your comments, please write:
  Publisher
  Thorndike Press
  10 Water St., Suite 310
  Waterville, ME 04901